C0-AXB-513

Objects of Desire

OBJECTS OF DESIRE

Conversations with Luis Buñuel

José de la Colina & Tomás Pérez Turrent

Edited and Translated by Paul Lenti

FRANKLIN PIERCE
COLLEGE LIBRARY
RINDGE, N.H. 03461

Marsilio Publishers
New York

Original Spanish title
Luis Buñuel: Prohibido asomarse al interior,
published by Joaquín Mortiz/Planeta, Mexico City, 1986
Copyright © 1986 José de la Colina and Tomás Pérez Turrent

Translation copyright © 1992 Marsilio Publishers, New York

Of the present edition © 1992
Marsilio Publishers
853 Broadway
New York, New York 10003

Cloth ISBN 0-941419-68-1
Paper ISBN 0-941419-68-X
LC 92-82642

PRINTED IN THE UNITED STATES OF AMERICA
All rights reserved.

Table of Contents

Objects of Desire

Introduction

Despite today's sophisticated special effects wizardry and the saturation of gory slasher films, we still cringe when Luis Buñuel draws a razor across a young woman's eyeball in his first film, *Un chien andalou* (An Andalusian Dog). Buñuel used this same razorlike perception in all his films to slice through conventional film expectations, with corresponding results.

A decade has passed since Luis Buñuel's death in Mexico City, yet his disturbing presence persists and continues to delight and shock us. Home video and film retrospectives now give us access to the major part of his oeuvre, allowing a new generation of film enthusiasts to view these individualistic works, with their obsessions and unexpected details.

Buñuel was well known in the film world for avoiding interviews. In his later years he once remarked, "I've said everything I had to say years ago and I haven't changed my mind." When his long-awaited autobiography, *My Last Sigh*, appeared in 1982, it charmed us with his distinct and Surrealistic vision of the world. Yet the filmmaker did not speak enough about his films. He resisted the propensity, common among directors, to theorize and discuss every symbol and nuance of his work. Not only did Buñuel resist, he deliberately avoided such commentary. To listen to him, he merely crafted stories, which viewers could interpret as they wished.

As a result of their long friendship with Buñuel, Mexican film critics and scriptwriters José de la Colina and Tomás Pérez Turrent proposed the idea of a book of interviews exploring his works. To their surprise, he accepted, and the three undertook a major film-by-film examination. The interviews were conducted from 1975 to 1977, and the transcripts were later submitted to Buñuel, who corrected and edited the text. Unfortunately, Buñuel died before the book was published.

The Spanish title of *Objects of Desire: Conversations With Luis Buñuel* is *Prohibido asomarse al interior* (Forbidden to Lean Inside), a title originally suggested for *Un chien andalou* — the reverse of the sign on Paris subway trains warning riders not to stick their heads or arms out the window. But it was Buñuel himself, as Pérez Turrent notes, who forbade all attempts "to peer into his interior." In fact, Buñuel was almost coy in his response to certain recurrent images in his films. These images, he tells his interviewers, "impose themselves on me and I insert them, but if I begin to give them meaning, I would take them out. When you two call my attention to them, I'm astonished. I tell you this sincerely." Yet the reader is also astonished; that is, if we are to believe that many of these details and images were not inserted deliberately.

Somewhere in this book, De la Colina says, "I hope this doesn't upset you, but *The Exterminating Angel* can be seen as a comedy." Of course, Buñuel wasn't upset. As he says later, "There is humor, to a greater or lesser degree, in all my films, even in *Los olvidados*." Humor has always been a fundamental aspect of Buñuel's work. At a recent New York screening of *The Exterminating Angel* and *El,* the audience laughed throughout, and it was hard to see either film as anything but a savage comedy on human foibles and bourgeois conventions. Yet this laughter was also provoked by the disturbing nature of the films, both of which are upsetting parables that touch a human nerve. Such laughter is an effort to dispel our unease with ourselves.

There is also abundant humor in this book, which recreates the intimate ambiance of three old friends sitting around discussing films. This relaxed intimacy is imparted to the reader. We take pleasure in Pérez Turrent's exclamation that Little Pedro's mother arises like an apparition of the Virgin of Guadalupe in *Los olvidados*, and in De la Colina's comment that the mannequin's lost limb in *The Criminal Life of Archibaldo de la Cruz* prefigures Tristana's amputated leg. Both De la Colina and Pérez Turrent know the films well, and their familiarity with Don Luis gets them results that few other interviewers could ever extract from this sphinxlike Spaniard, whose wit frequently emerges as the enigmatic equivalent of Mona Lisa's smile.

This notorious wit, sometimes darkly sardonic, sometimes subtle and ironic, sometimes even bordering on slapstick, invites viewers to share a certain disdain for society and bourgeois aspirations and values. It is the revelation in the parallel "parable" of *Nazarín*, in which we ask ourselves how Christ would be received were he alive today. Who else would have dared to make a comedy about heresies in the Catholic church from the fourth to the ninth centuries, as Buñuel did in *The Milky Way*? When confronting production problems on *That Obscure Object of Desire*, would any other director have chosen two actresses to play one role?

Buñuel reveals that his working methods, stemming from the automatic writing of his Surrealist days and his trust in his own intuitive temperament, were nearly agraphic in nature. The entire film, including the editing, was already in his mind as he worked, filming quickly, seldom shooting retakes or cutaways. He also discloses that many of the most disturbing images in his films were improvised during the production without advance thought. "In principle, when you make a film or write a book," he says, "you must put in whatever you want." Later, he adds, "An author has two ways of developing a narrative: either he can impose an intellectual or moral direction on it, or he can allow things to arise according to how they happen and how he feels or thinks them."

As might be expected, Buñuel's obsessions and fetish imagery supply ample fuel for discussion. Surrealism taught Buñuel to lift his self-censor, allowing startling images and unrestrained desires to flow into even the most conventional narratives of some of his midperiod Mexican films. Yet he roundly rejects any "delirium of an interpretation" here, though Pérez Turrent and De la Colina continually hound him with examples and force him to admit that yes, they could be keys to his subconscious, even as he claims to be "nonpsychoanalyzable." As Buñuel says, "I have always been faithful to certain principles of my Surrealist period and these have to come into play."

Above all, in these pages we confront Buñuel's power of observation, the understanding of human nature focused on small gestures and details that bring life to otherwise conventional moments. There are many such gestures and details throughout Buñuel's films. Yet despite his depiction of human folly and his cynical world view, Buñuel was a humanist who was truly moved by man's failures and efforts to live with his own defective nature. We find this compassion in many of his most personal films, the imperfect priest in *Nazarín,* the unsuccessful old lover in *Viridiana,* the pitiful condition of Don Lope in *Tristana.*

When Buñuel died in 1983, Pérez Turrent and De la Colina published an excerpt from the book in the Mexico City daily *Novedades.* I had always been an enthusiast of Buñuel's films, and this was my first encounter with the book. At the time I worked with José at *Novedades* and saw Tomás frequently, since we both wrote about cinema for Mexico

City daily newspapers. I even translated the excerpt as a posthumous tribute to Buñuel in the newspaper's English-language publication, *The News*. Three years passed before the book was finally published, and five more years went by before I saw Tomás in Havana and asked if an English-language edition were in the works. When he said no, I offered my services.

As Pérez Turrent points out, there are many similarities between this book and *My Last Sigh*. Buñuel's work on this book no doubt sparked many memories that eventually gave form to the autobiography he later "wrote" with his long-time collaborator, French scriptwriter Jean-Claude Carrière. As he was fond of noting, Buñuel usually dictated his ideas to a writer, who helped shape the material. Although we do get some information on his life and friends, his tastes and opinions, in this book the two interviewers focus the discussions on Buñuel's thirty-two films.

The greatest pleasure in translating this book was the opportunity it gave me to review all of Buñuel's films, this time with an eye to the text. Sometimes, through faulty memory, the interviews diverge from what is seen on the screen. But more often, small details that had previously been overlooked came to life and took on new significance, especially when seen in the context of Buñuel's overall oeuvre.

Like an actor, a translator must get close to the text, examining nuances, tones of voice, and other technical aspects. Yet beyond mere technical concerns, the real interest in this project was the opportunity to get close to Don Luis vicariously, to attempt to discover how this man would have spoken if English had been his native tongue. In this, I hope I have done him justice. Here is the book in English. As De la Colina says to Buñuel in one of these interviews: "All of this tells us something about you. What does it tell us? I don't know, but it tells us *something.*"

I wish to thank the following people for their invaluable advice and assistance on this translation: Roger Atwood, Jordi Torrent, Ottoniel Castañeda, John Madden, Walker Simon, Jesús Bottaro, Adrienne Mancia, Roberto Rochín, Eduardo Marín, Pancho Shiell, Cologero Salvo, Charles Silver, Fred Lombardi, José "Chema" Prado, Ron Littke, Frankie Westbrook, Benita Hack, Gerardo Dapena, Juan García de Oteyza, Esther Allen, Alberto Isaac, Pearl Hanig, Jennifer Apostal, Gary Crowdus, and, of course, a special thanks to Teresa.

Paul Lenti
1992

THE HISTORY OF THIS BOOK

I

I knew who Buñuel was from the moment cinema became something besides entertainment for me. One day I saw him in Paris on the Champs-Elysées. I knew that he was about to begin filming *Diary of a Chambermaid;* I accosted him; I told him that I was Mexican and worked at the Cinémathèque Française, that I had belonged to the *Nuevo Cine* group, and that I wanted nothing more than to work on the production of his latest film as a *stagiaire* (a type of unpaid trainee). Don Luis explained to me that because of union regulations this was impossible. But, if I wanted, I could visit him at the Billancourt Studios when they returned from filming on location. The visit never took place.

After returning to Mexico in 1968, I had the opportunity to meet Don Luis formally through Arturo Ripstein and Gustavo Alatriste, and I began to frequent his house with Ripstein, Rafael Castanedo, José de la Colina, Emilio García Riera, Alberto Isaac, and other friends related to cinema.

At that point, much had been written about Buñuel, some very good things and some not so good. After having read *Bergman on Bergman,* a book of interviews with the Swedish filmmaker (another director about whom much had been written) by Stig Björkman, Torsten Manns, and Jonas Sima, I came to the conclusion that the only possible book on Luis Buñuel would be an interview with two or three people. José de la Colina had the same idea. For a long time we had enjoyed Don Luis' hospitality and friendship, but knowing his aversion to interviews, we didn't dare approach him with our project.

In June 1972, when I was returning from the Cannes Film Festival, Don Luis allowed Alexis Grivas and me to visit him in Paris at the Billancourt Studios to film a report on the making of *The Discreet Charm of the*

Bourgeoisie. We arrived on the appointed day, Grivas with his Eclair 16 camera and I with the Nagra. Buñuel consented to our filming and even allowed his voice to be recorded. This report was broadcast in Mexico on Channel 11, on the program *Tiempo de Cine,* where De la Colina, García Riera, Fernando Gou and I all worked.

So we learned that it was not entirely impossible to go ahead with our project. But we did not immediately raise the question. We knew Buñuel detested interviews, that he felt a horror of the electronic apparatus called a tape recorder and of the "phallic" shape (he said) of microphones. One day around the end of 1974, at one of the meals at Don Tino's Charleston restaurant that had already become rituals (Buñuel's mere presence was enough to keep Don Tino from ever charging us), which was attended by Emilio García Riera, Alberto Isaac, Francisco Sánchez, José de la Colina, me, and perhaps some other friend whom I no longer remember, between the roast goat and the wine, we proposed our project. To our great surprise, Don Luis accepted immediately. He was a little more reticent when we mentioned that a tape recorder would be a witness to our conversations: "I don't think it will work out," he told us, "but let's try. If the book of interviews comes out well, I won't feel obliged to give any more; if someone asks for one, I'll simply give them the book."

The first interview took place on January 15, 1975. Don Luis began to regret having considered the project, particularly because of the tape recorder. De la Colina convinced him to go ahead with it, telling him that it was a very small and discreet Sony tape recorder without a microphone. The first interviews ended in February when Don Luis traveled to Europe.

We started meeting again at the end of 1975 and the beginning of 1976. Most of the conversations took place at his home on the Cerrada de Félix Cuevas in Mexico City. When Don Luis constructed the house in the 1950s, this was a quiet residential neighborhood located on the outskirts of the city. It is now a noisy area, full of businesses and incessant traffic.

Our meetings always took place in the bar in his home: a bar, three armchairs and a Paris subway map on the wall. A coffee pot, a good supply of whiskey, gin, and beer, and the constant barking of Tristana, Buñuel's small dog.

In 1976, Don Luis invited us to spend several days at a resort hotel at San José Purúa, some 250 miles from the capital. He wrote many of his scripts there with Luis Alcoriza, Julio Alejandro or Jean-Claude Carrière (some sequences of *Robinson Crusoe* were also filmed there).

The object of the trip to San José was to finish recording the conversations for the book.

Everyone knew him at the hotel, knew who we was, even the young waiters, who at least had seen his photograph in the newspaper *Esto.*[1] It was a fruitful stay: we worked thoroughly, talked a lot, and discovered many new things about our interviewee.

We thought then that we had finished. And it hadn't been easy. Buñuel is not a filmmaker who enjoys theorizing about his work. When he talked about cinema, he did so in terms of concrete facts: the placement of the camera, the position of the actors, production incidents, etc. On the other hand, perhaps as a result of his fundamental modesty, he was very defensive, totally forbidding any attempts "to peer into his interior." The process of the book was a veritable struggle, a constant pursuit in which he often came out victorious. De la Colina says that in a certain way it was like a series of "assaults." And we weren't only talking about Buñuel's memories, friends, tastes, and phobias; rather, we were eviscerating — if only in small part — the mechanisms of his cinematic technique. It often fell to De la Colina to play the devil's advocate.

We agreed that nothing would be published without his having read the transcripts of our conversations and made any changes and corrections he considered pertinent. But the transcription process dragged on longer than we had foreseen. During this delay, we had to admit that because of our respective occupations, we couldn't dedicate any more time to the book, but we were also held up by the various secretaries who tackled the job, the majority of whom resigned almost immediately after starting. To cut a long story short, after two and a half years of this, we ended up having to do the transcription ourselves, and even having to redo the parts already done by the secretaries.

In the meantime, Don Luis had traveled to Europe several times. When, in 1977, he made another film, *That Obscure Object of Desire,* we almost didn't dare ask him for a new interview about it. He asked about the book and how the transcription was advancing. Finally, in 1979, four years after having initiated the project, we brought him the first part, already edited and needing only his corrections. But the process was still long; our occupations kept us from dedicating the few necessary months to the work. When the manuscript was more than half corrected, Jean-Claude Carrière came to Mexico to propose *My Last Sigh,* Buñuel's auto-

---

1 *Esto,* a Mexico City daily specializing in sports, with an emphasis on soccer.

biography. It was 1981. Six months later, Carrière's book was published.

Our book bears some relationship to *My Last Sigh* (it is the same person saying the same things), but ours is fundamentally centered on cinema. In a certain way, the two books complement each other.

Our one regret is that Don Luis never saw the book published. Often during our conversations, he expressed his doubts: "Who would be interested in a book about my films?" He asked us to make it as short as possible so it would not be "so" boring. When he corrected the final version, it seemed to him that it wasn't bad after all, and that perhaps many people might be interested in it.

Tomás Pérez Turrent

II

In 1949, when I was fifteen years old, I was already an almost full-time movie fan. When the Mexico City newspapers announced that Luis Buñuel required nonprofessional young actors for a film called *La manzana podrida* (The Rotten Apple), I thought this would be an opportunity to observe a *maudit* filmmaker at work, one who was discussed in books on cinema, but of whose work I had, as yet, seen nothing. I sent my photographs and information to Ultramar Films and a couple of weeks later I was summoned, along with other aspiring applicants, to a screen test at the Tepeyac Studios. I can barely remember how I acted out the two typed pages of text that corresponded to the role of "Pedrito." The camera's gaze made less of an impression on me than the gaze of that robust man with the demeanor of a boxer or a teamster, the head of an excavated statue (as Ramón Gómez de la Serna said), and a strong voice with an Aragonese accent. He seemed like a hunter stealthily observing his prey. Buñuel was then close to fifty years old and his fame as an avant-garde filmmaker was almost something of the past.

It was several years before I met Buñuel again, because I wasn't chosen for *The Rotten Apple*. The film, whose final title was *Los olvidados* (The Young and the Damned), premiered in 1950 and was violently attacked in the Mexican press. A Sunday newspaper published a letter of mine, brimming with citations from André Breton, de Sade, Lautréamont, and other literary references that I used to defend the film and its creator.

I saw Buñuel again when he presented an anthology program of his works at the film club of the Latin American French Institute, to which the first generation of Mexican cinephiles owes a great deal. The program consisted of *Un chien andalou* in its entirety, the final reel of *L'Age d'or*, and some sequences from his Mexican films: the dream sequence from *Los olvidados*, the erotic reverie in the bus from *Mexican Bus Ride*, the delirious ending from *El* (This Strange Passion), and the butchers' sequence from *Illusion Travels by Streetcar*. I greeted Buñuel, who did not remember me. The writer Max Aub informed him that I had written the letter defending him and his film, and Buñuel was amazed that I was so young: he had thought it was written by someone his age. Suddenly, he remembered me: "Good heavens! I know you. You were going to play Pedrito. I had selected you for the role but the producer didn't want you because you didn't look Mexican enough."

At Max Aub's invitation, I attended several lunches at a French restaurant with some noted Spanish and Mexican intellectuals, and there I met Buñuel again. The civilized ritual of eating and drinking in cordial companionship, the fellowship of the table, had an essential importance for the future director of *Tristana*, a film in which *Cahiers du Cinéma* found a large number of gastronomic references. At the second meal, as we were eating our desserts, all the waiters and even the captain and the cook came up to ask him for his autograph. Bewildered and amused, he gave it to them, and finally asked what was happening. "You know," he was told, "for a hundred autographs like yours, we can get one of María Félix's." After puzzling over this for a moment, Buñuel began laughing. The joke had been set up by Max Aub; at the next meal it would be Don Luis' turn.

Toward the end of the 1950s, a small number of Mexican cinephiles, film critics, and aspiring filmmakers (who would later form the *Nuevo Cine* group and publish a magazine of the same name) used to visit Buñuel at his home on the Cerrada Félix Cuevas. We would drink, Buñuel more than anyone else, though the alcohol never seemed to affect his faculties. Despite this, one day there was an incident. He and I got into an argument over pornography. Out of a hackneyed desire to shock him in the Surrealist manner, I defended it. Buñuel, who had already begun critically revising some of the postulates of Surrealism, rejected pornography because he said it had lost its subversive virtue and had been converted into an object of commerce and a new "opiate" of the masses. The alcoholic fervor heated the argument. Buñuel called me a reactionary, and I responded by saying he was the reactionary and that he would end up like Dalí, within the bosom of the Catholic church. I think the comment about Dalí bothered him most: "Do me the favor of leaving this house," he told me. Hurt and furious, yet feeling that the Buñuel of the 1920s was with me, I left the house. I had already turned the corner when Buñuel caught up with me, accompanied by Emilio García Riera and González de León. "Listen, Colina," he told me, "these are stupidities on both our parts; it's the wine. Let's forget it and have another drink." I still felt that the Buñuel who had filmed *Un chien andalou* as a "call for murder"[2] was at my side; at that moment, I believed myself to be more of a Surrealist than André Breton himself. "I'm sorry, Don Luis," I told him, "but you have disappointed me." He replied, "In that case, there is nothing more to talk about. Good-bye and a very good night."

A short time later, at a private screening of *Viridiana,* we greeted each other and spoke with our usual cordiality. Buñuel had lunch with the *Nuevo Cine* group several times, and we published a monograph of our magazine on him, the first of its kind in Spanish, or perhaps in any language. We used to go to a restaurant that specialized in roast goat; Don Luis ordered, and recommended that we order, goat brains served in a skull that had been cut in half. I think this little detail, a mere gastronomic preference, would excite those who cultivate the legend of the de Sadian Buñuel, the priest of black masses and participant at diabolic banquets.

Nuevo Cine dissolved, but some of its members continued to meet with Buñuel two or three times a year. We understood that he honored us with his friendship, and we never dared take advantage of the situation to advance ourselves journalistically. For that reason, Pérez Turrent and I almost fell over when, during an after-dinner chat, he accepted our proposal to record a series of interviews about his work. But, even though we had his approval, the business was not easy, as Pérez Turrent remembers. This was not because of the increasing deafness of our interviewee, which, when all is said and done, was not the principal obstacle, but rather because Buñuel, who claims to be "nonpsychoanalyzable," was also not very "interviewable." He resisted explaining his films and even though he categorically denied that they lacked meaning, he neither affirmed nor denied our interpretations. During entire sessions, or on certain points, he was totally noncommittal. It was also disconcerting. At times he asked us to erase from the tape or cross out of the typed transcript a confession that seemed trivial to us, while on the other hand he let pass things we would have sworn he would object to. Often he gave us most during his digressions, on the margins of the subject, even while beating around the bush. He would return to some matters almost obsessively: the destruction of the environment, the proliferation of noise, political polarities, ideological fanaticism, terrorism, the commercialization of the personality and of eroticism, etc.

2 From the published preface to *Un chien andalou, La révolution Surréaliste* 12 (Dec. 15, 1920).

During the interviews (some fifty taped hours in all), Buñuel's small dog Tristana never left his side, seated on the sofa with her head resting on her master's knee. Tristana, on whom Buñuel would play innocent tricks, finally died completely blind. Buñuel wept when she died. She was replaced by another dog of the same breed that they called León, and at times when Buñuel was distracted, he called it Tristana or Tristanita.

Shortly before dying, Buñuel went about preparing for his last moments: he met with us, his friends; he gave each of us something that had accompanied him for years; and he said good-bye with a very precise request that we no longer come to call. It was a modesty in respect to his own end. He had already warned us what his attitude would be when the moment arrived, and at times he added, "You won't talk with me any longer then, neither through a medium nor through a Ouija board." But when, with incredibly exact foresight, he thought that the moment was very close, he no longer joked; his words were serious but without solemnity.

I want to finish these lines with a very precise image of him:

When we recorded the last interviews, Buñuel invited Tomás and me to spend five days at a resort hotel in San José Purúa. We tacitly agreed to respect our personal timetables and habits. He always got up earlier than we did, and when we got together at breakfast, he had already walked around the grounds. We accompanied him on one further round, and the septuagenarian Buñuel frequently left us behind and panting for breath. He would eat two hours before we did. One afternoon we left the restaurant to look for him on the terrace that directly overlooked a ravine full of exuberant tropical vegetation. We stopped respectfully about thirty yards away from him, without knowing why. He was seated next to the railing, his profile to us, breathing in rather than seeing the landscape under the midday sun. His presence alone was intensely impressive. He had filmed some scenes from *Robinson Crusoe* in that exact place, and that was how he looked: like Robinson who had returned to his island and was carrying on a silent dialogue with it, on the edge of history and until the edge of time.

José de la Colina
April 9, 1985

Objects of Desire

Conversations with Luis Buñuel

1: EARLY YEARS; CALANDA; MADRID; THE RESIDENCIA DE ESTUDIANTES

LUIS BUÑUEL: Let's put a little rum in our coffee like they do in Spanish country towns. It gives coffee a nice smell.

JOSE DE LA COLINA: Well, Don Luis, shall we begin?

BUÑUEL: Let's give it a try.

COLINA: What was your hometown Calanda like during your childhood?

BUÑUEL: It was completely feudal. The town church bells only rang to announce deaths, births, Mass, and the Angelus. I can also remember all the plaintive lamentations that used to accompany burials. "Ay! My dear son, I'll never see you again!" Always that feeling of death everywhere.

TOMAS PEREZ TURRENT: Tell us a little about your family.

BUÑUEL: I come from a bourgeois family. When my father returned from Cuba, he moved to Calanda to recapture the happy times of his youth. After only a year there he got bored, so we packed up and moved to Zaragoza. But we still spent our summers in Calanda. We were a whole tribe of summer vacationers: parents, seven brothers and sisters, the servants, and family friends. A very religious family, of course.

COLINA: What were your father's politics?

BUÑUEL: He was a liberal of the day, but not a revolutionary. Some years he took Communion, others he didn't. And, like any good bourgeois, he was frightened by the political situation at the time: the general strikes, revolution.

COLINA: Did he talk about politics with you?

BUÑUEL: No, never. My father was always a very severe and fair man. I loved him a lot and he treated me well, but he always kept a certain distance. He used to tell me about things that happened when he was young, and he took a great interest in my studies, but he never discussed religious or social issues with me ever, not even when I was older. I sometimes went with my father on his walks, when we would look over some of his olive groves. I remember one day there was a horrible smell in one of the groves...the smell of putrefaction. "What could it be?" My father stayed behind, smoking a cigarette. When I looked between the olive trees, I saw an immense animal being devoured by enormous vultures that looked just like priests. It turns out that when beasts of burden died, the peasants would leave them out in the open so that when they decomposed, they would enrich the soil. Later, when I was in my twenties, I killed a donkey with a rifle just so I could wait for the vultures.

TURRENT: Did you notice class differences?

BUÑUEL: Poor people used to come by the house to beg, and we usually gave them small change and some rolls. Girls came with their little brothers hanging on their backs, flies covering their eyes and glued to the corners of their mouths.

COLINA: In the past, there's been a lot of talk about your studying with the Jesuits. There is a curious story about you in one book: it seems your father punished you because at the Jesuit high school in Zaragoza you said that you found...

BUÑUEL: That I found a rat in my soup? Actually, I found a piece of an apron. The Jesuits have been accused of a lot of things. For example, I never saw one case of homosexuality, neither among the students nor between students and priests. But the Jesuits were very strong on vigilance. Every eighty or one hundred students formed a brigade. There were full- and part-time boarders, "privileged" kids from good families, and day students, who were miserable wretches we almost never talked to.

TURRENT: Then the class system was reflected there?

BUÑUEL: Yes, very much so. A class system perfectly defined either by aristocracy or wealth.

TURRENT: Since you spent most of the year in Zaragoza, what was it like?

BUÑUEL: A very backward nineteenth-century provincial capital.

COLINA: Was there a workers movement?

BUÑUEL: Zaragoza was known as "the pearl of unionism." From my balcony, I once witnessed a charge of the Civil Guard: two thousand workers and two squadrons of guards clashed face to face in the Plaza de la Constitución. The workers shouted "Down with this!" and "Down with that!" Then the commander of the Guard signaled his trumpeter and the horsemen charged the demonstrators. The Guards were very professional and completely untouchable

COLINA: Did you go to the movies as a child?

BUÑUEL: Yes. I even saw a film with sound and color at the Coine Cinema in Zaragoza: a pig sang a song with a stovepipe hat on his head, wearing a police commissioner's sash around his waist. It was a cartoon, so badly painted that the color was smudged outside the lines of the drawings; the sound came from a gramophone.

COLINA: What was the first film you remember seeing?

BUÑUEL: It was about the murder of a paralytic and it made a big impression on me at the time. It was about a couple who lived in a house isolated somewhere in the country: you saw the cripple sitting in an armchair and his wife. The wife killed him. Later, the cripple's ghost appeared in the armchair and the woman made horrified gestures.

TURRENT: Did you have religious doubts at that time?

BUÑUEL: I believed everything entirely, but I began to lose my faith when I was around fourteen or fifteen. There was a famous publishing house, Editorial Sempere, founded by Blasco Ibáñez, which published books by Spencer, Darwin, Kropotkin, Nietzsche, etc. And I read them all. Above all, I was influenced by *The Origin of Species,* which made me take "a sharp turn." My father also gave me a lot of books to read: Quevedo, Pérez Galdós, and *Gil Blas* by Santillana... He had a certain self-educated culture. I always saw him reading Spanish classics, never cheap novels.

COLINA: But I suppose you liked adventure novels?

BUÑUEL: Yes, when I was around twelve or thirteen I used to read adventure books about Sherlock Holmes, Ito Naki, Nick Carter, and other detectives, and above all Salgari. I had to read these books in secret because I was forbidden to read such things. The priests thought those kinds of books were inappropriate because they made kids live in a fantasy world at the expense of their studies. Sometimes I would get into trouble just so I'd be punished by having to stay at home, so I could read and I wouldn't have to go out with the family.

COLINA: Did you have a vocation?

BUÑUEL: I don't remember. Perhaps none. If by vocation you mean willpower, then I've never had a "vocation" ever.

COLINA: But you studied music and played the violin.

BUÑUEL: I studied the violin on my own when I was eight or ten years old. What a horrible instrument! In Zaragoza I took lessons at home.

When I finished high school and my father asked me what I'd like to study, I told him I wanted to go to the Schola Cantorum. In reality, I wanted to escape from my family and from Zaragoza. My father told me I would starve to death if I followed a career in music and to consider something more serious. "Okay," I told him, "the natural sciences...entomology." He advised me to study agro-engineering, which was compatible with biology and could also be useful at his country properties.

TURRENT: Why did you choose entomology?

BUÑUEL: I don't know. Perhaps it's because all living creatures fascinate me. I began reading Fabre's wonderful books. I'm passionate about insects. You can find all of Shakespeare and de Sade in the lives of insects...

COLINA: We touch upon another Buñuelian legend: is it true you once fainted when you saw a spider?

BUÑUEL: *(Laughs)* No. But it's true I'm afraid of spiders. My entire family is. I'm both afraid and fascinated by them, and I know a lot about them.

TURRENT: We were talking about how you were sent to study in Madrid.

BUÑUEL: I was seventeen years old. Though I was first in my class in biology, I failed mathematics three years in a row. So, I abandoned my agronomic studies and went into natural sciences.

TURRENT: What did you think of the differences between Zaragoza and Madrid?

BUÑUEL: Ah, it was wonderful to be in Madrid and suddenly be free. My parents went with me to see where I was going to live. My mother distrusted *pensiones*. A friend of my father advised them to place me in the Residencia de Estudiantes, which was an English-style institution, very modern and very liberal, with playing fields, library, and laboratories. My parents were delighted. The only thing my mother didn't like was that we were free to go out at night.

COLINA: At the Residencia you met many of those who would later make up the Generation of '27?

BUÑUEL: Yes. The group formed immediately. We would all meet in one of our rooms to drink tea, argue, and read poetry. At times, Federico García Lorca and I would improvise plays and even operas! There were about ten or twelve of us: Federico, Emilio Prados, José Moreno Villa, and others. Moreno Villa and I were the oldest in the group. Later Salvador Dalí and Pepín Bello arrived...

COLINA: What cultural movement interested you then?

BUÑUEL: That was the time when Ultraism[1] was created...around 1919, if I remember correctly...and those involved included Guillermo de la Torre, Humberto Rivas, Jorge Luis Borges, Barradas, Chabás, and Pedro Garfias. We were interested in everything, particularly in social issues. Once we joined a demonstration outside the city jail protesting the death penalty. It was at the time of the Expreso de Andalucia trial, which created quite a stir in Spain because one of the murderers was the son of a Civil Guard colonel. Later, in the '20s, we were very involved with the union question.

COLINA: The C.N.T.?[2]

BUÑUEL: Yes, and also the anarchists. There were a few anarchists among the Ultraists, such as Pedro Garfias and Angel Samblancat. I sympathized with the anarchists. We would get together at cafés like Platerías, which is where we met Santaolaria, who put out a newspaper that espoused "anarchic" ideas, as they were called then. At that time, people like me who were interested in the socio-political aspect of the period couldn't help being drawn to anarchism.

COLINA: The Generation of '27 can't be separated from the Residencia de Estudiantes. Could you talk a bit more about it?

BUÑUEL: I lived at the Residencia de Estudiantes from 1917 to 1924, the year I left for Paris. Those seven years were very important in my development. I passed from agronomy to the natural sciences and finally to philosophy and literature. Though I studied very little, I still managed to finish the course in two years rather than four. The most important thing was hanging out at cafés and talking with friends. Those gatherings of warm friendship...it was stupendous! We used to do all sorts of crazy things: we would go out in disguise or travel to Toledo on a five-day drunken spree; we would even kiss the cobblestones of Toledo.

COLINA: Is it true you picked fights with the cadets from Alcazar?

BUÑUEL: We did fight with the cadets but, depending on your point of view, we didn't provoke them. The Military Academy was located in Toledo, which at times caused friction between cadets and the locals.

1 Ultraism was a poetic movement launched in Spain in 1918, which dealt with modernity expressed through pure images, without rhetoric or sentimentality. Its members included Spanish and Latin American writers such as Rafael Cansinos-Asséns, Guillermo de la Torre, Xavier Bóveda, Mauricio Bacarisse, Jaime Torres Bodet, Pedro Garfias, etc.

2 C.N.T.: The National Workers Confederation, an anarchist workers' union whose influence waned following the Spanish Civil War.

Once there was a major clash. We were at the Posada de la Sangre, which was later destroyed during the Civil War. This was the same building described in Cervantes' story *La Ilustre Fregona* (The Illustrious Kitchen Maid). Not so much as a brick had been changed since that time; it was marvelous. From the balcony, we saw some cadets chasing a few of the locals and we insulted them.

TURRENT: What caused those clashes?

BUÑUEL: It was usually over some girl or some incident in the street that left a cadet looking foolish. Then the entire academy had to go out to avenge their fellow cadet.

COLINA: I've been told that for a joke you used to dress up as priests.

BUÑUEL: Yes. We wore all sorts of disguises: street sweepers, university assistants, priests, etc. It was an amusing way to study the social classes. One day I went to a theatrical costume shop and dressed up like a priest, complete with shovel hat, long cloak, and cassock. I was walking down the street carrying another costume under my arm for García Lorca, who was waiting for me at the Residencia, when suddenly I came across a pair of Civil Guards. I started shaking because anyone caught disguised as either a priest or a soldier could be tossed in jail for five years. Another time, when I was disguised as an official from the health department, I arrested a fellow student from my regiment on Montera Street because he had neglected to salute me. Although we were both only artillery soldiers, he hadn't recognized me — what a difference a uniform makes!

TURRENT: Then it's true that you did your military service?

COLINA: There's a photo of you as a guard in a sentry box.

BUÑUEL: Yes. It was at the time of the catastrophe at Anual.[3] Since my regiment wasn't assigned to go to Africa, I was allowed to shirk my duty in Madrid. Those who could afford to pay 10,000 pesetas served for only five months, while any unfortunate soul without the money had to serve the entire three years. Don Miguel Primo de Rivera recommended me to the colonel of the First Regiment of Madrid, which was a reserve unit and therefore wasn't sent to Africa. We were part of the quota of one hundred soldiers stationed there who stood guard at headquarters or the national palace.

COLINA: Were you and Dalí friends by then?

3 On July 21, 1921, twelve thousand Spanish troops perished in the Battle of Anual, when Rif chieftain Abd el-Krim forced Spain to withdraw from its possessions in northern Morocco, terminating the Rif War of 1919-21.

BUÑUEL: We were great friends. Even then he showed all the potential for everything he later became, both good or bad. He was a hard worker: he would go to the Academy of San Fernando and spend the entire day painting. When I first met him, he wore a velvet jacket that hung to his knees, a large artist's shawl, an old broad-brimmed hat, with a long mane of hair — something unheard of at that time — and leather leggings. We all liked him very much.

COLINA: I've read that you were all influenced by José Ortega y Gasset.[4]

BUÑUEL: Not greatly. In any case, only some of us. Instead we were very influenced by the French: Apollinaire, Cocteau, etc. We also adored Russian literature. At that time, there were two excellent Spanish translators of Russian literature. André Breton and the Surrealists later admired our knowledge of Russian novels. I had read almost all the Russian writers from the nineteenth century and the beginning of the twentieth.

COLINA: Who were your favorites?

BUÑUEL: Leonid Andreiev's *Sasha Yegulev,* although later, when I lived in Hollywood in the '40s, I reread it and found it weak. I also read Garin, Lermontov, Chekhov, Turgenev, and Dostoevsky, of course.

COLINA: And Galdós?

BUÑUEL: We were very anti-Galdós at the time. I began reading him in the '30s on my first trip to the United States.

COLINA: And the writers who were part of the Generation of '98?

BUÑUEL: We admired some of them: Ortega, Miguel de Unamuno, Ramón del Valle-Inclán. The admirable thing about Valle-Inclán is his use of language: archaisms, neologisms, Mexican words, invented words. Apart from that, I don't think much of his plays. Of course we liked his *esperpentos*[5] a lot. We were less interested in other writers such as Pío Baroja y Nessi. As I said, we were very influenced by the French and we looked to other horizons. We were very, excuse the word, avant-garde.

COLINA: In his book *Vida en claro* (A Clear Life), Moreno Villa noted that you were also very interested in sports; he used to see you out in the cold Madrid mornings carrying a vaulting pole over your shoulder.

BUÑUEL: Yes, I was something of an athlete.

---

4 José Ortega y Gasset (1883-1955), Spanish philosopher and essayist.

5 Valle-Inclán coined the word *esperpento* to describe certain short, expressionistic dramas he wrote, as well as the mingling of horror and satire, caustic humor, and grotesque deformation that characterized them.

TURRENT: ...and a champion boxer?

COLINA: And you even earned the title "The Lion of Calanda."

BUÑUEL: You've confused everything. I almost became an amateur boxing champion, but in the finals I was pitted against some guy named Naval. And while I was stronger and better, he attacked me furiously and I could barely manage to cover myself. The title you mentioned came from the days when we fought other kids in the streets and we all used different nicknames: "The Desert Tiger," "The Lion of Calanda," etc.

TURRENT: You must have been interested in cinema while at the Residencia?

BUÑUEL: Only as entertainment. We liked American comedies. García Lorca, Rafael Alberti, Dalí, and I used to go to the movies to laugh at Buster Keaton, Ben Turpin, Ambrosio. But we loved Keaton the best. We didn't care if cinema was art or not. But we did enjoy comedy and the poetry that is revealed in it. Lorca and Alberti even wrote poems about the comedians in American films.

2: PARIS; *EL RETABLO DE MAESE PEDRO;* FRITZ LANG'S *DER MUDE TOD;* THE SURREALISTS

TOMAS PEREZ TURRENT: We come now to your trip to Paris in 1925, and your work in experimental theater with *El retablo de Maese Pedro.*

LUIS BUÑUEL: During a student excursion to Salamanca, we were accompanied by Américo Castro,[1] who told me that French universities were looking for Spanish instructors. Since this interested me, he advised me to stop studying agronomy and switch to philosophy, history, and literature. I've already told you how I changed my field of study and that my father died in 1923 believing I was studying natural sciences. The well-known Spanish pianist Ricardo Viñes told me about a performance of Manuel de Falla's small chamber opera, *El retablo de Maese Pedro.* The premiere had been performed entirely with puppets, but I suggested that the opera could be performed using both puppets and human actors, so there would be a distinction between flesh-and-blood characters and the puppets, as in the *Quixote.* Under the musical direction of Willen Mengelberg, the opera was to be performed in Amsterdam, with comic opera singers, including the celebrated Vera Janocópulos. I was given the post of artistic director. I had no experience other than those "operas" we used to improvise for fun at the Residencia de Estudiantes. I made a mistake in the lighting: I didn't give enough depth to the stage at first. The rehearsals lasted a month. The work was performed for two days in Amsterdam; I corrected the lights for the second performance. Working as a *régisseur* was an audacity for me, but I believe the idea of combining puppets with flesh-and-blood actors seemed good.

JOSE DE LA COLINA: Yes, because Falla's work dealt precisely with Don

1 Américo Castro (1885-1972), Spanish critic and historian.

Quixote and his companions meeting up with Maese Pedro's marionette theater, and what happened when Don Quixote confused the puppets with real human beings.

BUÑUEL: Don Quixote thought the puppets were real and drew his sword to defend Don Gaiferos and Melisenda. The puppeteer tried to calm him: "Be careful, Don Quixote, because this isn't real and we earn our living with these dolls." But for Don Quixote, illusion was greater than reality and he ended up destroying the little theater.

TURRENT: Was this your only work in theater?

BUÑUEL: Here in Mexico, in the 1950s, I directed Zorrilla's *Don Juan Tenorio* for the Day of the Dead. I wanted to do a traditional *Tenorio,* old fashioned, the way they performed it in Spain to celebrate the Day of the Dead, the way we used to see it when I was young. Only I gave it a bit more movement. I used both professional actors and friends; we did it for fun and nostalgia. I played the part of Don Diego and Luis Alcoriza played Don Luis. At another theater very close by, Alvaro Custodio directed a more modern version of the *Tenorio* with sets by Leonora Carrington, in which the characters didn't talk directly to one another but instead walked from one side of the set to the other.

TURRENT: After *El retablo,* did you think about going into the theater?

BUÑUEL: I still didn't have a definite vocation. I had written poems at the Residencia de Estudiantes, but I was and am a bit agraphic; I find it difficult to communicate through writing. One day at the Vieux Colombier, I saw Fritz Lang's *Der müde Tod.*[2] Have you seen it? Do you remember the story?

TURRENT: Yes. A girl loses her beloved to Death and begs Death to return him to her. Death gives the girl three tests, three tragic adventures in different countries and time periods.

BUÑUEL: That's it. What impressed me was not the three interpolated stories, but the figure of Death, his arrival at a Flemish village, the dialogue with the girl, the Wall of the Dead. It was a revelation for me. I wanted to make films. Jean Epstein was filming *Les aventures de Robert Macaire* at the Albatros Studios in Montreuil and had an acting school. I went to see him and he took me on as what we now call a *stagiaire,* and later as an assistant on *Mauprat* and *The Fall of the House of Usher.*[3] I

2 *Between Two Worlds/Beyond the Wall* in the U.S., *Destiny* in the U.K., Fritz Lang, 1921.
3 *Les aventures de Robert Macaire* (1925), *Mauprat* (1926), and *La chute de la maison Usher* (The Fall of the House of Usher, 1928), dir. Jean Epstein.

did everything from extra to assistant, whatever needed to be done. But before finishing the second film, I quit. I've told the story many times, so I'll be brief. I had inflexible ideas and tastes where cinema was concerned. We were working at the Epinay Studios, and one day we went out to the country to film some exteriors. Epstein told me, "Buñuel, Abel Gance is coming to do some tests and you can stay to help him." I replied, "If it has to do with Gance, I'm not interested." "Excuse me, what did you say?" "I detest his films." He said, *"Qu'un petit con comme vous ose parler comme ça d'un homme aussi grand que Gance!"* ("That an insignificant idiot like you dares to speak like that about a man as great as Gance!"). He added, "Buñuel, we are finished. If you want, I'll give you a ride back to Paris in my car." En route, he kept giving me advice: "I see you are very Surrealist. Be careful with the Surrealists, they are very crazy."

TURRENT: And were you a Surrealist at the time?

BUÑUEL: No, but the Surrealists interested me. Around the time I arrived in Paris, there was a banquet that the Closerie des Lilas offered for the writer Madame Râchilde,[4] who was very old by then. Two Surrealists were at the banquet; I'm not sure whether Benjamin Péret was one of them. Many writers spoke, then Madame Râchilde said, "And the Surrealists have nothing to say?" One of them stood up and said, "Madame..." and slapped Râchilde's face. What a brawl! Some people grabbed chairs, others bottles. It was a huge scandal and the café was closed for three months. That night, after the scuffle, I happened to walk by there; I saw the broken glass, policemen. People said, "It was the Surrealists." But it wasn't until two years later that I found out what Surrealism really was.

COLINA: But you had read the Surrealists?

BUÑUEL: I was just beginning to read them. Especially Benjamin Péret, whose poetic humor filled me with enthusiasm. Dalí and I read him, rolling on the floor with laughter. There was something in his work, a strange and perverse little engine, a delicious, convulsive humor. I tried to do something similar in my film *The Phantom of Liberty*, but without succeeding.

COLINA: I think there is one very obvious link between your films and Péret's poetry: gastronomy.

4 Madame Râchilde, pseudonym of the French hack, erotic novelist Marguerite Eymery (1860-1953) who, with her husband, Alfred Vallette, was a lifelong friend of Alfred Jarry, publishing his works, frequently receiving him in her home, and caring for him in his final poverty-stricken years. He immortalized her in his works, and she wrote an insightful biography: *Alfred Jarry ou le surmâle des lettres*.

BUÑUEL: That is one link, but there are many others. I admire Péret's variety of points of view. What a recreation of reality! Blind people, for example Péret wrote, *"N'est-ce pas vrai que la mortadelle est faite par des aveugles?"* ("Isn't it true that mortadella sausage is made by blind people?") What extraordinary exactitude! I know blind people don't make mortadella... And yet, they do. One can see them making it.

COLINA: I suppose you've read Ramón Gómez de la Serna,[5] who also has that kind of humor and poetry.

BUÑUEL: The first film I was given a chance to direct — the project I quit for *Un chien andalou* — I wrote with Ramón. It was called *El mundo por diez céntimos* (The World for a Dime). It showed how to make a newspaper, selling it in the street, the people who read it. The articles in the paper consisted of eight stories by Ramón. I worked with him for two days: I only gave some shape to the storyline, which was by Ramón. But then the project with Dalí arrived.

COLINA: The first question that arises is: why the title *Un chien andalou*? In his book, Aranda[6] said that some of you wanted to make fun of the Andalusian poets at the Residencia de Estudiantes.

BUÑUEL: That's not it at all. People find whatever allusions they want when they're determined to find references to themselves. Federico García Lorca and I were angry at each other for several years. When I was in New York in the 1930s, Angel del Río told me that Federico, who had also been there, had told him: "Buñuel has made a tiny pile of shit called *Un chien andalou*, and the Andalusian dog is me." But that wasn't it. *Un chien andalou* was the title of a book of poems I wrote. Dalí and I had thought about calling the film *Es peligroso asomarse al interior* (It Is Dangerous to Lean Inside), the reverse of what is always printed on train windows: "It is dangerous to lean outside." This seemed too literary to us. Then Dalí said, "Why don't we use the title of your book?" And that's what we did.

---

5 Ramón Gómez de la Serna (1891-1963), prolific and original Spanish writer whose works spanned almost all literary genres. He is considered a precursor of the avant-garde movement during the first decade of the century, especially for his *greguerías*, short prose pieces seldom more than two lines that mixed humor and metaphor.

6 Francisco Aranda, *Luis Buñuel: A Critical Biography* (New York: Da Capo Press, 1975).

3: *UN CHIEN ANDALOU* (AN ANDALUSIAN DOG) AND THE SURREALIST TRIAL

TOMAS PEREZ TURRENT: How did the project for *Un chien andalou* (An Andalusian Dog) first come about?

LUIS BUÑUEL: I became very interested in cinema around 1927 or 1928. I put together an evening of French avant-garde films in Madrid, and the program included Cavalcanti's *Rien que les heures, Entr'acte,* by René Clair,[1] and I can't remember what else. It was a huge success. Ortega y Gasset called me the next day and told me, "If I were young, I would dedicate myself to cinema." Juan Ramón Jiménez[2] was also *ébloui.* It was a great revelation because, though we were familiar with American movies, avant-garde films had yet to arrive in Spain. Later, while spending Christmas vacation with Salvador Dalí in Figueres, I suggested making a film with him. Dalí told me, "Last night I dreamed about ants swarming in my hand." And I said, "Well, I dreamed that I sliced someone's eye open." We wrote the script in six days. We understood each other so well that there were no arguments. We worked by accepting the first images that came into our minds while systematically rejecting anything that emerged from our culture or education. They had to be images that surprised us and we both accepted without argument. For example: the woman grabs a racquet to defend herself from the man who wants to attack her. Then he looks around, searching for something (now I am talking to Dalí): "What does he see?" "A flying frog." "Bad!" "A bottle of cognac." "Bad!" "Alright, I see two ropes." "Okay, but what comes after the ropes?" "The fellow pulls them and falls, because something very heavy is tied to them." "Good, I like that he falls." "With the ropes

---

1 *Rien que les heures* (1926), dir. Alberto Cavalcanti; *Entr'acte* (1924), dir. René Clair.
2 Juan Ramón Jiménez (1881-1958), Spanish poet and recipient of the Nobel Prize for Literature in 1956.

come two large gourds." "What else?" "Two Marist brothers." "And afterwards?" "A cannon." "Bad. A luxurious armchair." "No, a grand piano." "Very good, and on top of the piano is a mule... No, two rotting burros." "Magnificent!" That's how it would go; we had to suggest irrational images with no possible explanation.

TURRENT: Nevertheless, critics have attempted to find a logical explanation for it.

BUÑUEL: A cavalry captain in Zaragoza, a German professor, and many others have all coincided in the same explanations. "The man advances toward the woman: this is the sexual impulse; the ropes are moral impediments; the two cork mats: life's frivolity; the two gourds, testicles; the priests, religion; the piano, love's lyricism; and the burros, death." These images shouldn't be explained, they should be accepted for what they are. Do they repel me? Do they move me? Do they attract me? That should be enough.

JOSE DE LA COLINA: There appear to be certain analogies or metaphors. For example, the cloud that passes in front of the moon corresponds to the blade that cuts the eye. Naturally, one is inclined to explain this symbolically: it is a prologue that invites the audience to close their eyes, which only see appearances and facile poetry, and to attempt instead a profound vision, a Surrealist vision.

BUÑUEL: I don't deny that the film can be interpreted as you have just done. "Let's close our eyes to apparent reality and look inside the spirit." But I put the image in because it came to me in a dream and I knew it would repulse people.

TURRENT: What was it really? A cow's eye?

BUÑUEL: A calf's. With the hairs removed and made up.

TURRENT: Did Dalí participate in the filming?

BUÑUEL: No, I filmed it by myself. Dalí has come to say that every day during the filming I asked his advice about what to do. What a charmer! Dalí had told me to send him a telegram when I was about to finish. Two days before finishing, I telegraphed him and he came to the studio to watch the filming of the final scenes. The next-to-the-last scene was the one with the pianos and the burros.

COLINA: In *The Secret Life of Salvador Dalí*, he says he prepared the burros for that scene.

BUÑUEL: Yes, that he did do. I had two burros killed and stuffed with straw before making the film. Dalí added some fish to simulate putrification.

TURRENT: How was the film financed?

BUÑUEL: My mother had given me 25,000 pesetas (five thousand *duros*). She had given each of my sisters 10,000 *duros* so they could get married, and I asked for only 5,000 to make the film. In Paris, I ended up spending half this amount on cabarets and dinners with friends. And when I had only 12,500 pesetas left, which at that time was a lot (because the franc was very low: a bottle of champagne cost only one peseta), I decided to make the film, because I am a responsible man and didn't want to cheat my mother. I rented the Billancourt Studios; I paid the actors very little (but I did pay). I was my own producer for the first and only time in my life.

COLINA: Were there any union problems at the time you made the film?

BUÑUEL: None that I know of, no. Besides, there wouldn't have been any union problem because I was a "capitalist producer."

TURRENT: What was the first scene you shot?

BUÑUEL: It had to be something easy. I was afraid to start and I told myself, "Begin with the easiest." I believe it was the balcony scene, the one where I appear with the razor.

TURRENT: How did you put the crew together? For example, did you know Pierre Batcheff?

BUÑUEL: I met him when I was an assistant to Henri Etiévent and Mario Nalpas in a film with Josephine Baker, *Siren of the Tropics*. He was not just a handsome leading man, he was cultured and had intellectual inclinations. One day, Josephine Baker arrived at the studio at five in the afternoon when she had been told to arrive at nine a.m. She was fit to be tied because one of her little dogs had gotten sick, and she broke the mirror in her dressing room. This kind of thing made Batcheff furious. I commented, "That's cinema." He answered, "Maybe your cinema, but not mine." I told him he was right and we became friends. And so I called him for *Un chien andalou*. I had to look for the other actors. Fano Mesan, who plays with the severed hand in the film, was a girl who used to drink coffee with us sometimes in Montparnasse; she always dressed as a boy until one day she arrived dressed as a girl. The female lead was Simone Mareuil, who twenty or thirty years later committed suicide like a Buddhist monk. She poured two cans of gasoline on herself, lit a match, and began running through the woods covered in flames. Batcheff also committed suicide.

COLINA: How did you direct the actors?

BUÑUEL: I didn't let them see the script. I only told them, "Now look out the window; there is a military parade," or, "There, two drunks are fighting." In reality, that scene was linked to the scene about playing with the amputated hand. Neither the camera operator nor any of the crew knew anything about the story line.

COLINA: Nevertheless, the final result is very faithful to the script. When did you improvise?

BUÑUEL: No, I didn't say I improvised. I cut things out, here and also in *L'Age d'or*, but I didn't improvise. I knew more or less what I was going to do. For me, the script has always been the basis. What happens is that one detail can change everything. I can cut out a scene because I am very economical, and I have an intuition for what is necessary and what is superfluous. I take the script as the basis, because a film is only what you see on the screen. A bad script can be made into good film, depending on who makes it. On the other hand, sometimes very good scripts can be made into absolutely terrible films.

TURRENT: Carlos Velo told us a story about the ants that swarm in Batcheff's hand.

BUÑUEL: I had been to the Sierra del Guadarrama where there were very fat ants with red heads, which came out very well in close up. I asked a friend, Maynar, to send me some and he took them to Velo, who sent them to me in Paris in a piece of a rotting tree trunk inside a can.

TURRENT: Velo says those ants could also have been found in the French moors.

BUÑUEL: In Provence, surely. But I didn't know any entomologists in France.

COLINA: Who were the seminarians tied to the piano?

BUÑUEL: Miratvilles and my *régisseur*. In another shot, they were Miratvilles and Dalí. That scene was the only one the censors ordered me to cut: "*Couper les deux curés que l'on traine.*" ("Cut the two priests who are being pulled.")

TURRENT: The film still makes people shudder, even today.

BUÑUEL: The day following the first screening of it, the owners of Cinéma des Ursulines told me, "We're sorry. The film was well accepted yesterday, but we can't take it because the censors won't pass it." Then the people at Studio 28 asked me for it. They gave me 1,000 francs for it and it showed there for eight months. There were faintings, a miscarriage, more than thirty complaints were lodged at police headquarters. Today, times have changed. The Surrealists didn't attend the first screening.

Neither did Dalí, who had gone to Cadaqués to paint. My first contact with the Surrealists was with Louis Aragon and Man Ray in the restaurant La Coupole. I had finished the film and discovered that Man Ray was about to show *Le mystère du château de dé*,[3] which had been financed by the Vicomte de Noailles. Fernand Léger introduced me to Ray. I told him, "I believe you're about to show a film. I also have one that lasts twenty minutes and I would like you to see it." He introduced me to Aragon, who was at the bar. The next day the two of them saw my film and said they liked it very much. It premiered that evening and was attended by *le tout Paris*. As a precaution, I carried — I have told this story many times — stones in my pockets. The film was projected while I manned the gramophone. Arbitrarily, I put on an Argentine tango here, *Tristan and Isolde* there. Afterwards I intended to offer a Surrealist demonstration by throwing rocks at the audience. The applause disarmed me. The next day there was a lot of talk about the film, I was written up in the newspapers. I went to the Cyrano and there I was introduced to André Breton and the rest of the Surrealist group.

COLINA: Is it true the Surrealists put you on trial because *Un chien andalou* was so successful?

BUÑUEL: The trial was not because of that, although a few Surrealists did say that if a film directed against the public was so successful there must be something suspicious about it. The trial was for something else, the publication of the script in a magazine.

TURRENT: In the *Revue de Cinéma*. But what bothered the Surrealists about that?

BUÑUEL: The magazine had asked for the script and I gave it to them. A little while later, I joined the Surrealist group. There was a magazine in Brussels called *Varieté* that was going to devote an issue to the Surrealists, to be edited by them. Paul Éluard asked me for the script to *Un chien andalou* and I told him, "I'm very sorry but I gave it to the *Revue du Cinéma*." They asked me to withdraw it. "Impossible, I gave my word." They told me, "One's word does not count." I considered this to be unfair. "Fairness does not exist," Breton said. *"Il faut choisir: avec la police ou avec nous."* ("You must choose: with the police or with us.")

COLINA: That was the time of the Surrealists' greatest intransigence. Did you accept?

BUÑUEL: Completely. I had surrendered all my activity and hope to

3 *Le mystère du chateau de dé* (The Mystery of the Chateau of the Dice, 1929), dir. Man Ray.

Surrealism. That trial was a very grave matter for me. You two can understand: the Catholic church and the Soviet Union have been intransigent and they are still there. Aragon was the prosecutor and he went at it like a wild man, saying, *"Et bien, mon cher ami, je trouve tout ça detestable. Nos camarades..."* etc. ("Now then, my dear friend, I find all this detestable. Our comrades...") In the end, they suggested I go to the plant where the magazine was printed and destroy the lead plates it was printed from. "But I don't know where the lead plates are," I said, "and I might break the wrong thing. I don't know." They insisted and I obeyed. I bought a hammer that I hid under my raincoat as if it were a revolver, and Éluard and I went to see Gallimard, because the presses were located at the magazine offices. "I came to protest the publication of *Un chien andalou*," I told him. Gallimard was perplexed: "But you gave it to me voluntarily..." "Yes, as a matter of fact I did, but I have thought it over and have decided I want to withdraw it." "But it has already been printed and I can't do anything about it." We said good-bye to him, and I had to write a letter to twenty Parisian newspapers protesting that "I was a victim of abuse on the part of Mr. Gallimard. This capitalist...," etc. And the script also appeared in the next edition of *La révolution Surréaliste* with a note that said, "This is the only authorized publication of my script."

COLINA: Breton was very demanding. At the time when Dalí and you joined the group, the expulsions had already begun.

BUÑUEL: Yes, there had already been many. There were already about ten outside of the movement: Robert Desnos, Pierre Naville, Jacques Prévert, Georges Ribemont-Dessaignes, who published a *cadavre exquis* written against Breton. Alejo Capentier, who was unknown at that time, also signed it. It said, *"Breton est une ordure"* ("Breton is garbage") and other insults. At that time, I had been with the group for a year.

COLINA: Besides you, the remaining members were Dalí, Aragon, René Char, Éluard, Max Ernst, Péret, Francis Ponge, George Sadoul, Tristan Tzara, René Crevel, and others, who signed the *Second Surrealist Manifesto* and launched a new magazine called *Le Surréalisme au service de la révolution.* You all appear in a photo-montage, your portraits bordering the image of a nude woman with the caption...

BUÑUEL: Yes, all of us with our eyes closed and the woman in the middle, and a caption that read: *"Je ne vois pas la femme cachée dans la forêt."* ("I do not see the woman hidden in the forest.")

4: *L'AGE D'OR* AND THE ENSUING SCANDAL; THE MARQUIS DE SADE; THE DRUMS OF CALANDA

JOSE DE LA COLINA: How did it come about that the Vicomte de Noailles financed *L'Age d'or*?

LUIS BUÑUEL: After the premiere of *Un chien andalou*, Cocteau, who was enthusiastic about the film, advised the Vicomte de Noailles to call me and give me another project. Zervos, the editor of *Cahiers d'art*, told me, "Go see him. De Noailles is an extraordinary man, a marvelous Maecenas." Finally, one day when I went to see Zervos about something else, Noailles was there. He told me, "Cocteau, Auric, and Poulenc are all crazy about your film. Would you like to direct another one for us?" Two days later he sent the assistant director of the Musée de l'homme to my hotel to invite me to eat at his house. Sitting around the table after dinner, he insisted: "We would like to make a film with you...two reels, just like *Un chien andalou*. We have a commitment with Stravinsky, who is in Nice. You make the film and he will write the music." I turned him down because I didn't want to work with geniuses. Very kindly, Noailles told me, "Okay, make the film anyway you want, with or without music. Whatever you want." I thanked him and began to prepare *L'Age d'or*.

TOMAS PEREZ TURRENT: Did you begin writing it with Dalí?

BUÑUEL: By that time Dalí and I had ended our friendship. It happened after we worked together for three days. He was already very influenced by Gala. Whatever else she was, Gala would become Dalí's great love, but her influence on him was enormous and bad. Of course, they are really twin souls. So, just as *Un chien andalou* was a fraternal collaboration — resulting from friendship more than anything else, from an understanding so great we hardly ever argued about anything — with *L'Age d'or*, he now wanted to follow a very aestheticist line. After a couple of days I told him, "It looks to me like we can't continue. You are very influenced by

Gala (whom you know I can't stand), to the degree that there is a type of barrier between us as friends." I left and worked by myself. Gala and he spent their time travelling around Spain, and while I was still writing the script, he sent me a card proposing several ideas.

COLINA: Did you regret breaking off your friendship with Dalí?

BUÑUEL: A lot, because we had been great friends. At that time Dalí was a charmer. He came to Paris to see *Un chien andalou* with his sister and his aunt; every time they had to cross a street, the aunt, who was in the middle, would take Dalí's and his sister's hands and say, "Come on, children!" and then they would all run across the street. At that time, Dalí lacked any practical sense whatsoever. When I joined the Surrealist group, I showed them some photographs of his paintings and I was upset because they didn't like them. When Dalí arrived, I introduced him to the group and then they were impressed by his paintings. Within a short time, he was one of the most prominent Surrealists. The bad part was that Gala was a negative influence on him. When he introduced me to her, I have to admit she did not make a very good impression on me, but he was fascinated. Dalí is very asexual, almost androgynous, like the angels. And because of Gala, he ended up falling out with a lot of people. For example, he continues to be on bad terms with his sister María... Well, at the end of that summer, our friendship came to an end.

TURRENT: And when you began writing *L'Age d'or*, did you use the same system of free association of ideas you used in *Un chien andalou*?

BUÑUEL: No. I had about thirty gags: the cart that passed through the middle of a drawing room, the gamekeeper who kills his son for no reason, the defenestrated bishop, etc. Dalí had a few others, such as the man with the stone on his head, but we discovered that we disliked each other's ideas. "This is very bad," he would tell me. And I would say, "And this, it's terrible." There was no longer any *entente*. And besides, the first film and this one were different. There was no narrative line in *Un chien andalou*, and in *L'Age d'or* there was, a type of narrative very similar to that in *The Phantom of Liberty*, one that passes from one thing to another through some small detail.

COLINA: Did you film the documentary about the scorpions?

BUÑUEL: No. It was stock footage. I took four shots from the stock footage and included them. I wasn't bothered by the technical aspects of it, the photographic differences between the documentary — which was very old, from the days of silent movies — and the rest of the film.

COLINA: Yes, you can see that the shots of the scorpions were filmed on old orthochromatic film.

BUÑUEL: And with bad photography, but that's why I liked it. I wanted to do anything except please.

TURRENT: How much did *L'Age d'or* cost?

BUÑUEL: I can't remember very well. It must have been very cheap, about 260,000 old francs.

COLINA: Were all the people in the party sequence professional actors?

BUÑUEL: There were actors, extras, and a few friends, like Madame Victor Hugo, who was accompanied by the Catalan ceramicist Artigas, the one with the large moustache. Max Ernst and Pierre Prévert also acted in the film, appearing in the scene with the bandits. The crippled bandit is Pancho Cosío, a Spanish painter who died recently.

COLINA: Where were the scenes of the bandits shot?

BUÑUEL: At Cap de Creus, north of Cadaqués, close to the French border.

COLINA: That landscape is very beautiful and vigorous: the architectural form of the rocks and the calm sea under a full sun. Dalí has often painted at that spot. How long was the filming?

BUÑUEL: It lasted twenty-four days, or something like that.

COLINA: Did you use direct sound?

BUÑUEL: A technician from Berlin did the sound. The soundtrack was synchronized, not like now, but by guesswork.

COLINA: There is a formal brashness to the relation between the image and the soundtrack.

BUÑUEL: Yes, there is an idea that was later abused in cinema: the off-camera voice. The characters are seated in a garden, but the dialogue indicates they are in a bedroom: *"Approche ta tête, ici l'oreiller est plus frais... Tu as sommeil?"* (Move your head closer, the pillow is cooler over here. Are you sleepy?")

COLINA: And a very strong phrase: *"Quel joie d'avoir assassiné nos enfants!"* ("What a joy to have murdered our children!")

BUÑUEL: Yes, and they say that as if they were in bed. It was the first time spoken thoughts were used in film.

COLINA: The final scene is an homage to the Marquis de Sade. When did you read him?

BUÑUEL: A short time before making *L'Age d'or*. He impressed me a lot. During lunch at Tual's house, Robert Desnos talked to me about de Sade, whom I had never heard of. He gave me *120 Journées de Sodome* (120

Days of Sodom), the same copy Proust and Gide had read, because at that time de Sade's works were out of print. The edition was by a German professor, who only printed ten copies in 1905, and that was the only copy in France. In Sade I discovered a world of extraordinary subversion, one that included everything: from insects to social customs, sex, theology... In short, I was utterly dazzled.

COLINA: I would say there is an echo from de Sade's *Dialogue Between a Priest and a Dying Man* in *Nazarín*. The priest talks of heaven and the girl says, "Heaven no, I want Juan."

BUÑUEL: It's possible, even though in the *Dialogue* the dying man wins the priest over, while in *Nazarín* the girl continues to say, "I don't want heaven. I want my lover. I love the earth. I love Juan." It's a bit different, even if it is in the same spirit.

TURRENT: In *L'Age d'or*, there is a social criticism that is not evident in *Un chien andalou*.

BUÑUEL: There is no social criticism of any kind in *Un chien andalou*. In *L'Age d'or*, yes. There is a *parti pris* attack on what can be called bourgeois ideals: family, fatherland, and religion.

COLINA: Apparently, you considered giving the film a title taken from the *Communist Manifesto*: "In the icy waters of selfish calculation." It is when Marx says, more or less, that the bourgeoisie sacrificed the old ideals of the aristocracy for its own interests.

BUÑUEL: We thought of that title after the scandal and subsequent banning of the film. In order to continue showing it, the thought occurred to us to camouflage it with another title. It's a phrase in which Marx and Engels speak almost favorably of feudalism in comparison to the bourgeoisie. So we showed the film with this title, but the censors banned it anyway.

TURRENT: Did the censors discover that the title came from Marx and Engels? They seem to be very well read!

BUÑUEL: They became aware of the camouflage, of what the film was, and that it contained enough elements to warrant censorship.

TURRENT: Were you in Paris at this time?

BUÑUEL: No, in Hollywood. The de Noailles were charming aristocrats, liberal people, and for that reason they financed films without knowing very well what they were about. When I finished the film, I was invited to Hollywood. The de Noailles were delighted because all their friends and acquaintances adored cinema. They gave a private screening at ten a.m.

at the Panthéon cinema, close to the Sorbonne, with a rigorous guest list: Countess So-and-So, Princess Such and Such... *Le tout Paris!* The de Noailles received everyone at the door of the cinema as if they were in their own home: *"Bonjour, Madame la Marquise... Bonjour, Marie-Laure..."* Later, as they were leaving, the guests were indignant and didn't even say good-bye. De Noailles was expelled from the Jockey Club, of which he was president: out! The Pope was on the point of excommunicating him. Not me, who was unknown, but him, who had paid for this. De Noailles' mother had to go to Rome to resolve the matter there. It was a scandal. They were perplexed: "But, what did we do?" they kept asking. Within the intellectual atmosphere in which they lived, among the leading artists, they didn't think they had done anything so terrible. They were dumbfounded to see people leave the premiere without even talking to them.

TURRENT: So Prefect Chiappe banned the film?

BUÑUEL: First there was the attack by the Jeune Patriots and the Camelots du Roi.

TURRENT: Was the film exhibited commercially?

BUÑUEL: It had already been shown commercially at Studio 28. One night, one or two hundred fellows from the extreme right attacked the cinema. They brought axes and smoke bombs. They destroyed the seats and slashed a Dalí, a Tanguy, and other paintings that were on exhibit in the vestibule... I was in Hollywood, and I found out through the *Los Angeles Examiner.*

COLINA: Then you left for Hollywood shortly after finishing the film?

BUÑUEL: I went to Hollywood in November 1930. I found out about the scandal ten days after my arrival.

TURRENT: There is a specific reference to it in *Diary of a Chambermaid.*

BUÑUEL: No. There is only a right-wing demonstration.

TURRENT: But the protesters shout, "Long live Chiappe!" — the police prefect.

BUÑUEL: That's true. A coincidence.

COLINA: Returning to the innovations in the film, there are scenes where the sound deliberately clashes with the image. For example, in the protagonist's bedroom.

BUÑUEL: Yes. The wind starts coming out of the mirror and you hear a cowbell and the dog barking. From there, I intercut to the main character, at whom some dogs are barking in the street.

COLINA: Why did you chose Gaston Modot for the character?
BUÑUEL: I knew him from our group in Montparnasse. Modot had been a painter and companion of Picasso in 1912. He liked to play the guitar and was very pro-Spain. I noticed him because he was an actor, and a very good actor, too.
COLINA: I think his character is very different from the character in *Un chien andalou*. In the first we have a handsome type, "spiritual," who reminds me a bit of Antonin Artaud. In *L'Age d'or*, the character has the demeanor of a prim-and-proper rich kid, with a carefully trimmed moustache, hair combed with the part in the middle, etc.
BUÑUEL: Who? Modot? I can no longer remember how his hair was combed. But it's true: they are two very different characters.
TURRENT: And the actress, Lya Lys?
BUÑUEL: I chose her. She wasn't an actress and she was monstrously difficult to work with, but she was well liked and even got a contract from Hollywood to turn her into a "starlet." She failed there, even though she was very beautiful.
COLINA: Who played the orchestra conductor?
BUÑUEL: An old White Russian from around there. He was very brutish. I don't remember his name. I couldn't get everything I wanted from him. And I must say I didn't like how some things turned out. For example, the cross that comes out at the end. I had envisioned it as a cross covered with women's hair, blond and dark heads of hair, splendid; but it turned out hair only looks like that when it surrounds the head; hair hanging down stays limp like a horse's tail. I would have had to put up a sign: "This is a woman's head of hair."
COLINA: But in any case, the image is upsetting.
BUÑUEL: Yes, and it was accompanied by a Spanish *pasodoble*, *Gallito*. *(He hums it.)*
COLINA: Now that you mention *pasodobles*, I am reminded that you have never included bullfights in your films.
BUÑUEL: There is a bullfight in *La fièvre monte à El Pao*, but you can hardly see it. It is in the background of a scene. I have little use for the Spain of bullfights and *olé*.
COLINA: Didn't you once plan to make a film with the bullfighter Ignacio Sánchez Mejía? Aranda printed one of your letters in which you mentioned it.
BUÑUEL: I don't remember. Ignacio was a friend of all the poets of my

generation. He liked to mix with intellectuals, he bought drinks and dinner from time to time. An intelligent guy, interesting.

COLINA: Perhaps you would have had bullfights in the film you were planning to make about Goya.

BUÑUEL: That, yes. It was to have celebrated the centenary of Goya's death, and how happy I am not to have made that film, because of how it would have come out! I had submitted the project to a commission from Aragon and they accepted it. I went to Madrid to see Valle-Inclán, who also worked on the project, and I found myself at the Fine Arts League. He told me, "Well, I thought of making a film about Goya, but since you are the man of cinema, I think I will let you do it." Later, the project fell apart. By the way, there is another film I'm also glad not to have made: *Les caves du Vatican* (Lafcadio's Adventures). I worked with Gide for three days on it. Gide had written a pro-Soviet Union book and, to return the favor, they proposed filming *Les caves* in Moscow. Aragon and Couturier suggested that I direct it. I worked with Gide for three days, from five to seven p.m. And since I hadn't directed anything other than *Un chien andalou* and *L'Age d'or*, you can imagine what *Les caves du Vatican* would have been like directed by me in Moscow. Fortunately, the project was soon canceled.

TURRENT: A while ago when you cited the phrase about blind people and mortadella sausage, I remembered that there is a very sadistic scene involving a blind person in *L'Age d'or*.

COLINA: Blind people appear frequently in your films. The eye that is cut in *Un chien andalou*, the blind man who is kicked in *L'Age d'or*, the terrible blind man in *Los olvidados*...

BUÑUEL: And the blind men at the end of *The Milky Way*. The blind man who is miraculously cured, says: "Many thanks, Lord. A bird just flew by. I knew it because of the noise of its wings."

COLINA: And even when there are no blind people, there are images of aggression against eyes. For example, in *El*, Arturo de Córdova tries to blind the eyes he suspects are spying on the bedroom, and in *La mort en ce jardin*, they stab the jailer's eye with a penholder. Why this obsession?

BUÑUEL: I am not preoccupied by my obsessions. Why does grass grow in the garden? Because it is fertilized to do so.

COLINA: The "de Sadian" castle in the final scene of *L'Age d'or* is constructed with a very phony-looking set and façade.

BUÑUEL: Yes, very bad. Its fakeness is apparent even from far away. It looks like a toy, doesn't it?

TURRENT: And who played Christ?

BUÑUEL: Lionel Salem, who also played that role in French films made for Holy Week.

COLINA: The drum roll, is that from Calanda?

BUÑUEL: Yes, but they weren't Calanda drummers. For the recording, we used drummers from the Republican Band. There were twelve of them and I showed them how to play in the style of Calanda.

TURRENT: Is it true that you played those drums until your hands bled?

BUÑUEL: That happens in Calanda. Now there are more drummers, around a thousand. They play for twenty-four hours straight without stopping. And by the end the skin on the hands breaks and blood flows through the sheer force of gravity; that's why you see the drums marked by large blood stains. The drummers walk around town, beginning at twelve o'clock on Good Friday and they do not stop until noon on Holy Saturday. In fact, the tradition is not that old.

COLINA: Listen, Don Luis, returning to Sade, do you find anything reprehensible in his works?

BUÑUEL: Why?

TURRENT: Well, some people have presented Sade as a man who *a priori* justified concentration camps and Nazi crimes.

BUÑUEL: But, those are different things. Sade only committed his crimes in his imagination as a way to free himself of criminal desires. The imagination can permit all liberties. It is quite another thing for you to commit the act. The imagination is free, but man is not.

5: AN ERRANT SURREALIST IN HOLLYWOOD; *LAS HURDES* (LAND WITHOUT BREAD); THE BREAK WITH THE SURREALIST GROUP

JOSE DE LA COLINA: After *L'Age d'or*, you went to Hollywood?

LUIS BUÑUEL: Yes. The First Congress of Intellectuals was going to take place in Kharkov, and Aragon, Sadoul, and I thought about attending. Then Mr. Lorentz — who was in charge of Metro-Goldwyn-Mayer in Europe — called me and said, "Your film caught my attention. But you must see what it's like to make a film with everything Hollywood has to offer. You will get two hundred dollars a week just for observing how they work there. You'll spend a month in the studios, another in the editing room, etc., and later we'll see if you'll make a film with us." I told the Surrealists, "I can go to the Soviet Union whenever I want; I'll never go to America. I prefer to go to Hollywood now, as a representative of Surrealism." So Aragon and Sadoul went to Kharkov and I went to Hollywood. I was introduced to a supervisor from MGM who saw my contract and asked me where I would like to start. I said in the soundstages to observe a film in production. He looked at what appeared to be a strategic military map that he had in his office: "Stage 24. Would you like to go there?" He gave me a card with my name on it, and I went to the studio where they were doing a close-up of Greta Garbo. I kept myself at a respectable distance in order not to disturb anyone. Garbo, whose makeup was being touched up, glanced over and saw me. She spoke to some fellow with a small moustache, who came over and said something to me in English, but I didn't speak English, and he took me by the arm and threw me out of the studio. Well, I never went back, ever. But every Saturday I went to cash my check and eat at the studio restaurant. This was during Prohibition. (I knew a very good bootlegger who had had three fingers amputated, and he taught me how to tell if gin is real. He would shake the bottle and if it made bubbles, it was good; if not, it was poison. A small flask could cost five or six dollars.) One Saturday at the studio, I ran into Mr. Kilpatrick, who was an assistant producer, and he told me to go to a projection room to see a screen test of Lily Damita: "See if she speaks Spanish well." I answered, "Tell Mr. Thalberg that even though I'm Spanish, I'm here in the French section and I don't feel like listening to some whore." I considered this an appropriate answer coming from an errant Surrealist like myself. The next day my friends told me, "Well you've done it now. That is something you don't do here." The day after that I went to see Mr. Lewin and told him, "After what happened yesterday..." "What happened yesterday?" "In brief," I said, "I am here with a six-month contract. I have been here four. Pay me one more month and I'll leave." He accepted and I returned to Europe in April of 1931. (I had left in November 1930.) When I arrived, Aragon and Sadoul had already returned from Kharkov and the French authorities were going to try Aragon for his poem *Red Front*. I spoke with de Noailles and he gave me money so that Aragon could flee France. He went to Russia. For their part, Sadoul and Caupenne had written an offensive letter to a recent graduate of the Saint-Cyr military school. They caught Caupenne and made him apologize in front of everyone standing in formation at the Saint-Cyr school. De Noailles gave me four thousand francs for Sadoul, who fled to Russia so he wouldn't be arrested.

COLINA: What did you do when the Republic was proclaimed in Spain?

BUÑUEL: I arrived in Spain several days before the proclamation, a spectacle that moved me. Fifteen days later I returned to Paris and rejoined my friends. I was disoriented, but I didn't want to make any more films; the whole milieu repelled me: the public, the critics, the producers, etc.

COLINA: In what year did you return to Spain, after Hollywood and Paris?

BUÑUEL: I returned around 1934 because I had sciatica and wanted to recover. Warner Brothers offered me a job supervising their films in Spain. I was paid magnificently without having to do hardly anything. Warner had thirty films a year to dub into Spanish. I only chose the voices, corrected the dialogues, and then verified that the synchronization and sound were good. I was working at that when the revolution began in Asturias in October.

TOMAS PEREZ TURRENT: Let's retrace our steps, since *Las Hurdes* is from 1932. How did the project for *Las Hurdes* come about?

BUÑUEL: It came about because I had read the doctoral thesis of Legendre, director of the French Institute of Madrid. An admirable book, I still have it in my library. For twenty years Legendre spent every summer in Las Hurdes to conduct a complete study of the region: botanical, zoological, climatological, social, etc. A marvel! Later, I read some articles about the place that the Madrid magazine *Estampa* published when the king visited there.

COLINA: There is also an essay by Unamuno, in which he says, more or less, that within the Hurdanos' extreme need you can see the Spaniards' soul and dignity naked...

BUÑUEL: I was able to film *Las Hurdes* thanks to Ramón Acín, an anarchist from Huesca, a drawing teacher, who one day at a café in Zaragoza told me, "Luis, if I ever won the lottery, I would put up the money for you to make a film." He won a hundred thousand pesetas in the lottery and gave me twenty thousand to make the film. With four thousand I bought a Fiat; Pierre Unik came, under contract from *Vogue* to write an article; and Eli Lotar arrived with a camera loaned by Allegret.

COLINA: Acín gave you twenty thousand pesetas without making any demands about the film?

BUÑUEL: No, none of that. He told me, "If you return some of the money, so much the better..." Of course the film didn't make any money. Later, during Franco's 1936 uprising, he and his wife were shot by the rebels. First they took his wife prisoner and announced that they would shoot her if he did not turn himself in to the authorities. Acín presented himself. The next day he and his wife were both executed.

COLINA: How was the filming of *Las Hurdes?*

BUÑUEL: Eli Lotar, Pierre Unik, and Sánchez Ventura helped me. Las Hurdes was four hours by car from Madrid. It was a desert, but I found some Hurdanos who spoke French.

COLINA: Where did you stay?

BUÑUEL: At Las Batuecas. It is a paradise valley. Only one kilometer away, the Hurdano hell begins. We stayed at an inn that had been a convent managed by a Carmelite brother, who had stayed on as a layman. We slept there and left very early in the morning to film.

COLINA: In one scene the text reads, "At times, a goat falls from the rocks," but in the bottom corner of the image we see smoke from a gunshot. In other words, the goat didn't fall by accident.

BUÑUEL: Since we couldn't wait for the event to happen, I provoked it by firing a revolver. Later, we saw that the smoke from the gunshot appeared in the frame, but we couldn't repeat the scene because it would have angered the Hurdanos and they would have attacked us. (They don't kill goats. They only eat those that fall by accident.) Since the Hurdanos didn't have any firearms, I used a revolver because I couldn't find a rifle.

COLINA: The contradictions of cinema: to show the Hurdanos' poverty, you add to it by killing a goat.

BUÑUEL: It's true, but we were trying to show an image of life among the Hurdanos and we had to show everything. It's a very different thing to say, "At times a goat falls," than to show it as it really happens.

TURRENT: Did you ever return to Las Hurdes?

BUÑUEL: Many times, until the Civil War broke out. I was going to buy the monastery at Las Batuecas. It had nineteen chapels on its grounds and a marvelous convent in ruins, with an inn that could accommodate up to twenty people. Everything was wonderfully preserved. On July 14, 1936, I went to Salamanca and talked with the owner of the monastery, who was asking only thirty thousand *duros* for that wonderful property: the best orchard in Spain, with natural springs of medicinal waters. When I returned to Madrid so my mother could give me the money, the war broke out. If the Civil War had caught me at Las Batuecas, I wouldn't be here with you now to tell about it. I would have to speak to you through a Ouija board.

TURRENT: And have you been back there more recently?

BUÑUEL: Yes, some years ago I went to Las Hurdes. It had changed somewhat because it had become part of Franco's favorite region. There was electricity in some towns and they made bread everywhere.

COLINA: You film people were outsiders to the Hurdanos; they didn't receive you badly in 1932?

BUÑUEL: No, I brought a recommendation from Pascua, the Health secretary, and from Don Ricardo Urueta, the Fine Arts director, who were Republicans and very good friends of mine; they had given me permission to make an "artistic" film about Salamanca and a "picturesque" documentary about Las Hurdes.

COLINA: But how were your relations with the Hurdanos...?

BUÑUEL: They were good.

COLINA: What was the reaction to the film?

BUÑUEL: It was banned. Very worried, Ramón Acín asked me to do something about it. I went to see Dr. Gregorio Marañón, who was head of the government's local administrative bureau for Las Hurdes, and I asked him to see the film so that he could authorize its exhibition. We saw it together at a private screening at a cinema on the Gran Vía. Afterwards, Marañón stunned me. He said, "You went to La Alberca, and the only thing that occurred to you to do was to film a horrible and cruel party where they rip the heads off of live chickens. La Alberca boasts the most beautiful dances in the world and its peasants dress in magnificent costumes from the seventeenth century. And I want to tell you something, Buñuel, I've seen a good many carts full of wheat driving by in Las Hurdes." I told him, "Carts full of wheat in Las Hurdes? But I have been in seventeen *alquerías* where they didn't even know what bread is. You speak like a member of Lerroux's cabinet[1]... Good-bye." And the film continued to be banned.

COLINA: Marañón always took that kind of position. In his prologue to Cela's *La Familia de Pascual Duarte,* Marañón attacks the Spanish picaresque novel because it gives Spain a "bad image."

BUÑUEL: Don't you see that I'm right? Such blind nationalism is repugnant coming from a scientist like him. To say that the dances from La Alberca are the most beautiful in the world! It's the same as those who proclaim that their country has the world's most beautiful women and its bravest men. Lerroux's government issued a communiqué to the Spanish embassies in every country instructing them to lodge an official protest before the government of any country where *Las Hurdes* was shown. Later, during the war, Franco's rebels had a file on me which stated that I had made a film that was defamatory to Spain and that if I were arrested, I was to be taken to the Generalísimo's headquarters at Salamanca. The file was found at a Civil Guard barracks that the Republican troops took.

TURRENT: Did you use a script for *Las Hurdes?*

BUÑUEL: No. I visited the region ten days before the filming started and brought my notebook. I would jot down: "goats," "a child sick with malaria," "anopheles mosquitoes," "there are no songs, there is no bread," and I shot the film pretty much in agreement with those notes. I edited the film without using a moviola, on a kitchen table with a magni-

---

1 Alejandro Lerroux y García (1864-1949), Spanish politician, a radical and anticlerical revolutionary. During the Second Spanish Republic, he attacked the right wing during the so-called "Bienio Negro" (1934-36), when the Republican government passed through a reactionary phase.

fying glass and, since I still didn't understand much about cinema, I eliminated many of Lotar's good images because the photograms looked *flou*. I didn't know that movement can somehow reconstruct the image. So, by not having a moviola, I lost some good shots.

COLINA: Did the Hurdanos ever see the film?

BUÑUEL: Some of them saw it in Paris. There was a neighborhood in Saint Denis where fifteen thousand Spaniards lived. I showed the film and afterwards five Hurdano workers came to speak with me cordially. They liked the film very much.

TURRENT: Did you feel that the film was very different from *Un chien andalou* and *L'Age d'or*?

BUÑUEL: It was very different and yet, nevertheless, it was a twin. To me, it seemed very much like my other films. Of course, the difference was that this film was based on a concrete reality. But it was an exceptional reality, one that stimulated the imagination. Furthermore, the film coincided with the social concerns of the Surrealist movement, which were very intense at that time.

COLINA: Why did you use music by Brahms?

TURRENT: The Fourth Symphony. It drew a lot of attention because it's very romantic music.

BUÑUEL: There are only a handful of musical works that are etched in my brain in an obsessive way, and I've always searched for a way to use them in my films (even though I very rarely use music). They showed *Las Hurdes* in New York at a documentary makers' association, and this accompaniment caused a sensation. To me, it seems to go very well with the film. Why did I use it? It's something irrational, something I cannot explain.

TURRENT: Did you use it as a counterpoint or to create a distance?

BUÑUEL: I don't know. I heard it mentally while I was editing the film and felt it would go well with it.

TURRENT: Don't you think the fact that the commentary is in French and spoken by a Frenchman makes the film very neutral?

BUÑUEL: Yes. But also because the text itself is already very neutral. Pay attention to the end: "After so much time in Las Hurdes, let's now return to Madrid." That's how the commentary is, very dry, very documentary-like, without literary effects.

COLINA: I understand the sound was added much later.

BUÑUEL: Yes, since the film was banned during the so-called Black

Biennium, it was not given a sound track...

COLINA: The Black Biennium: the two years of the Republic when the right wing won the elections.

BUÑUEL: Yes, with Lerroux and Gil Robles. Later, in 1936, the war broke out, and then the Republican government gave me money to add a sound track. The ban was only during the Republic's reactionary phase.

TURRENT: Many people have said, and I agree, that *Las Hurdes* is like a response to *Un chien andalou* and *L'Age d'or*.

BUÑUEL: It's in the same line. The first two are imaginative, the other is taken from reality, but I feel it shares the same outlook.

TURRENT: But while the first two are films of revolt, *Las Hurdes* explains the reason for the revolt. You also changed genres and made a documentary. What were your ideas about documentary filmmaking?

BUÑUEL: I had no preconceived idea. I visited the region, read the book by Legendre, and since cinema is my means of expression, I made the film without *parti pris* of any sort.

COLINA: Is there some reason that one of the characters in *The Phantom of Liberty* is named Legendre, like the author of the book about Las Hurdes?

BUÑUEL: Is there a character named Legendre? Then I must have used it like any other last name.

COLINA: A case of involuntary memory?

BUÑUEL: It is a family name that appears with some frequency in France, and I didn't use it with any intention. It is as if I were to make a film about the army with a colonel named De la Colina. I hope you wouldn't take offense.

TURRENT: Don Luis, by filming reality as you see it, do you believe you faithfully follow the Surrealist spirit?

BUÑUEL: Yes, yes, yes, of course. We're talking about a tendentious film. Such poverty doesn't exist in Las Hurdes Bajas. Of the fifty-two communities or *alquerías*, as they call them, there are around thirty that have neither bread, nor chimneys, nor songs. I photographed Las Hurdes Bajas in passing, but almost the entire film occurs in Las Hurdes Altas, which are mountains like infernos, a series of arid gulches, a bit like the desert landscape of Chihuahua, but much smaller.

TURRENT: I read one critic who said that the film is a declaration in favor of euthanasia.

BUÑUEL: Of euthanasia? *(He laughs.)*

COLINA: Did the Surrealists see the film?

BUÑUEL: I don't remember. Perhaps when it was shown in France. I was already outside the group.

COLINA: Did you leave the group voluntarily?

BUÑUEL: Completely voluntarily. Aragon, Sadoul, Unik, Maxime Alexandre, and I all left at the same time.

COLINA: Aragon and Sadoul had parted from the group because they were already in the Communist Party, but as far as I know you never became a militant Communist.

BUÑUEL: No. I was a sympathizer, no more. Especially during the Spanish Civil War.

COLINA: Then why did you break with the group?

BUÑUEL: I was more uncompromising about more things than they were. I believe in intransigence. When I saw an enormous portrait of Éluard or of Breton in a bookstore on the Boulevard Raspail, it infuriated me. They put out *Minotaure,* a luxurious magazine. All this began to bother me. They gave themselves a lot of publicity. Before, they had fought publicity; now they fell into it. That was one of the reasons that led to my break. Later, they reacted very badly to the Fascists' attack at the Place de la Concorde in 1934. I remember I went to see Dalí the next day. He was sculpting a woman with enormous buttocks in clay. I said to him: "Did you see what happened in the street? It's terrible, something has to be done." He answered, "I don't give a damn. These buttocks interest me more." That is: the total separation of life and art. They were already falling into exactly what they had criticized so much. I always continued my relationship with Breton, but I broke with the group.

TURRENT: Returning to *Las Hurdes,* did the documentary footage on the mosquito have the same intention as that of the scorpions in *L'Age d'or?*

BUÑUEL: No. I put it in as one more element of information, to demonstrate that malaria was a component of Hurdano poverty.

COLINA: So, this bug isn't gratuitous the way the scorpions were in *L'Age d'or.*

BUÑUEL: No. Nothing is gratuitous in *Las Hurdes.* It is perhaps the least gratuitous film I have made.

6: *WUTHERING HEIGHTS;* FILMOFONO; THE SPANISH CIVIL WAR; RETURN TO HOLLYWOOD; THE FINAL BREAK WITH DALI; THE MOVE TO MEXICO

JOSE DE LA COLINA: During the 1930s, Pierre Unik, Sadoul, and you adapted *Wuthering Heights*, a book the Surrealists liked very much.

LUIS BUÑUEL: Yes, we were attracted to everything about savage love, *l'amour fou.* We also liked *Là-bas,* by Huysmans, a spiritual return to the Middle Ages, the evocation of the figure of Gilles de Rais. De Rais is wonderful, isn't he? A Christian knight and comrade of Joan of Arc, who committed those terrible crimes, and then when they punished him, the people cried with him and even forgave him. But *Là-bas* posed the problem of recreating the Middle Ages, an era that is both barbarous and delicate and one that I love, but to make a film — it would require a lot of production.

COLINA: Had any producer offered to make *Wuthering Heights*?

BUÑUEL: No. I proposed it (and it's one of the few times I have proposed a film) to Noailles, who recommended me to a very rich lady, whose name I can't remember at the moment; she was a sort of Egyptian princess: a Soraya of those times, let's say. I gave up on the project because I realized it could end up as a commercial film, something I detested because I was already a Surrealist, body and soul. For me, Surrealism was not an aesthetic, just another avant-garde movement; it was something to which I committed myself in a spiritual and moral way. You two can't imagine the loyalty Surrealism demanded in all aspects of life. Actually, after *Las Hurdes* I didn't want to make any more films, in order not to fall into the industrial production trap.

COLINA: But at that time you were working on dubbing films.

BUÑUEL: That, yes. I did it to make a living while doing something that would also allow me to acquire technical knowledge. It was useful when I later worked as an executive producer in Spain. With dubbing — from

English into Spanish — my job consisted of translating and measuring texts so that the words corresponded to the lip movements of the English-speaking actors. Later, I was promoted to director of dubbing, which at the time was something that paid very well. I had that job for two years.

COLINA: Did you consider abandoning all your artistic and intellectual activities?

BUÑUEL: I was more concerned with the political and social situation of Spain and the problems of the Republic. Besides, Jeanne and I had gotten married in 1934.

TOMAS PEREZ TURRENT: The dubbing into Spanish, was it done in France or Spain?

BUÑUEL: Warner Brothers sent me to Spain as a supervisor. It was the time in my life when I was paid the most money for doing nothing, or practically nothing.

COLINA: And the four Spanish films you made?

BUÑUEL: Those from Filmófono? My name doesn't even appear in the credits. Two were directed by Sáenz de Heredia, one by Marquina, and the other by Grémillon. I was only the executive producer: I supervised the script, the work at the studio, the sound recording... My job was to keep an eye on the production so it would stay within the budget. The first film, *Don Quintín el amargao*, was a tremendous success.

COLINA: An indiscreet question: did you feel like you were abandoning your Surrealist conscience when you made those films, which are a bit like the "tourists' Spain," with folklore, sentimental speeches, etc.?

BUÑUEL: Yes, I had a guilty conscience. Even though I neither wrote nor directed those commercial ventures and only participated on a technical level, I was contributing to the kind of films I hated.

COLINA: Which is to say, the Spain that you rejected: the large estates, the castanets, the *señoritismo* tradition...

BUÑUEL: Well, I don't think I went that low. *(He laughs.)*

COLINA: It is one of my provocations, Don Luis.

BUÑUEL: I know, I know...!

COLINA: I believe the tone of those films is reminiscent of Arniches, who is an interesting author.

BUÑUEL: Yes, the films were a bit like Arniches.[1] In a certain way, I

1 Carlos Arniches y Barrera (1866-1943), playwright who raised the quality of a minor Spanish genre, the *sainete*. He was very successful with both critics and the general public. His works are characterized by a sharp observation of popular life, sentimentality, an ear for the spoken language, and light good-natured humor.

always liked Arniches, even though I didn't agree with the type of society he presented in his *sainetes*. Two of the Filmófono films were adapted from Arniches: *Don Quintín* and *¡Centinela alerta!*

TURRENT: Why did you hire Jean Grémillon[2] as director?

BUÑUEL: We hired very cheap directors. Luis Marquina, who went from sound engineer to director, was paid a thousand pesetas. He was the son of the poet.

TURRENT: But why Grémillon?

BUÑUEL: Grémillon adored Spain. I wrote to him: "Dear Jean, make a film with us and spend a month and a half in Spain." He accepted, came to Spain, and, with admirable skepticism, made a film. One day he told me, "I won't be there tomorrow, Luis. I have to go to the dentist." I said, "Very well, but what are we going to do with this scene?" "Do whatever you want." So I directed the scene. While making the film, we poked fun at ourselves frequently.

COLINA: And how did the films do commercially?

BUÑUEL: The first two were an enormous success. The third was not. The last one, *¡Centinela alerta!* (Guard Alert!), was finished during the war.

COLINA: Because of that and also the title, one tends to think the film is *engagé*.

BUÑUEL: But it had nothing to do with that. It was a sort of musical comedy featuring the singer Angelillo.

COLINA: I read that in the second Filmófono film, *La hija de Juan Simón* (Juan Simón's Daughter), you appear singing in a jail. What did you sing, *jotas* from Aragon?

BUÑUEL: None of that is true. Neither in jail nor in freedom, nor anywhere else have I sung *jotas*, nor do I sing at all.

TURRENT: I saw those films here in Mexico in my childhood, around 1943. I can hardly remember them.

BUÑUEL: I gave the films to Mexico's National Cinémathèque. When I came here there were ten very damaged prints of *Don Quintín*. Of those ten, I managed to splice together one decent print.

COLINA: When you returned to Spain, how were things with your friends from the Residencia de Estudiantes?

2 Jean Grémillon (1901-1959), considered by the French as one of their most personal directors. Despite making such acclaimed films as *Remorques, Lumière d'été,* and *Le ciel est a vous,* he frequently found it difficult to get funding. Grémillon was president of the Cinémathèque Française from 1943 to 1958.

BUÑUEL: It was the time when Federico García Lorca's plays were given large premieres, and he and I saw each other with some frequency. But I no longer went to the *peñas* at the cafés.

COLINA: What was the political climate in Spain?

BUÑUEL: Until 1927, the so-called Generation of '27 was not politicized. As the Republic took shape, there was a great change: everyone began to take sides. For example: Giménez Caballero and Eugenio Montes became Fascists, Alberti became a Communist, and with the approach of the Civil War people talked about nothing but politics. The situation was asphyxiating. There was a feeling that things would explode.

COLINA: Did you participate actively in politics?

BUÑUEL: Very little; I did do something, but I prefer not to deal with it here.

COLINA: I believe you were in Madrid when the Falange was born.

BUÑUEL: That was in 1931. I brought *L'Age d'or* to Madrid. Friends and acquaintances had raised five hundred *duros* to pay for the print, the trip, customs duties, etc. The entire Madrid intelligentsia attended the film's only screening. In a book, Agustín de Foxá tells how he and Alberti were walking to see *L'Age d'or* when they encountered two youths who told them they were going to José Antonio Primo de Rivera's rally. Foxá changed his plans, went to the rally, and left it an enthusiastic Falangist.

COLINA: When the war broke out, where were you?

BUÑUEL: In Madrid. Writers, artists, and intellectuals joined together immediately in defense of the Republic. I also offered my services to the Republican cause. I never got as far as putting my feet in a trench, because after two months I was sent to the Spanish Embassy in Paris as a cultural attaché. For that reason, I made frequent trips between Spain and France.

COLINA: What was your job in the Republican "war film" effort?

BUÑUEL: Among other things, I was put in charge of film propaganda at the embassy. Le Chanois edited a film[3] with material I had received and supervised. Some books have claimed this film as mine, but that is not the case.

COLINA: What did you think of Joris Ivens' film *Tierra de España* (The Spanish Earth, 1937)?

BUÑUEL: I don't know what I would think of it now, but at the time the

---

3 *España leal en armas/España 1937* (1937), a four-reel documentary with material filmed by Roman Karmen. The film was directed and edited by J.P. Dreyfus, pseudonym for Jean Paul Le Chanois, with commentary written by Pierre Unik and Luis Buñuel.

film seemed very good. It showed that our army was not made up of murderers, but disciplined people with a political sense.

TURRENT: And Malraux's film *L'Espoir?*

BUÑUEL: I didn't work on that at all. The one who worked with Malraux
was Max Aub.[4] We paid for the film there in Paris, and I sent the money.
I liked it a lot, except for the last part. That final moment, when thousands of peasants were mobilized and formed a kind of enormous funeral
march because of the death of an aviator is not believable. Can you imagine it: so many men mobilizing just to bury one more soldier! Beautiful
framing, an interminable line of peasants zigzagging through the mountains, a flag... Cheap cinematic eloquence... On the other hand, I did like
the episode about the peasant who was taken up in a plane to observe the
Teruel territory. The peasant knows the area like the back of his hand
because he has always lived and worked there, but he knows it from down
there, at the height of a man. And, of course, he can't recognize anything
from the air and is of no help. That is very authentic. It moved me.

COLINA: During the war you made your second trip to Hollywood.

BUÑUEL: They were going to make two or three films there about our
war favorable to our cause, and the Republican government sent me there
as a supervisor. This was some ten months before the end of the war.
Metro was going to film *Cargo of Innocents,* which dealt with Spanish
children who came as refugees by ship from Bilbao to the United States.
They also made *Blockade,* with Henry Fonda.[5] They were well-intentioned films — with errors perhaps — and they didn't want to take a
stand on certain political questions, but they were favorable to us. The
mere fact that a film was not against us was good. But there was also pressure on the U.S. government not to help us. Hemingway and Ivens told
me that they had lunch with President Roosevelt; the interview was very
moving and Roosevelt told them that, while his heart was with us, the
U.S. Catholics were applying pressure on the government not to take
sides. I believe he was sincere. We had many sympathizers in Hollywood,
including people who were not political but were indignant over the
injustice. In Hollywood, they wrote up a declaration in our favor which,
by the way, Charlie Chaplin totally refused to sign. Well... when I arrived,

---

4 Max Aub, Spanish writer of French-Jewish origin (1903-1970). His highly regarded work
  covered all genres; in Mexico, he wrote screenplays for quality commercial films. He died
  before finishing his monumental book on Buñuel, a mixture of biography and essay; his
  notes were published in 1984 under the title *Conversaciones con Buñuel* (Madrid: Aguilar).
5 *Blockade* (1938), dir. William Dieterle.

I introduced myself to the producer Frank Davis, who was very much a leftist, and I told him that since I was paid by my government, I wanted to work for them for free as a technical adviser. The Hollywood films that dealt with our war contained incredible mistakes and they had to be corrected. Davis accepted, but the movie was ultimately suspended because the U.S. film producers' association agreed not to make any films on the subject, either for or against the Spanish Republic. I wrote a letter to our government's ambassador in Washington, placing myself at his disposal to go to the front when my contingent was called up. I was waiting for his response when we lost the war. I found myself in the United States without work. I couldn't work in cinema because I had a bad reputation in Hollywood. My earlier experience, as you remember, didn't exactly recommend me. I also didn't feel like it... After the way our war had ended, few things interested me. I could live thanks to a few dollars some friends and my wife's sister sent me, telling me to pay them back whenever I could. And I was left there, trapped.

TURRENT: How did you begin working at the Museum of Modern Art?

BUÑUEL: Dick Abbot and Iris Barry took me to New York. I left my wife and two-year-old son in California. The Second World War had begun, and they had founded the Office for Coordination of Inter-American Affairs, sponsored by Rockefeller; I was installed at the museum to work on documentaries in an office for Allied film propaganda for Latin America. This interested Roosevelt a lot and, thanks to Iris Barry, I began working there. I edited scenes from Leni Reifenstahl's *Triumph of the Will* along with a film about the invasion of Poland for Roosevelt and the senators.[6] It made quite an impression: there were at least three reels of S.S. forces goose-stepping to music by Wagner. It was gut-wrenching, and even more so when you had to see the images again and again on the editing table. A nightmare. René Clair told me, "It would be better not to show this film because the effect would be terrible. It gives the impression that Fascism is invincible." Clair was horror-stricken, but Chaplin laughed uproariously; apparently he found Hitler very funny. The film was shown in all Latin American countries for free, at schools and clubs, etc. It was withdrawn at the end of the war: the winds had changed and it no longer seemed convenient to attack Fascism.

TURRENT: Did you have any plans for a film of your own?

6 *Triumph of Will* (1939), a 9-reel montage composed of material from Leni Riefenstahl's *The Triumph of the Will* (Triumph des Willens, 1935) and Hans Bertram's *Baptism of Fire* (Vuurdoop, 1939). See Buñuel's filmography.

BUÑUEL: I had two projects. At that time, many of the Surrealists were in the United States: Breton, Marcel Duchamp, Ernst, Yves Tanguy... Also the painter Ferdnand Léger, the anthropologist Claude Lévi-Strauss... A short time ago Delphine Seyrig told me, "When I was a girl, I sat on your lap at our house in New York. I remember you very well because of your bulging eyes." I saw Léger and Duchamp and we planned to make a pornographic movie that we would film on a terrace in New York. We thought it would be a scandal. Nowadays, scandal isn't what it used to be: now it only serves to fatten dozens of producers. I also had a project about schizophrenia: a film about how the disease begins, how it develops, and how it is cured. But some psychoanalysts are very reactionary. Mr. Schlesinger wanted to make a film with me. He knew a psychoanalyst, Dr. Alexander, director of a clinic in Chicago. Alexander wanted them to show him *Un chien Andalu,* and afterwards he wrote Schlesinger a letter: "We were scared to death watching Buñuel's film. It is abominable: instead of curing complexes, it creates them." And there the project ended.

COLINA: That reminds me of Freud's rejection of the Surrealists.

BUÑUEL: Jung saw *Un chien andalou* (in Zurich, I believe) and said that it was a case of *dementia praecox.*

TURRENT: Did you see the other Surrealists in New York?

BUÑUEL: Yes. At the house of a millionaire whose name I no longer remember, during the black-outs that sometimes happened while we were playing the "game of truth," which consisted of questions and answers. There were Breton, Leonora Carrington and her husband, the Mexican poet Renato Leduc. Leonora, who was a beautiful woman, gazed at me with affection and said, "You look so much like the orderly I had at the mental institution in Santander!" At times, the millionaire owner of the house would offer some timid comment about art or literature, and Breton, who was always so intransigent, would say to him, *"Monsieur, vous nous emmerdez. Sortez d'ici!"* ("Sir, you're pissing us off. Get out of here!"). And the millionaire would leave his own home.

COLINA: In some interviews, you said *The Secret Life of Salvador Dalí* — which Dalí, who had already become *Avida Dollars,* in Breton's anagram, had written himself — was the reason you left the Museum of Modern Art. It's a surprising fact. How did it happen?

BUÑUEL: A certain Prendergast, who represented Catholic interests in Washington, after reading what Dalí had said in that book... Have you two read it?

COLINA: I have here a paragraph by Dalí: "Buñuel filmed *L'Age d'or* alone, practically leaving me out altogether." Later: "Buñuel finished *L'Age d'or*. I was terribly disappointed. The film was no more than a caricature of my ideas. He attacked Catholicism in a primitive manner and with no poetry whatsoever. Nevertheless, the film produced a considerable impression, particularly the frustrated love scene when the unsatisfied leading man was voluptuously sucking the big toe of the statue." In fact, it was the woman. I will continue reading a bit further on: "In the film, a luxurious automobile is seen stopping, the chauffeur dressed in livery opens the door and takes out a monstrance to deposit it in close-up in the street." Later, Dalí describes the screening when the Fascists attacked the cinema. And, some paragraphs lower, he adds: "I accepted the responsibility for the sacrilege, even though it was not my intention." And, in a footnote: "Later, when Buñuel expunged his most frenetic passages from *L'Age d'or*, with the goal of adapting it to Marxist ideology..." Dalí accuses you of, well, sacrilege and of being a "red."

BUÑUEL: Yes. And this Prendergast, who knew nothing about me until he read the book, spent a year pressuring the museum to throw me out. One day an article in the *Motion Picture Herald* reported, from what I remember: "This strange character, who works at New York's Museum of Modern Art, has made a scandalous film, one that provoked a right-wing attack on the cinema where the film was being shown, and the police had to be called in to break it up." This appeared the same day the Americans were disembarking in Morocco. When I saw Iris Barry — thanks to whom I was working at the museum, and who was also a very good friend of mine — she received me almost in tears, and told me some people had been trying for a year to get rid of me, and would have succeeded except for the directors and an in-law of Rockefeller — the architect of the Rockefeller Center — who opposed them. I said that at a time like that, with the Allies disembarking in Morocco, my case had no importance and I didn't want to cause problems. I tendered my resignation, they accepted it...and I ended up in the street. I had a wife and two sons and only three hundred dollars to my name. One day I talked with Dalí at the Sherry Netherland Hotel. "This happened to me and it is all your fault," I told him. "It seems like a dirty trick to me." He answered, "I wrote a book to put myself on a pedestal, not to put you on one." We continued talking a bit and finally I left without busting him in the face. And there our friendship ended definitively.

TURRENT: We understand that during this period you worked at the film unit for the Marine Corps.

BUÑUEL: After my departure from the Museum, I was contracted by Vladimir Pozner, who had been a director of cinematography in Moscow. Pozner was a very good friend of the head of Metro-Goldwyn-Mayer, where they dubbed propaganda films. *Le Génie* (the military engineers) made short films about azimuths, parallaxes, howitzers, etc., in various languages: English, Spanish, Portuguese... I did the Spanish voice-overs: "The azimuth rises twenty-five by thirty-three, it fires to four by five..." They paid me two hundred fifty dollars per reel. I spoke and spoke, and I must have done it badly because my pronunciation and my Spanish accent are ferocious for Latin America: I lisped every "z" and hissed every "j"! That enabled me to live for three or four months. Later, I went to Hollywood with a producer's contract from Warner. They calculated that the war was almost over and they wanted to make Spanish-language versions of their films for the European market, which would immediately open up. In other words, they wanted to make the same films they made in English, with the same script, the same shots, but substituting the English-speaking cast for one that spoke Spanish, as they had done in the 1930s. I was in charge of producing the Spanish versions. I arrived with a contract and spent a month without doing anything. In the end, Warner decided that since Europe would be avid to see real American films, it was better just to dub them, and besides it would be cheaper: Europeans would see Humphrey Bogart, not a substitute. I was named head of the dubbing section and assigned some thirty employees: writers, actors, etc. As with my job at Warner in Spain, I had very little work: simply revising the translation, measuring the movements of the lips, selecting the voices... I worked at this for a year and a half.

COLINA: Didn't you plan a sequence for a film by Robert Florey?

BUÑUEL: *The Beast With Five Fingers*. I wrote it in order to charge them for an entire sequence, even though it was not filmed (I needed money). I imagined a cut-off hand that had a life of its own. Later, they filmed it and didn't pay me anything. I wanted to sue the company but I was already here in Mexico and I decided against it. I received my salary at the company, but that was a job I did on the side. As you two remember, there was already a scene with an amputated hand in *Un chien Andalou*. I also used a severed hand that moved in *The Exterminating Angel*.

TURRENT: And didn't you want to go back to directing films?

BUÑUEL: At that time, it seemed difficult to me, but yes, I did. After seeing so many films being dubbed! But I thought I would never be able to make a film in Hollywood.

TURRENT: And so you came to Mexico...

BUÑUEL: When they suspended the production of films in Spanish, I spent eight months in Hollywood using up all the money I had saved. I had asked for citizenship papers and was going to become an American citizen. At a dinner at René Clair's house, Pierre Batcheff's widow, Denise Tual, who was beginning to produce films, told me that she had the film rights to *La casa de Bernarda Alba,* by Federico García Lorca. With the war recently over, the play had been performed with great success in Paris. Denise wanted to film it in France and I was to direct it. En route to France, we made a short trip to Mexico because Denise had to arrange some matters here, to talk with Oscar Dancigers,[7] etc. From the Hotel Montejo I called Paquito García Lorca, who was in New York with his parents and sisters. Paquito told us that he could get much more money for the rights to Federico's play in London, and that the family was not in very good financial shape. In that case, I told him, sell the play to the highest bidder. I told Denise, "The play is sold. We can't make the movie." Denise returned to Paris. At a dinner in the house of the Spanish architect Mariano Benlliure, the Mexican writer Fernando Benítez who was also secretary to the Interior Minister, told me that if I wanted to stay in Mexico he could help me with the paperwork. The next day I went to the ministry and Benítez introduced me to the minister, Héctor Pérez Martínez, a very friendly man, who was also a writer and favorable towards Spaniards. "Return to the United States and we will issue an order to the Consulate so you can come and live in this country." I went back to Hollywood, sold the furniture I had there, and when the papers arrived, I came to Mexico, this time with Jeanne and the boys. Dancigers had already contracted me to make a film...which turned out to be *Gran Casino.*

---

7 Oscar Dancigers, film producer born in Russia. After WWI he moved to Paris with his brother and acquired French citizenship. Fleeing from the Nazis, he moved to Mexico in 1940 and resumed his career, producing quality commercial films.

7: *GRAN CASINO; ILEGIBLE, HIJO DE FLAUTA;*
EL GRAN CALAVERA (THE GREAT MADCAP)

GRAN CASINO OR *EN EL VIEJO TAMPICO*

TOMAS PEREZ TURRENT: What did you think of the story line of *Gran Casino*? As one who was so intransigent a Surrealist in the 1930s, what did you think about making such a commercial film?

LUIS BUÑUEL: I thought it very bad, but I didn't give it much importance. Years had passed, we had lost the war, and I said to myself, "So much the worse!" Besides, I was interested in a career in cinema, working in the studio, the organization. On the other hand, since I had already been a producer at Filmófono and I knew the various aspects of the industry on different levels, I could work fast, which was how everyone was used to working in Mexican cinema. When I read the story of *Gran Casino*, which I adapted with Mauricio Magdaleno and Edmundo Báez — because I always worked on the scripts, even the bad ones! — I told myself, "This is a little adventure novel. Is there anything my conscience can't bear? No? Well then, let's get going."

TURRENT: For example, the film has no sentimentality.

BUÑUEL: And if it did, I took it out.

TURRENT: You even eliminated the inevitable kisses between the film's stars, and how you did it is famous: Libertad Lamarque[1] and Jorge Negrete[2] are enemies, but in one scene they begin arguing and start to fall

---

1 Libertad Lamarque: Born in 1908, singer-actress Lamarque was Argentina's most popular leading lady, usually in sentimental melodramas. She also acted in many Mexican films in the 1940s and '50s.

2 Jorge Negrete, Mexican actor and singer, and star of many popular ranch comedies where he played the singing-cowboy in a series of films idealizing Mexico's "charro" (cowboy) tradition. He played the epitome of the romantic rancher, an honest plain-speaking *macho*, a somewhat boastful, skirt-chasing adventurer prone to burst into serenade at the sight of a beautiful woman.

in love; just when they are going to give each other the inevitable kiss, the camera breaks away from them and frames a puddle of mud or tar. Negrete stirs this puddle with a small branch while the invisible kiss goes on offscreen.

BUÑUEL: There is not one kiss in the entire film. The scene you remember is handled so as to avoid the moment of conventional and mediocre love, the melodrama. Imagine the scene: "You want to kill my brother and for that I want to kill you. We hate each other, but deep down we love each other... My love!" And a kiss! It couldn't be. I gave Negrete a stick and told him to play around distractedly with it. Later I filmed a close-up of a hand stirring the mud or tar with the stick, and I intercut it into the love scene in order to clean it of mushiness.

JOSE DE LA COLINA: It's impressive because in love films you usually see the camera break from the lovers and frame some detail in the bedroom or garden, a clock or a flower or a moon...but a puddle of mud or tar! It seems like an internal criticism, as if you were saying to yourself, "This is a crock!"

BUÑUEL: I haven't seen the film again. Jorge Negrete didn't protest. Had he been paying attention, Negrete would have shot me.

TURRENT: Besides the scene with the puddle, I like it that, without worrying a lot about believability, every time Negrete begins to sing, the folk music trio Los Calaveras appears as if by magic and they wave to each other.

BUÑUEL: The stars were two singers so I had to put in songs. To me, filming songs seemed boring and I made sure to put in some details that amused me in order not to make a realistic film, accentuating its lack of logic and breaking the monotony.

TURRENT: During the filming, a journalist wrote a well-intended article — the man at least knew you had made *Un chien andalou* and *L'Age d'or* — in which he said you had many difficulties while working, that you were a "prisoner" of cinema.

BUÑUEL: Yes, there were difficulties. Tampico...at the time depicted in the story, before petroleum was nationalized, the oil companies were foreign and in Tampico there were many English and Dutch people, but the extras didn't give the impression of being foreign. I also had problems with the cinematographer, Jack Draper, who was — everyone knows — a bad-tempered and vulgar man. If Negrete hadn't intervened, it would have ended badly. I had no problems with the actors or technicians, although at times I didn't respect the 180-degree camera angles.

COLINA: You crossed the axis, as they say in the trade; that is generally considered a serious infraction of conventional film language, because it upsets spatial relations.

BUÑUEL: Yes, because supposedly in one shot the actor looks at someone else in the same direction as in another shot and by "crossing the axis," he looks elsewhere. But I often did this on purpose. That's their tough luck! I could care less. I was experimenting with changing angles.

COLINA: I was told that because of that the producer had to reverse the negative on one shot so the left passed for the right and the looks corresponded.

BUÑUEL: That wasn't *Gran Casino*; it was *The Great Madcap*. Originally, it was my assistant's mistake, but it was also mine and everyone else's. An actor followed a taxi with his eyes as it entered a street and his look didn't correspond to the car's direction. An error, not like in *Gran Casino*, when I told myself, "Down with 180-degree angles!" Now, after having made thirty films, I must confess I still have doubts about the relationship between looks in reverse-angle shots.

COLINA: There is a musical scene in *Gran Casino* that I think is very well filmed: Meche Barba's dance at the casino, between the people and tables. The camera follows her in one long take without cuts, adjusting to the movements of the dance.

BUÑUEL: I hadn't filmed anything in a long time and I was interested in discovering the secrets of film technique.

TURRENT: How did *Gran Casino* do commercially?

BUÑUEL: Badly, without being a catastrophe. I had spent three years without filming anything. I could live thanks to my mother, who sent me money. I have never instigated a film project; I have never gone to tell a producer, "I want to make this."

COLINA: But you had a project: *Ilegible, hijo de Flauta* (Ilegible: Son of Flauta), a very free-style Surrealist film. What a pity you never filmed it.

BUÑUEL: *Ilegible* was a novel by Juan Larrea.[3] Before it was finished, he lost it on a trip, but he told me the plot and I said we could adapt it into a film. Years later, before we made *Nazarín*, we were about to make the film with producer Manuel Barbachano. "At last we will make *Ilegible*," I wrote to Larrea. "Barbachano is giving each of us one thousand dollars.

---

3 Juan Larrea (1895-1980), Spanish poet, essayist and disciple of Apollinaire, was one of the founders of the "Creationist" movement.

I am sending the two thousand to you, because you need it more." He responded: "Delighted. That money comes to me like rain from heaven." I added four or five ideas to the story line, and he did the same. One scene needed thirty thousand people: the Jehovah Children — or Witnesses, I can't remember — congregate at Madison Square Garden and Ilegible and a friend pass by on horseback. I wrote to Larrea: "The Children of Jehovah scene is impossible; we can't go to New York to film and it's also not possible to have so many extras." And he answered back, "If you cut the Children of Jehovah, I forbid you to make the film." He told me it could all be done using trick photography. But how can you use trick photography in Mexico to create thirty thousand people? Since I didn't make the film, Larrea returned the two thousand dollars. What an incredible fellow! He lost both the film and the money over a few Children of Jehovah more or less.

EL GRAN CALAVERA (THE GREAT MADCAP)

BUÑUEL: I had been out of work for a long time and I didn't have a cent. Fernando Soler was going to act in and direct *The Great Madcap* for Dancigers, but he finally realized that it was too much work to do both things and asked for a director: any director, as long as he was technically competent. Dancigers called and asked me to direct the film. I accepted. The story line had been written by Luis Alcoriza and his wife Janet.[4] She had worked as an actress and dancer in Mexican cinema but had stopped and now wrote screenplays with Alcoriza. *The Great Madcap* is the only film I directed without ever working on the script. (I have worked with twenty-two writers.)

COLINA: I like *The Great Madcap*, it seems to me a very fresh film. How does it seem to you now? I would say it looks like you had fun shooting it at least.

BUÑUEL: I remember very little, and haven't seen it since it was made. I had fun because it excited me technically. I enjoyed myself with the editing, the construction, the camera angles... All of that interested me because I was still an apprentice in what I call "normal" cinema.

4 Luis Alcoriza, born in Spain in 1920, pursued a career as an actor, scriptwriter, and filmmaker in Mexico. His wife, the former Mexican film actress and dancer under the name Raquel Rojas, worked with him as a coscriptwriter using the name Janet Alcoriza.

TURRENT: Do you remember the opening scene? Legs intertwined and shoes of varying types on the floor of a cell at the police station...

BUÑUEL: That scene was improvised, because I don't think it was in the script. It occurred to me that we should get to know the character in an interesting manner. His shoes are elegant, expensive and they contrast starkly with the shoes of the bums or drunks who are in the cell. There is a short prologue: a "dandy" must be shown sleeping in the cell among these bums. I remember that word *dandy*, because I learned it then. It means the same as *señorito* in Spain, doesn't it?

TURRENT: It's a strange scene because we don't know what's happening, we only see a lot of feet. After the scene opens, we see the cell and the men sleeping on the floor. But at the beginning there are only feet.

BUÑUEL: I don't have a foot fetish, but feet appear in many of my films.

TURRENT: Antonio Bravo's character is wonderful. I imagine that you had a lot of fun with him. He is a man who, when he talks to Soler, alternates between using his first name and calling him sir, and he drops Latin words and phrases.

BUÑUEL: I don't remember that film very well. I remember that I was already an aficionado of what they call tracking shots. There are two or three in that film. Some people have said film technique doesn't interest me, but I remember at that time I was fascinated by it and I wanted to take advantage of its narrative possibilities. I always try to avoid reminding the viewer that there is a camera. On the other hand, I don't usually shoot cutaways, or what Mexican studios call "protection takes." And I've had to pay for it with lots of trouble editing! Even though, in general, thanks to habit, I seldom fail. In the drawing room scene in *El*, when the protagonist receives the woman who will later be his wife, I inserted a medium close-up of the woman that really pertained to an earlier sequence, with another stage setting and another dress. No one has ever noticed.

TURRENT: One week I saw *El* twenty times in a row because I was going to do a book, shot by shot with a transcript, and I never noticed that the shot did not correspond to the scene.

COLINA: During those years, Fernando Soler was a *monstre sacré* in Mexican cinema. Did he cause any problems?

BUÑUEL: On the contrary: we understood each other perfectly. He treated me as an experimental director and the filming went ahead without any hitches.

COLINA: Soler was a performer from the old Spanish school — principally comedy and *sainete* — somewhat conventional, but in my opinion a good actor.

BUÑUEL: Certainly, he was a good actor; he possessed the entire technical repertory of his craft, and I didn't have to give him cues for every gesture. So, I could take care of other details of directing the film.

TURRENT: There are some very good gags using the sound equipment the leading man carries in the truck. He and his girlfriend kiss and say amorous phrases in the truck that are overheard by everyone in the street because the microphone has accidentally been left on. The first time the truck appears, it is seen from above: the people and cars look very small. Some critics have tried to find a Surrealist tone to the advertising slogans that are announced over the loudspeaker: "Go to bed ugly and wake up beautiful using Sin of Syria cream." And you use the sound equipment again at the end, in a duel with the nuptial ceremony...

BUÑUEL: Yes. The girl is going to marry another fellow. The young man blocks out the priest's sermon and, with the loudspeakers at full blast, assaults the wedding. This ending isn't very original; I used something we have seen a thousand times in American comedies: a wedding that is interrupted just when the bride is going to say, "I do." I made the film in eighteen days.

TURRENT: Nevertheless, the experience of filming it must have been more enjoyable than making *Gran Casino*. It looks like you had more fun.

BUÑUEL: Yes, much more, because technically I felt more secure, more at ease. Remember that when I made *Gran Casino*, I had allowed too much time to pass without directing a film. I had made nothing since *Las Hurdes*, except the films when I was executive producer at Filmófono. With *The Great Madcap*, I had had some experience; I knew the medium better. I had a bad reputation because of *Gran Casino*, but *The Great Madcap* was a hit with the public and thanks to it I was able to continue making movies in Mexico.

8: *MI HUERFANITO, JEFE; LOS OLVIDADOS* (THE YOUNG AND THE DAMNED)

JOSE DE LA COLINA: Finally, we arrive at *Los olvidados*, the film in which Buñuel the filmmaker is reborn.

LUIS BUÑUEL: I was initially going to make another film. Juan Larrea and I wrote a synopsis for a commercial film, *Mi huerfanito, jefe!* (My Little Orphan, Boss!), which dealt with a young boy who sold lottery tickets. As you two know, in Mexico the last group of unsold lottery tickets is called "an orphan." Vendors offer them by saying, "Take my orphan, boss." Larrea found this amusing and thought it could be used as the title. I no longer remember the story. I proposed the film to Dancigers, who was in a good mood because *The Great Madcap* had done well at the box office. "It's not bad," Dancigers told me, "but it's a minor melodrama. Instead, let's make something more serious: a story about poor children in Mexico." I began to work with Luis Alcoriza, but he had another contract to fulfill at the time and so I continued writing with Larrea and Max Aub. I shouldn't say "write." I am almost completely agraphic and prefer to talk about my ideas and have them written up for me afterwards. The dialogue was reworded in a "low-class" Mexican Spanish by Pedro de Urdimalas, and with much success, by the way. Later, I don't know why, except for Alcoriza, the names of the other participants didn't appear in the credits.

TOMAS PEREZ TURRENT: Did you do any documentation for the story?

BUÑUEL: I went to Mexico City's poor neighborhoods accompanied first by Alcoriza and later by the art director, Edward Fitzgerald. I spent about six months getting to know those neighborhoods: I left very early by bus and would walk at random through the narrow streets, making friends with people, observing types, visiting people's homes. I remember I sometimes went to talk to a young girl who had infantile paralysis. I would walk along Nonoalco, the Romita Plaza, the slums in Tacubaya. Those places later appeared in the film and some of them no longer exist.

TURRENT: Did the idea of reforming minors interest you in the film?

BUÑUEL: No. I was interested in discovering characters and stories. I consulted particular cases with a psychiatrist at the Juvenile Court, with María de Lourdes Rico. I read the files on a great number of cases...fascinating! Also I used articles that appeared in the press. For example: I read they found the body of a twelve-year-old boy at a garbage dump, and this gave me the idea for the ending.

COLINA: The film was originally going to be called *La manzana podrida* (The Rotten Apple)...

BUÑUEL: I don't remember that.

COLINA: They published an open call in the newspapers: they were looking for boys aged twelve to eighteen years old who had finished elementary school; you had to bring a photograph so they could select those who would act in the film. I fulfilled all the requirements and went to call at the offices of Ultramar Films, on the Paseo de la Reforma, close to Chapultepec Park and above the Chapultepec Cinema.

BUÑUEL: That's right. We put in the elementary school requirement so that three thousand children wouldn't show up instead of the three hundred we could examine. We finally selected around twelve, and among them was you; you were to play the role of Pedrito. But the producers said you didn't look like a Mexican child, so we decided on Alfonso Mejía. It seems we ended your acting career...

COLINA: Just as well, because it didn't interest me, and besides I would have been a terrible actor. I had read histories of cinema, I knew you were the director of prominent films and I wanted to see you work. Twice I got up very early for screen tests at Tepeyac Studios. I talked to most of the boys who were tested, and found out that Roberto Cobo, the one who played El Jaibo, was a musical review dancer, that the boy who would play El Ojitos was an authentic peasant boy, and that Alma Delia Fuentes, who was so refined and so blond, was playing a poor girl from the neighborhood...

BUÑUEL: Yes, Roberto Cobo was a dancer in a chorus, one of those who are called "dancing boys" or something like that. When he answered the call, he was not known as an actor and he did very little film work after *Los olvidados*, except for a small role in *Mexican Bus Ride*.[1] Alma Delia

---

1 Roberto Cobo has actually appeared in many Mexican films. Besides his work in *Los olvidados,* Cobo is probably best known as "La Manuela" in *El lugar sin límites* (Hell Has No Limits, 1977), dir. Arturo Ripstein.

Fuentes was indeed blond and refined, but you can suddenly come across girls like that in the slums, can't you? The peasant boy had come to the city in almost the same way as his character in the film: he was a natural actor and no one had to show him how to act. Several real boys from the farm-school reformatory figured in the film, the others were already minor actors. I chose Stella Inda to be Pedro's mother and Miguel Inclán for the blind man.

TURRENT: Of course, the character of the blind man was criticized for not being a "Mexican character."

BUÑUEL: Someone told me he seemed more like a blind man from a Spanish picaresque novel, like the one in *Lazarillo de Tormes*. It's possible. He is greedy and cunning, villainous, but he also has his own characteristics: he is a one-man orchestra, something of a folk-healer, and he has respect for Don Porfirio[2]...and besides, he likes little girls.

TURRENT: The blind man may have characteristics from the Spanish picaresque tradition, but Miguel Inclán, a great actor who specialized in playing villains, gives them great reality and authentic "weight," and he also Mexicanizes them...

COLINA: By the way, you seem to take delight when they stone the blind man.

BUÑUEL: Delighted, me? No.

COLINA: ...Because you hear a light, almost mocking music a little while before the stoning, and when the blind man is already on the ground begging for pity, a rooster or a hen appears to be looking at him mockingly, and once again the music comes in with a kind of...hennish guffaw.

BUÑUEL: Yes, the music was like a minuet, gracious, cordial, and it finishes off with a sort of mockery. Today I wouldn't have put music in the film. There isn't any in my recent films. Some people have commented on the music in *Viridiana,* saying it is an achievement. But the music comes from a gramophone speaker clearly visible in the scenes. When I made *Los olvidados*, all Mexican films had to have music, if only for union reasons. The music was written by Gustavo Pittaluga, but since he was neither in the union nor a Mexican citizen, all of it was signed by Rodolfo Halffter and he was almost forced to leave the union because of it.

COLINA: To me, the musical sarcasm regarding the blind man doesn't

2 José de la Cruz Porfirio Díaz (1830-1915), Mexican general and president for virtually thirty four years of unchallenged rule that, although brought prosperity to the ruling classes, fostered an archaic social system. Díaz was overthrown by the Mexican Revolution of 1910.

seem bad. Convention would call for "compassionate" music, but the blind man in *Los olvidados* is a real bastard.

BUÑUEL: Yes, he is against the boys from the very beginning. And he has reactionary ideas: he would solve the problem of delinquency by shooting all of them. In the scene at the tortilla shop, he says something like, "What times we are living in! In my general Don Porfirio's day, anyone who stole so much as a loaf of bread would have been shot." In film, music can not only be easy, but deceptive as well. I don't like to use it.

COLINA: Since we've mentioned roosters and hens, why are there so many of them in *Los olvidados*?

BUÑUEL: I don't know. There's a realistic justification: Pedrito has barnyard birds and he takes care of them. Later, at the farm-school reformatory, he takes out his problems on them.

COLINA: How do you feel about roosters and chickens?

BUÑUEL: Now I feel rather fond of them. Before, I rejected them. I felt that a bird of any kind was a threatening element: an eagle, a sparrow, a hen. Why? I don't know. It's something irrational, perhaps related to my childhood. But I like nocturnal birds, especially owls.

COLINA: What you're saying is curious because when we see Pedro's body at the end, a rooster walks over his chest, as if to say the animal ultimately predominates over the human.

BUÑUEL: It's a natural moment because the boy dies in a place where animals are kept.

COLINA: But we also see the hens fluttering around in slow motion in Pedro's dream.

BUÑUEL: But there are many other elements: the mother is there, El Jaibo, the boy he kills, a piece of meat, flashes of lightning. By the way, I would like to have seen the piece of meat the mother offers hit by lightning, and I also wanted to have it rain in the room. But this was difficult to achieve, we lacked the technical means. I was very attracted to using *ralenti*, slow motion. Slow motion is used for the image of the dog that walks up the street when El Jaibo dies. I always liked *ralenti*, because it gives an unexpected dimension to even the most trivial gesture; we see details that we cannot perceive at normal speed.

TURRENT: Nevertheless, you've abandoned the use of *ralenti*. As far as I remember, you haven't used it in your recent films.

BUÑUEL: I no longer use it now because it is a clichéd way of enhancing something.

COLINA: In the dream, the mother (Stella Inda) gets on the bed and lifts her nightgown, jumps to the floor and runs toward Pedro. Her clothes and hair flutter around her and her steps are like a dance. A very beautiful image.

BUÑUEL: I don't look to beautify images. If it came out pretty, fine.

COLINA: The image almost suggests an apparition of the Virgin.

TURRENT: (Laughing) Of course, the Virgin of Guadalupe!

BUÑUEL: I never intended that consciously, of course. During my childhood with the Jesuits, I thought the Virgin was an enchanting image, and later I had her appear in *The Milky Way*, for example. But not in *Los olvidados*. Not consciously, at least.

COLINA: For me, that dream and the soldier's dream in *The Discreet Charm of the Bourgeoisie* are the best in cinema.

TURRENT: Perhaps even the technical imperfections helped give the sequence the texture of an authentic dream.

BUÑUEL: I admit that at times an error can eventually come out as an enhancing element in a scene, opening it up to other possibilities, but it's better to avoid errors. Anyway, something of what one intended always remains, even if the technique is not very brilliant.

TURRENT: Before coming here, De la Colina and I were talking about that dream and we remembered what Octavio Paz[3] wrote: that the scene synthesized the film's themes — hunger, crime, and the mother — in a kind of holy banquet.

BUÑUEL: Of course. Dreams concentrate elements that have affected us while awake, disguising them and presenting them to us in another manner. Pedrito was affected by Julián's death at the hands of El Jaibo, and he remembers that his mother refused to give him something to eat. For that reason, he dreams the murdered boy is under the bed; smiling tenderly, his mother offers him a large hunk of meat, and El Jaibo snatches it away...

COLINA: El Jaibo is a passionate person. I like it that he seduces Pedro's mother while sentimentally talking to her about his own mother. This intensifies in the scene when he dies and has a vision of a skinny dog walking up a street, when you hear a female voice saying, "How alone you have been, my son!"

BUÑUEL: El Jaibo does this (Buñuel slowly rolls his head), and at the moment of his death, the image freezes. I felt that there had to be some

3 Octavio Paz, 1991 Nobel Prize-winning Mexican poet and essayist. His essay "El poeta Luis Buñuel" was published in *Las peras del Olmo* (1957).

sort of vision there. Why does he remember his mother? I don't know. That is how I felt it. In *The Discreet Charm of the Bourgeoisie*, there is the dream of the lieutenant who looks for his mother, and she says to him, "Don't be afraid, my son. It's me!" These are things that move me and I put them in, without reasons. It is enough that they are felt as such.

TURRENT: Here is the dog we were missing in *Un chien andalou*. Why does this dog appear in El Jaibo's vision?

BUÑUEL: It could be any other animal, an elephant, for example. But a dog is what came into my mind.

TURRENT: No, an elephant would be a bit too arbitrary in the daily life of *Los olvidados*.

COLINA: And the dog seems to be El Jaibo's image of death.

BUÑUEL: Well, an elephant could also suggest death. Why not? Mental associations don't have to be realistic. For example, in the scene in *Un chien andalou* in which the protagonist pulls a series of things, anything you like could have been tied to the ropes: an umbrella, an empty taxi, an elephant, a thousand things. El Jaibo could have seen elephants at the movies or at the circus. I felt it had to be a dog.

TURRENT: And why the wet street?

BUÑUEL: Only for photogenic reasons. The street looked too gray and light; since we wanted a dark street, we wet it down to get more contrast.

COLINA: El Jaibo touches me perhaps more than the other characters. We understand that El Jaibo kills Pedro because, from El Jaibo's point of view, Pedro had informed on him, he lacked an essential loyalty.

BUÑUEL: You can find that loyalty in even the most lost individuals. And El Jaibo is not entirely bad, no. In my films, nobody is fated to be bad or entirely good. I am not...How do they say it now?... I'm not Manichean.

COLINA: The scene where El Jaibo seduces Pedro's mother suggests incest.

BUÑUEL: I won't argue with you about that, but I don't believe it was intentional. I remember I preferred to do no more than suggest that Pedro's mother sleeps with El Jaibo.

TURRENT: You don't even see the moment of copulation begin. The camera is placed outside the shack and shows a mountebank who makes some little dogs do a dance for some children, among whom are Pedro's little brothers...

BUÑUEL: I prefer suggestion in these cases. If I had shown directly that El Jaibo and the woman go to bed, it would have been very vulgar.

COLINA: There is perhaps more eroticism in the scene where El Jaibo contemplates the woman while she is washing her feet in a basin.

BUÑUEL: Her feet? Some critics call me a "foot fetishist." (He laughs.) It's true that feet appear frequently in my films. Ever since *L'Age d'or*, when the female protagonist sucks the big toe of a statue.

TURRENT: They are fetish elements: the woman's shoes in *El*, in *Diary of a Chambermaid...*

BUÑUEL: We all have our fetishes... although some of us exaggerate them, no?

COLINA: I believe even people on the production crew had some objections to the character of Pedro's mother.

BUÑUEL: Yes, there were objections, both during and after the filming. I had some problems with the people on staff. The hairdresser was offended when Pedrito comes home hungry and his mother refuses to give him food. "No mother would say that to her son in Mexico. It's degrading, I don't want to work on this film." She left the studio and handed in her resignation. I had to hire another. And some of the staff grumbled about certain scenes: "Mr. Buñuel, this is terrible garbage. Not all Mexico City is like this. We also have some beautiful residential neighborhoods like Las Lomas..."

TURRENT: They thought you "blackened" Mexico. Perhaps because of this, they put a "justification" at the beginning of the film. Did they impose that on you?

BUÑUEL: No. It was my idea, so that the film could be shown. Since I saw that it was a theme used in Mexican cinema at that time, it came to me to add this warning. I don't remember it very well... How does it go?

COLINA: I have the text here: "Concealed behind the magnificent buildings of our great modern cities, New York, Paris, London, are homes of misery that house children who are badly nourished, dirty, and uneducated, a breeding ground for future delinquents. Society tries to correct this evil, but the success of its efforts is very limited. Only in some near future can the rights of children and adolescents be revindicated so that they can be useful to society. Mexico City, a large modern metropolis, is no exception to this universal rule, and for that reason this film, based on fact, is not optimistic and leaves the solution of the problem to the progressive forces of society."

BUÑUEL: Despite that, the film bothered some people because they thought I deliberately blackened everything. But these objections were not only voiced by Mexicans. Did you know that my Communist friends in Paris were initially disgusted with the film? I remember a meeting on the Champs-Elysées with Sadoul, who was a very good friend of mine. Very saddened, he told me, "You can't imagine how bad your film makes us feel, because it has a bourgeois ideology. In it, you show that a bourgeois teacher and a bourgeois state are very humane because they reform children. In the scene where the policeman stops the pederast from taking the boy, you present the police as something useful. We are hurt by this: it saddens us. To us, it seems like a film in favor of bourgeois morality." Things changed when Pudovkin praised the film in *Pravda*. Some critics who had attacked the film later began saying it was very good.

TURRENT: Do you think Sadoul and these critics had misunderstood these scenes?

BUÑUEL: I think they were wrong. The director of a school for delinquent children or the mentally retarded can be a good man and give a boy an opportunity, while making a psychological experiment: "Take these fifty pesos. Go buy me a pack of cigarettes and bring me the change..." But a character like that does not stop the boy from turning into a delinquent. Pedrito wants to go back with the change, but he meets El Jaibo in the street.

COLINA: That is to say: the "oasis of kindness" is not enough. When they leave the institution, the kids find the same hard reality as always.

TURRENT: And the problem will not be solved by a good teacher, but rather by changing the social environment.

BUÑUEL: Perhaps it would have been more edifying if Pedrito, upon meeting El Jaibo when he left the farm-school, had said to him, "I have a very nice teacher, come and meet him," and El Jaibo had gone along and said, "Well, s'not so bad here," and became a good boy. But that doesn't seem very believable. It would also be a different film.

COLINA: Like the Soviet film *The Road to Life*.[4]

BUÑUEL: Yes, there all delinquent children end up becoming good. I believe that if, in bourgeois society, there is an understanding teacher who helps mentally retarded or delinquent children, this does not justify monstrosities of social injustice. I also don't believe that policemen individually always have to be villains. A cop can act as much like a policeman as he wants and tomorrow club some students who are demonstrating, but he can also be desirable on a day when you are assaulted and he

4 *The Road to Life* (Poutieva V Gizn, 1931), dir. Nikolai Ekk.

shows up to stop it. I put no love of the police in that scene that bothered Sadoul. Besides, the policeman did not arrest the pederast.

TURRENT: Afterwards, you could have shown the policeman blackmailing the pederast.

BUÑUEL: And that would also be a different film. But, so what! I wasn't making a film about pederasts and policemen.

COLINA: Tell us about other reactions to *Los olvidados*.

BUÑUEL: It premiered at Cine México on a Thursday — such is the custom here — and it was withdrawn that Saturday. Dancigers didn't want to attend the opening because he was afraid of the audience's response. He was a good friend, but these things gave him cold feet. I went to the Cine México that night and found a hundred people in the theater, and there was not one friend, not one acquaintance, not one cinema aficionado, not even the actors in the film. At the exit everyone looked like they were at a funeral. And immediately the press began to rail against it. There were protests from I don't know what society, the teachers union, from other unions. There were those who said, "You deserve Article 33 (which expels 'undesirable foreigners' from the country), you dirty Spaniard coming to insult Mexico." In the end nothing happened. I already had my Mexican citizenship.

COLINA: The critic Francisco Pina told me there was a somewhat stormy private screening.

BUÑUEL: Yes. Twenty people attended. There were intellectuals and artists: the Mexican painter Siqueiros, the Spanish poet León Felipe and his Mexican wife, Bertha, and Lupe Marín, wife of painter Diego Rivera. When the screening ended, Siqueiros was happy with the film, it seemed admirable to him. Crossing her arms, Lupe Marín looked at me and said: "Don't talk to me." Bertha — who had been at my house several times with León, and whom I had known since she worked for the Spanish Republic—approached me as if she wanted to claw my eyes out. "You are a wretch! You offend everyone. What you show in your film is not Mexico." But Siqueiros told me, "Very good, Buñuel. Let these old women say what they want and keep making movies." I could tell you other negative reactions. Jorge Negrete ran into me one day in the cafeteria at the film studio. He asked me indignantly, "Did you make *Los olvidados*? If I had been in Mexico at the time, you would never have made that film."

COLINA: That is significant. On screen, Negrete, the singing cowboy, represented a Mexico that was diametrically opposed to the one shown in

Los olvidados — the idyllic ranches, the men of honor, the *macho*. Besides, he was head of the Actors Association.

TURRENT: I think even today a film like *Los olvidados* could not be made in Mexico. In any case, it would be banned.

BUÑUEL: There was a lot of negative criticism. People argued with me over even small details. Palacios, the engineer... Do you remember him?

TURRENT: The man who was famous because he "invented" the star María Félix?

BUÑUEL: That's the one. Despite the fact that he was a friend of mine, he published an article against me in *Claridades*. He said things like, "Buñuel doesn't know the slightest thing about Mexico. In his film he shows miserable shacks with brass beds inside them." But if Palacios hadn't seen them, I had, many times. Even in the slums, the first thing a poor married couple buys is a brass bed. And, in a family with numerous children, you can find as many as three brass beds. A couple from one of those neighborhoods told me they didn't get married until they bought one of those beds.

COLINA: Reality has more than one image. Even today, you can see a forest of television antennas in the slums. It's typical of underdevelopment: in the middle of great poverty, you can find objects belonging to a completely different social level.

BUÑUEL: Exactly. I could give you many more examples of objections to the film, including some from before the filming, when we were still writing the story. We began with a different story line than the one that was filmed: some kids rummage through a mountain of garbage and discover the portrait of a sort of "nobleman," a Spanish gentleman, a magnificent fellow who has degenerated into a beggar in the Mexican slums. Pedro de Urdimalas, a Mexican scriptwriter, said he didn't want to work on a film in which Spain, the *Madre Patria*, would be offended. That's why his name didn't appear in the credits even though he added a very good popular Mexican flavor to the dialogue.

TURRENT: In a famous interview published in 1954 by *Cahiers du Cinéma*, you said Dancigers opposed your including certain irrational details in the film.

BUÑUEL: Yes, I wanted to include a couple of details that broke with conventional realism. When El Jaibo and Pedro go to visit the boy who will later be killed, in passing you would have seen behind the vacant lot, where there was a large building under construction — a Social Security hospital — a hundred-piece symphony orchestra installed within the metal structure. At Pedro's house, when the mother was cooking, at a certain moment you also would have seen her move aside a magnificent top hat. These things would have been seen in the blink of an eye and would only have been noticed by one spectator in a hundred, who would have been left in doubt, thinking it might only have been an illusion. They were elements of an irrational type, an attempt not to follow the story line to the letter, to achieve a "photographic" reality. But Dancigers told me, "Buñuel, I beg you, don't put those things in. I'm already making a lot of sacrifices for this film: there is a lot of garbage, unknown actors, etc..."

COLINA: I suppose that these absurd elements could have been justified *a posteriori*. Musicians at a construction site? It could have been explained as an official preopening of the hospital. The top hat? Pedro's mother could have a secret and rich lover...

BUÑUEL: No. They were *a priori* unjustified elements, irrational sparks, quick shots.

TURRENT: Despite the reactions against it, the film was shown at Cannes.

BUÑUEL: Yes. The head of the Film Institute in Mexico was an intellectual who liked the film and accepted it. They made one cut, nothing more, in the scene where the blind man is talking at the tortilla shop: a phrase without great importance. On the other hand, there in France, the Mexican ambassador was the poet Jaime Torres Bodet, who did not offer me much support, and had even less support for the film, but his secretary was Octavio Paz, who was in favor of it; despite the post he held at the embassy, he wrote a text for the presentation of *Los olvidados*. I had met Octavio only a short time before...when I showed the film in Paris to my Surrealist friends. They liked the film, even Breton.

TURRENT: For the international press, we could say that *Los olvidados* was Buñuel's "resurrection."

BUÑUEL: Indeed it was. I had spent many years without making anything worth noting. But, despite its imperfections, *Los olvidados* was already something. Something lived there; the film lived.

TURRENT: After the prize at Cannes, *Los olvidados* was rereleased in Mexico and had more success.

BUÑUEL: It was rereleased at the Prado Cinema and ran there for six weeks. It is a film that has gone on making its own way. I see it still gets shown a lot at cinema clubs, on television. In France they gave it an appalling title...

TURRENT: *Pitié pour eux* (literally, Pity for Them).

BUÑUEL: Horrible. Something like "Forgive them, God!" Imagine what the books say: "Buñuel, director of *Pitié pour eux.*" How embarrassing!

9: *SUSANA* OR *DEMONIO Y CARNE* (THE DEVIL AND THE FLESH)

LUIS BUÑUEL: I have been reviewing the notes on my productions and I see I made *Los olvidados* in February 1950 and *Susana* in June of that year.

TOMAS PEREZ TURRENT: Some film books note that playwright Rodolfo Usigli worked on the dialogue.

BUÑUEL: Jaime Salvador, Manuel Reachi, and I wrote the screenplay that was based on a story by Reachi. Rodolfo Usigli[1] revised the dialogue.

TURRENT: I imagine that the producer, Sergio Kogan, wanted to make a film to show off his wife, Rosita Quintana.

BUÑUEL: I think so. There was a three- or four-page synopsis: a "bad" girl arrives at a ranch and seduces the father of the family, the son, the foreman. It developed along those lines.

JOSE DE LA COLINA: Then it was an "exemplary tale" with a moral lesson?

BUÑUEL: Very moral, because the seductress is punished in the end. I feel I didn't emphasize the irony enough, the joke.

TURRENT: On the contrary, it's very apparent.

BUÑUEL: Perhaps the public takes the story too seriously, especially the ending.

TURRENT: In an essay titled *Buñuel or the Antiphrase,* a French critic compared *Susana* with Flaubert's *Dictionary of Accepted Ideas.*

BUÑUEL: The film can function in different ways, depending on whether the audience is naive or malicious. Some find it a naive film, others find it morally repugnant. I find the protagonist's eroticism very simple, a bit silly.

---

1 Rodolfo Usigli, successful Mexican playwright, poet, and essayist (1905-1979), whose only novel, *Ensayo de un crimen* was later adapted by Buñuel in 1953 as *The Criminal Life of Archibaldo de la Cruz.*

COLINA: But that eroticism also has humor. Every time Susana lowers her neckline to seduce a man, she seems to parody Goebbels: "When I hear the word morality, I take out my tits."

BUÑUEL: There are things I improvised during the filming. One of my favorite scenes is the one with the spider. There is a tremendous thunderstorm and we are at the women's correctional institution. Susana is frightened and prays to God: "Lord, even though I'm bad, I'm also one of your creatures." Lightning flashes and in the light, the shadow of the bars looks like a cross. A spider walks over this shadow cross. Finally, there is a "miracle." Susana shakes the bars, which yield easily.

TURRENT: Because "the ways of the lord are infinite and his designs impenetrable."

BUÑUEL: It seemed to me I should have made the story less simple and introduced more visual ideas such as the spider, or substituted one erotic object for another. In one scene, Fernando Soler, who has just been aroused by Susana, sees his wife arrive...and it is his wife he kisses passionately while thinking of Susana... I remember certain Surrealist meetings; at one of them we had a questionnaire on eroticism. I asked if one erotic object could sometimes be substituted mentally for another; if, for example, you could make love to your wife while thinking about a lover or a prostitute or a sexy little maid you had seen walk by in the street. At this meeting of friends, almost everyone responded yes, that they had imaginarily exchanged one woman for another while making love.

COLINA: Arriving at the ranch, Susana acts like a subversive erotic element.

BUÑUEL: Yes. Her arrival provokes a series of actions that were impossible to imagine happening there. It's an honest family without ill will, and the father, mother, son, and foreman are wholesome people. Susana appears like a seductive devil...

TURRENT: Everyone changes, and even the mother, the one who seems to have most resisted the evil, ends up lashing at Susana with a whip while smiling sadistically.

BUÑUEL: But at the end, everything is back in order and happily resolved: birds sing, father and son are reconciled, even the mare is healed and gives birth to a colt, and Susana has been arrested and taken to jail. The ranch becomes a paradise again!

TURRENT: As a matter of fact, order triumphs. But it is a disturbing ending because the mare begins to trot again and life reappears. The ambiguity of this so-called soothing ending is as magistral as the endings of *El* and *The Criminal Life of Archibaldo de la Cruz*.

BUÑUEL: I made *Susana* in twenty days. Theoretically, I would like to make it again with the resources and the freedom I have now. Among the things I improvised to enrich the story is the scene when Susana seduces the son inside the well. The eroticism, so simple in this scene, is intensified perhaps because of the notion of hiding. The idea came to me from the chapter about Montesinos Cave in *Don Quixote*,[2] although there is no eroticism there.

TURRENT: What would you change in your new version of *Susana*?

BUÑUEL: I would try to make it more interesting. There would not be any pornography, but there would be a more sophisticated and less conventional eroticism.

COLINA: Perhaps it seems conventional at first glance, but some very interesting things happen "below the surface." What is important is the "latent content," as Breton would say.

BUÑUEL: What do you two make of it?

TURRENT: There is a complete Buñuel menagerie: the spider, the rooster, the mare; the flock of turkeys at the end are like the sheep in *The Exterminating Angel* — they signify the "return to order."

COLINA: Susana arrives at the ranch dragging herself in the mud, almost reptilian like a Biblical viper. And almost every time we see Fernando Soler with the girl, he has a pistol or a shotgun in his hands: an obvious phallic symbol, as a psychiatrist would say.

BUÑUEL: I am an aficionado of firearms; to keep the dialogue from being too static, I had Soler cleaning his guns. Perhaps you can say that there is a phallic symbol hidden there in that innocent detail: the image of the penis. But it was unconscious.

COLINA: It doesn't matter. The latent meaning works in favor of this symbol.

BUÑUEL: Besides, who knows if my attraction to firearms symbolizes a desire for phallic reassurance.

COLINA: I think when you read the script, surely you realized immediately that it was full of melodramatic conventions. And you played them all the way, you went to the extreme on purpose.

---

2 In *Don Quixote de la Mancha*, Don Quixote descends into an uninhabited cave; when he returns, he tells of meeting with various characters and having adventures described in books about knighthood.

BUÑUEL: Of course I knew it and played them all the way. But I didn't try to be astute by going contrary to what was dictated by the story. I don't like giving winks to those in the know.

TURRENT: And don't you think that by taking those conventions to the limit, you were pushing them to the point of absurdity and would contradict them?

BUÑUEL: Naturally. What happens is that it isn't a deliberate thing on my part. The subconscious comes into play, and certainly I don't trust reason and culture. There are images that suddenly spring to mind without having meditated on them. In all my films, even in the most conventional ones, there is that tendency to be irrational, to behave in a way that can't be explained logically.

COLINA: But you can employ a cultural element in a certain ironic or parodic sense. A short time ago we were talking about the fact that the scene inside the well was suggested by the Montesinos Cave episode in *Don Quixote*.

BUÑUEL: That's different. I don't exclude *a priori* anything that originates from culture, if it's a memory taken from my personal experience. Above all, that scene inside the well came to me because Susana and the boy have to see each other somewhere in secret. Then I remembered the niche that was inside Montesinos Cave.

COLINA: Let's continue our discussion of eroticism, which is the film's engine. There is a very beautiful and exciting moment when the whites and yokes of some broken eggs run down Susana's thighs.

BUÑUEL: Like the milk that drips off the girl's legs in *Los olvidados*. We always return to these fixed images, don't we? Without noticing, we repeat ourselves. It's very attractive to me to see thighs with something viscous running down them because the skin is brought closer; it's as if we were not only seeing them but touching them.

COLINA: But there is something else about the broken eggs. In Mexico, we call testicles "eggs."

BUÑUEL: Also in Spain. I looked for a way to enrich the scene because in the script the characters were just talking and talking. So I made the foreman hug Susana tightly in such a way as to break the eggs she had collected in her skirt, and the yokes and whites run down her legs.

COLINA: In effect, a sensuality very rarely achieved in cinema with such tangibility. And the fact that that part of the actress's body is very powerful adds a lot to the scene: the legs aren't statuesque but very full, very carnal.

TURRENT: The tangibility of Susana's skin is also found in the scene at the beginning. After the "miracle" that gets her out of jail, Susana escapes, dragging herself through the mud, sopping wet, and that is how she appears at the ranch, it is how Fernando Soler first contemplates her. Her clothes are soaking wet, sticking to her body.

BUÑUEL: I like that; I also had the innocent bride get soaking wet in *Mexican Bus Ride*. The water makes her clothes cling to her body, emphasizing it more than if she were nude.

COLINA: Details that turn out to be more erotic than total nudity.

BUÑUEL: Naturally. A woman in a black lace chemise with gartered stockings and high-heeled shoes is more erotic than a naked woman. Total nudity is generally pure, not erotic.

COLINA: One erotic scene in *Susana* is presented through intermediaries. Susana is taking her clothes off in her room and her somewhat blurry silhouette is perceived through a translucent window. The three male characters, Soler, the foreman, and the son, all spy on her, each one not knowing the others are present. That moment is intense and significant because it's as if the three gazes were intertwined into one, into a single desire, and finally into the gaze of the audience.

BUÑUEL: All I remember about that scene is the sneakiness. The three men all say they are going to sleep, but hide from each other in order to spy on Susana. And it is raining cats and dogs. The rain gives the space more "body."

COLINA: From what I remember of that scene, it's filmed in only one movement of the camera and has great intensity: as if a third dimension, one of desire, had been achieved.

TURRENT: The takes in the film are long, very simple, functional.

BUÑUEL: I use long takes to eliminate editing. They make a film more fluid, wouldn't you agree? Of course, it's more difficult to do one continuous tracking shot than to do three short ones: if you have to film rapidly, it's a bit of a luxury. A tracking shot has to be more calculated with the action and the set, but it is richer. If you examine my films, you will notice there are not a large number of shots.

TURRENT: *Susana*, like your other films that follow conventional story lines, seems to be a house you build...only to knock down in the end.

BUÑUEL: That's very perceptive. Yes, I accept that. But when I made these films I was also conscious of my responsibility to comply with the producer's wishes and not deliberately to "boycott" them. Apart from that, I can have a bit of fun and add some things to amuse my friends. They aren't "winks," because I detest filmmakers who seem to be saying, "Look how clever I am." Let's say I put in some memories I share with a few people, innocent clues. If there are jokes in *Susana*, I had to be very careful that the entire film didn't end up as a joke.

COLINA: I would say you don't knock the house down; rather, you lock it up, leaving the characters smothered in their conventional, stupid happiness in a type of semifeudalism... and after the denouement, Susana is, in her own way, the "exterminating angel."

TURRENT: The old proverb-spouting, well-meaning servant closes the window saying, "Sir, it's better to live like this in the blessed peace of God." It seems characteristic of your humor to offer such an obviously conformist moral.

BUÑUEL: Your interpretation can be valid because you know I don't think like that character, but also because the audience leaves the cinema convinced it has seen a very moral story, isn't that so? The important thing is that the film moves each spectator, it suggests something.

COLINA: The poet Tomás Segovia says in more or less these words: "The poem is not what is written, but rather what happens between what is written and the reader."

BUÑUEL: That is really good, and it's perhaps even more true in cinema. When you see a film with friends, the divergent commentaries are surprising. Sometimes it seems that each person has seen a different film. And there are some people who see symbols everywhere. Those people frighten me, they do.

COLINA: I remember one critic said that *The Exterminating Angel* was an anti-Communist film because the menacing bear that appears for a moment in the Nobile's house represented...the Soviet Union!

BUÑUEL: *(Laughs)* And another critic said it was really a pro-Communist film because the bear had entered to free the servants. But the bear represented nothing more than a bear, and, by the way, he never managed to eat anyone.

TURRENT: I would have liked Susana to triumph in the film because, for me, of all of them, she is the only sympathetic character.

BUÑUEL: I would have liked that, too, but that must remain a secret.

TURRENT: Do you accept that *Susana* is a philosophical story?

BUÑUEL: Philosophical, no. A story, yes.

10: *LA HIJA DEL ENGAÑO* (DAUGHTER OF DECEIT); *UNA MUJER SIN AMOR* (A WOMAN WITHOUT LOVE); *SUBIDA AL CIELO* (MEXICAN BUS RIDE)

LA HIJA DEL ENGAÑO (DAUGHTER OF DECEIT)

TOMAS PEREZ TURRENT: According to filmographies, 1951 was a very active year for you. You made three films: *Daughter of Deceit, A Woman Without Love,* and *Mexican Bus Ride.*

LUIS BUÑUEL: That title, *Daughter of Deceit,* was the producers' mistake. If they had left the original title, *Don Quintín el amargao,* all Spain would have gone to see it because Arniches and Estremera's play is very well known to the Spanish public. But the producers didn't want people to think they were producing a remake. They showed the film at a third-rate cinema and it was poorly attended, which made me happy because it is a film that didn't work out for me.

JOSE DE LA COLINA: Did you follow the script of the film you produced for Filmófono in 1935?

BUÑUEL: Yes. I had a print of that film here in Mexico, a print salvaged out of the best parts of ten damaged prints. Several friends and I, all Spanish refugees, saw it three or four times at the small screening room at the Directors Union. I remember that Eduardo Ugarte, Luis Alcoriza, Ignacio Mantecón, Moreno Villa, and several others came to see it. We had fun together; the film brought back nostalgic memories because the protagonist bragged and joked around in typical Madrid fashion.

TURRENT: But this had to be translated into a Mexican version.

BUÑUEL: Of course. I did some work on the adaptation that Alcoriza and his wife made. They Mexicanized the story, but in general, Don Quintín was still the same person: a Mexican *macho* instead of a Madrid *echao pa'lante.*[1] But there is very little I can say about that film, because I remember almost nothing about it. It was a "bread-and-butter" film, made so we could eat. Certainly, I tried to make it professionally.

UNA MUJER SIN AMOR, OR CUANDO LOS HIJOS NOS JUZGAN (A WOMAN WITHOUT LOVE)

TURRENT: *A Woman Without Love* or *Cuando los hijos nos juzgan* (When Our Children Judge Us) is the only film of yours in which I find nothing of interest.

BUÑUEL: Me neither. It's the worst one I made. It was based on de Maupassant's *Pierre et Jean,* which Cayatte[2] had filmed very well. I had to shoot it in twenty days, and with less money. I would have liked to see William Wyler make a film under those conditions! In fact, we followed Cayatte's film almost shot by shot, which provided a minimum guide to work with at the studio. We had to film quickly, so I avoided cutting as much as I could and that helped me later when I was editing. Editing a film used to take eight days of work. Now, as I've told you, I do it in two or three. This means I had to come into the studio very well prepared, especially because it's not my practice to shoot cutaways.

SUBIDA AL CIELO (MEXICAN BUS RIDE)

COLINA: *Mexican Bus Ride* seems to be an amusement with some elements of melodrama. It's a minor work perhaps, but it has a lot of life and holds up very well. Now that it's shown on television, have you seen it again?

BUÑUEL: I don't watch television. Well, sometimes my wife calls me if something interesting comes on, but it's only for a moment and I never feel like watching something from the beginning to end.

COLINA: Nevertheless, someone told me that one day you were watching *The Great Madcap* on television and when they cut to a commercial, you said, "I didn't film that."

1 Colloquial spelling for *echado para adelante,* or literally "thrown forward." Though not precisely a *macho,* the term is very Spanish and refers to a somewhat flagrant individual, a swaggerer possessing a dauntless and adventurous attitude.
2 *Pierre et Jean* (1943), dir. André Cayatte.

BUÑUEL: Yes. It was the scene when Fernando Soler comes home drunk and becomes furious with his wife's guests. Soler had a menacing look and suddenly...a furniture store appeared! It's an outrage. They ruin whatever they want in order to make us buy some stupidity: the news, a film, everything.

COLINA: Who had the central idea for *Mexican Bus Ride*?

BUÑUEL: Manuel Altolaguirre.[3] He had taken a trip from Acapulco to Zihuatanejo with his wife, María Luisa. Several things similar to what happened in the film happened to them — for example, the bus got stuck in a river...

TURRENT: Altolaguirre not only came up with the idea, he was also the producer. How much money did he put into the film?

BUÑUEL: Altolaguirre didn't have any money. The money was from his wife María Luisa's family. But we ran out of cash before the end of the filming to the point that they held the production manager's assistant hostage at an Acapulco hotel. María Luisa was an incredibly foolish woman. Because we had no money we couldn't shoot the end of the story, and I can no longer remember what it was. I keep all my scripts, but not that one. I suppose the National Cinémathèque has it.

TURRENT: Even under those difficult conditions, don't you think it's a very free film?

BUÑUEL: Taking those limitations into account, yes, like almost all the films I've made.

COLINA: Some of its limitations give the film a naive charm. For example, the almost unbelievable miniature of the place called precisely *Subida al cielo*. There are mountains, the bus that ascends, the storm...and it all looks like a toy.

BUÑUEL: Yes, the miniature was no larger than this room. Am I to blame? I wish they had given me a model like the one I saw in Hollywood in the '40s. You can't imagine it: the entire studio covered with a back-drop that represented the sky, perfect reproductions of mountains, a hotel, airplanes flying on invisible cables. A marvel! They told me it had cost two hundred thousand dollars.

TURRENT: Or rather, twice the cost to make your entire film.

BUÑUEL: Yes. *Mexican Bus Ride* must have cost one million two hun-

---

3 Manuel Altolaguirre (1905-1959), Spanish poet who belonged to the Generation of 1927. Although his literary output was slim, his reputation has grown over the years. He flirted with cinema both as a producer and a director, and shortly before his death he directed the poetic *El Cantar de los cantares* (Song of Songs, 1959), using texts by Fray Luis de León.

dred thousand Mexican pesos,[4] and that was because we filmed on real locations and had to move the equipment and the people involved in the production to Cuautla and Acapulco.

COLINA: Lilia Prado shook up our adolescence with this film. She is one of the most erotic presences in Mexican cinema.

BUÑUEL: Manuel Altolaguirre told me, "Look, I am going to introduce you to a girl who might do..." He brought her to the studio and introduced her to me. A lovely girl, very likable. She was a rumba dancer and very naive, as you will see from a story I'll tell you. I selected the other actors myself.

COLINA: Many of us agree that Esteban Márquez, the actor who played the protagonist, is very bad.

BUÑUEL: He was a boy who had never made a film before, and who had a florist shop with his mother. He lied to me and told me he had studied with Seki Sano, the renowned Japanese theater director and acting teacher. After finishing the film, I ran into Seki Sano and told him, "I made a film with a student of yours, Esteban Márquez." He said, "He's not one of my students; I never accepted him." Besides, Márquez was naive, like Lilia. On the first day of shooting I played a joke on them. I called them aside and told them, "Look, you two, since we're not working much with the union, we have permission to charge the actors a hundred pesos for every close-up we take. I wanted to warn you before we begin shooting. If you want your face in close-up it will cost you a hundred pesos. Ten close-ups, a thousand pesos. How many do you want, Lilia?" "Well... let's say eight or ten." "Very well. And you, Márquez, how many?" "Me, as many as you want, but many, many." They thought it was true! Very naive. Lilia was very young, but she never gave me any problems during the filming. Márquez did. Fortunately, there were some good actors, for example Miguel Dondé, who played the role of the politician.

COLINA: Since he looked a lot like President Miguel Alemán, it was said you put a little political commentary into it. Did you choose him for his looks?

BUÑUEL: I believe so. Because the character participates in a rather turbulent political demonstration, the resemblance could be amusing. But that was all; no political commentary, in reality.

COLINA: The film gives the impression you improvised a lot.

BUÑUEL: Sometimes... For example, remember the scene when the bus

4 Approximately ninety-five thousand dollars.

gets stuck in the river and needs some tractors to get it out? It came to me during the shooting to have a little girl arrive with an oxcart and, with hardly any effort, manage to get the bus out of the jam. Later, this is the girl we see dead in the coffin the father carries on the bus. I've seen people get on a bus with a child's coffin here in Mexico when there was no automobile available. And in reference to that scene, you see how we made films in Mexico at that time: we went on location for three days and nights at the Iztapalapa cemetery to film a sequence in which a mobile cinema showed a film at the same time as the little girl was buried (Altolaguirre had once seen this coincidence at a small-town cemetery). Everything was ready to film. The sequence presumes that, at the same time dirt is thrown on the girl, a newsreel with scenes of the atomic bomb is being projected on the cinema screen. We arrived at the location with the entire crew at ten o'clock at night, and Pizarro, the production manager, told me, "Mr. Buñuel, because of union regulations we have to finish shooting by two a.m." "But listen, I have three more days of shooting." "I'm very sorry." And since we had to finish by two a.m., I filmed only one shot: the bus arrives, they take out the girl's coffin and carry it into the cemetery amidst music and fireworks. Nothing more.

COLINA: The dream sequence, or rather daydream, is very important. In it, the protagonist reveals his Oedipal complex: he adores his mother, he throws his wife in the river... Did you or Altolaguirre write the scene?

BUÑUEL: Altolaguirre gave me nothing more than the general storyline: a very eventful trip on the Guerrero coast, a story of inheritance, a mother who is going to die. Juan de la Cabada[5] did some good work on the story, along with an intelligent and likable woman from Guerrero, who gave the dialogue a popular flavor; I don't know why she wasn't given credit in the film. I don't know if the dream you mention is in the script, but it's totally mine. I always try to put everything in the script because the technical demands of a production make it very difficult to improvise while you work. Though I did improvise that dream.

COLINA: The dream presents an excellent concept, very simple and very graphic. The mother is peeling an orange or an apple in a rocking chair on a pedestal, and the fruit's peel forms a ribbon that stretches all the way to the protagonist, who holds the end in his mouth. It's a metaphor for the umbilical cord.

---

5 Juan de la Cabada, Mexican short-story writer from Campeche; his work as a scriptwriter includes two films by Buñuel: *Mexican Bus Ride* and *Illusion Travels by Streetcar*.

TURRENT: And further about the daydream in the bus: the protagonist dreams he is making love with Lilia in the middle of a jungle that grows inside the vehicle and some sheep pass between them.

BUÑUEL: Those moments came to me while we were shooting. I didn't want to present a strict realism. I was also fascinated by putting in scenes in which nothing important happened. You two remember the admirable sequence of the maid in Vittorio de Sica's neorealist film *Umberto D*. The maid simply entered the kitchen, lit the fire, killed some roaches with some water, served the old man a glass of milk, and nothing more. Told like that, it has no interest whatsoever, does it? Yet on the screen it ends up being incredibly interesting. Almost an entire reel, and it is brilliant.

TURRENT: Indeed, it has been said that you were inspired by Italian neorealism when you made *Mexican Bus Ride*.

BUÑUEL: No. The one film of mine that has some relation to Italian neorealism would be, *Los olvidados*. I had seen De Sica's *Shoeshine* before and the much-praised *Road to Life,* that Soviet film about reforming children. I liked *Shoeshine* a lot, but in principle, I don't like Italian neorealism. Only a few films from that movement satisfy me: *Umberto D., Bicycle Thief,* a few of Fellini's... I believe reality shouldn't have only one dimension; it should have as many dimensions as possible.

COLINA: Even though the bus trip in *Mexican Bus Ride* is real, you are left with the impression that something fantastical has happened.

BUÑUEL: Perhaps it is because the number of incidents that would normally happen on several journeys are collected into a single trip. Reality is not usually so concentrated.

TURRENT: Do you remember *Le voyage surprise,*[6] a film by Pierre Prévert that also dealt with a very eventful bus trip?

BUÑUEL: I haven't seen it.

COLINA: Could it be said that *Mexican Bus Ride* is the first Buñuelian comedy?

BUÑUEL: If you say so... But is it a comedy? I don't know.

COLINA: It seems to me that one feels a certain happiness in *Mexican Bus Ride*, a humor without shadows.

TURRENT: But there is the girl they carry in the coffin.

COLINA: Yes, but even death is accepted as something inevitable in this film.

BUÑUEL: I already told you that episode came to me from something sim-

6 *Voyage-surprise* (1947), dir. Pierre Prévert.

ilar I saw on a bus. In the film, the father opens the little window of the small coffin, shows the dead girl's face, and asks the other passengers, "Wasn't my little girl pretty?"

TURRENT: How did the film do?

BUÑUEL: I don't know. Manolito Altolaguirre took it to Cannes and one critic said it deserved the Palme d'Or because of the possibilities it opened up to film. I think he exaggerated.

COLINA: Well, perhaps not. It won the International Critics Award for the Best Avant-Garde Film.

BUÑUEL: I think so. It must have had something.

11: *EL BRUTO* (THE BRUTE); REALITY AND IMAGINATION; PORNOGRAPHY

JOSE DE LA COLINA: Where did the story of *The Brute* come from?

LUIS BUÑUEL: Luis Alcoriza brought me an idea about an old man, owner of a tenement house, who wants to evict his tenants for business reasons. They organize in their own defense, and to block them, the landlord uses his strong man, a very powerful and very brutal man.

COLINA: Whose idea was it that this brute be a butcher at the Rastro slaughterhouse?

BUÑUEL: I don't remember. I added the landlord's father and also a scene between Katy Jurado and a rooster that I improvised during the filming.

COLINA: The scenes at the Rastro, Mexico City's principle slaughterhouse, have received a lot of attention. How did you find out about that place?

BUÑUEL: When we wrote the script, I went there at four in the morning to witness the slaughter of bulls and calves. I became friends with the butchers and sometimes went to drink *pulque* with them. I also watched them work. For example, one of them had a large knife, an ox would pass and slash! — the animal fell dead, without the man even interrupting his conversation with me. An incredibly precise way of wielding the knife; it gave me the shivers, but for him it was strictly routine. The most impressive thing was when the poor resigned lambs, which didn't even bleat, thronged into the passage that brought them to where they had their throats cut. One would pass and slash! Then another, slash! Some would continue to shake for a good time afterwards. And the stench of blood: Horrible! It was terrible for me.

TOMAS PEREZ TURRENT: Very few of those details remain in the film. Why?

BUÑUEL: I don't like those things. They impress too easily. They come off like Peckinpah.

COLINA: The image of the Virgin at the slaughterhouse has been called a "Surrealist wink."

BUÑUEL: The idea came to me while we were filming the scene, and I asked them to bring in a Virgin of Guadalupe. There was lot of tequila and wine. The bullfighter Dominguín and the writer Renato Leduc, who were friends from the bar where bullfighting fans usually gathered, were also there. The butchers invited us to eat the night before the bullfight, which was the next day or several days later. I remember that all the butchers were very anti-Communist. "We are Mexicans," they said. "We don't want exotic theories." Entering the slaughterhouse, you would see the image of the Virgin of Guadalupe on her altar in a vestibule, always surrounded by flowers and candles. On Virgin of Guadalupe Day, the butchers lit up the altar and had a marvelous party. Everyone spent thousands and thousands of pesos that they had saved specifically for that day, they invited their friends and many people. The Virgin was part of their lives and she accompanied them in their labors. I was afraid that showing this would seem disrespectful, but no one here in Mexico protested.

TURRENT: Do you think Pedro Armendáriz's character corresponded to some of those butchers?

BUÑUEL: Armendáriz dominated the character, but I had some problems with him because he put on a long-sleeved shirt when he was supposed to wear a short-sleeved one. He thought the short-sleeved one was for queers.

TURRENT: I think he also refused to say some lines of dialogue for the same reason.

BUÑUEL: In the scene where the neighbors are chasing the Brute and he evades them by jumping an adobe wall and hiding behind a door, he finds himself with Rosita Arenas and puts his hand over her mouth so she won't scream. The Brute has an icepick stuck in his back and says to the girl, "Take that out of my backside." Armendáriz refused to say that line because it included the word "backside." We left it as, "Take that out."

COLINA: The Brute is a very simple character.

BUÑUEL: That's why he's called "the Brute." But he isn't a bad man. For example: he takes care of some relatives who sponge off of him like parasites. And he is capable of feeling love and tenderness.

TURRENT: He is a pure man, an innocent who can be manipulated.

BUÑUEL: But he is also a beast. I have absolutely no sympathy for bestiality.

TURRENT: But the Brute is "pure."

BUÑUEL: I don't like his form of violence. It has nothing to do with what de Sade depicted in his books. (By the way, I am a sadist, not sadistic.) The Brute does not kill out of fidelity to any ideas, but only because his master orders him to.

COLINA: Some critics say the Brute finally suffers a "crisis of conscience" and confronts his boss, taking sides with the victims.

BUÑUEL: But it's not like that. The landlord insults him — "Bastard, damn you! You tried to rape my woman!" — and then tries to kill him. They struggle and the Brute kills the landlord. It's not that the Brute has become socially aware, no.

TURRENT: One scene caught my attention: the Brute, who is a force of nature, extinguishes a candle very delicately with his wet fingers instead of simply blowing it out.

BUÑUEL: A brute can be very fine and delicate in some things. On the other hand, this gesture is nothing extraordinary. Many people are in the habit of putting out a candle like that: I myself have done it. But in prison you can come across a man who has killed his entire family and who is perhaps doing very delicate needlework.

TURRENT: The two female characters, played by Rosita Arenas and Katy Jurado, are two very contrasting women.

BUÑUEL: Yes. One is an innocent girl and the other is a full woman. Meche is virginity, submission to the man, and the other is a voracious female who does what she wants.

COLINA: Katy Jurado's character, Paloma, is the more complex and duplicitous one, and she is very sensual. Why is she called Paloma? Usually a *paloma* (dove) is an image of innocence and she is exactly the opposite.

BUÑUEL: That name is not deliberate. I don't like those contrasts. I am incapable of making Paloma a woman who is just anyone. That's easy — as if an executioner were named St. Francis. Perhaps the character is called Paloma because I remembered a friend's daughter or a woman friend, or for the Virgin of the Paloma.

COLINA: Paloma is not a simple character. She is a "bad" woman, selfish, predatory, etc., but seen in another light, she is a woman who fights the world with her own weapons, has a frank sensuality, sleeps with whomever she wants... On the other hand, Meche, the good girl, seems too servile, too passive...

BUÑUEL: Meche is like that because sweetness and innocence attract me.

COLINA: There are also the Brute's relatives, his "parasites." I remember that an irate leftist Mexican critic protested about this image of a poor family.

BUÑUEL: Some poor families are parasites, others no. I don't generalize or try to demonstrate anything.

COLINA: That critic said you didn't know how to portray the people, that instead of the people, you show the *lumpen*. And that you attack workers.

BUÑUEL: I don't think so. I don't intend to treat workers either well or badly. Just because a family is working class doesn't make me feel either sympathy or antipathy. My sympathy would depend on how each one is as a person. Besides, I see these things with humor. In *The Exterminating Angel*, the woman with cancer tells the doctor, "Will you really take me to the sanctuary at Lourdes? I want you to take me there and buy me a washable plastic Virgin." A bourgeois person says that, and I present it with a certain humor. I am impartial. Another example, from the same film: some bourgeois people are talking about a catastrophe in which many people were injured. "But they were just common people," says one of the characters, "and those people don't suffer, they are like animals. Once I saw a mule with its feet broken and it was completely impassive, with no expression of pain whatsoever. On the other hand, you remember Prince Divani, what majesty he had facing death. The masses don't feel anything, they are like mules..." I'm not the one who is attacking the masses, it's the character. One further example: in *The Discreet Charm of the Bourgeoisie*, Fernando Rey calls to his chauffeur: "Come here, have a drink with us." The chauffeur throws down the drink in one toss, without savoring it. "Thank you, you may now leave," Rey tells him, and later comments to the other bourgeois characters, "You see what a lack of refinement? No regime, no matter how advanced, can give the masses the necessary refinement." This would supposedly be another of my attacks on the people. But it is not mine, it comes from one of my characters and I view it humorously.

COLINA: But in *The Brute* we're not dealing with some character's commentary: you show us a really abject and rapacious family, a bit like the destitute people in *Viridiana*.

BUÑUEL: I'm not dealing with "the people" in *Viridiana*, but rather with beggars. Besides, despite everything, those beggars are men of good will. They're not bandits, they don't intend to destroy their benefactor's house. They enter it out of curiosity, see the tablecloths and the silverware, and decide to eat like princes. Afterwards, they will wash the tablecloths and the silverware and nothing will have happened. But they get drunk and lose control of their actions. Nor am I attacking beggars here. What happened to them could easily happen to many others.

TURRENT: People say that whenever you show a blind man in one of your films, he is always evil. But that's because they prefer to believe that all blind people are saints.

BUÑUEL: I believe people are bad because their own deficiencies make them that way. But in which other films do I present a blind person as bad? The blind man who was kicked in *L'Age d'or* is neither good nor bad, and yet the protagonist kicks him. The protagonist did that, not me. In reality, I have never had a bad experience with a blind person. But in my imaginary world, a blind person can be like a threatening bird. Why? For me it is instinctive and I can't avoid it.

COLINA: It is curious, because it could be said that you are making a distinction between reality and imagination, life and art...

BUÑUEL: You have touched upon something important. In fact: the imagination is one thing and life something else. No one can teach my imagination anything because I know everything, at least I hope I know everything. With life, it's different. In my life, I have never been a man of action, but I am one in my imagination. And for that reason, I can imaginarily attack. As I am greeting someone in real life, I can entertain the fantasy of killing him. They are two distinct levels: the real social action on the one hand, and on the other, the imaginary, the dreamed. In *L'Age d'or*, I tried to offend the public because it seemed necessary for me at that time. Nevertheless, when I had to cut a dead calf's eye in *Un chien andalou*, I had to work myself up to do it. Painlevé,[1] who made documentaries about nature — some wonderful films with scenes of life at the bottom of the ocean — thought I loved to cut up eyeballs. I went to see one of his films that he dedicated to me: "To Luis Buñuel, with affection. Jean Painlevé." The camera filmed the cadaver of a woman about eighty years old, whose nose was stretched out with a pair of tweezers, and they were sectioning it with a saw in order to exhibit the veins, the bones. Horrified,

1 Jean Painlevé, French documentary maker who founded L'Institut du Cinéma Scientifique.

I fled, and I said to Painlevé, "Do you think that just because I sliced an eyeball open in a film I enjoy these things? I do them for ideological reasons. But an operation horrifies me. I can't stand the sight of blood."

COLINA: Can you say then that our imaginations free us of our fears, our desperations, our unrevealable desires?

BUÑUEL: In principle, when you make a film, or write a book, you must put in whatever you want. The imagination is the only terrain where man is free.

COLINA: We have already spoken a bit about this, in regard to Sade. He brought to the field of the imagination things that were inadmissible in real life.

BUÑUEL: That's right. They have never attributed more than two crimes to the Marquis de Sade. They said that he poisoned two women at a brothel in Marseilles. The truth is that neither of the women died: they had stomach pains and nothing more. They also say that he found a beggar woman on the outskirts of Paris whom he took up to a garret and whipped. This was not proved. In any case, these things would be innocent compared to everything he imagined. And few people know that he was accused of being counterrevolutionary at the Convention because he was against the death penalty.

COLINA: At one point we mentioned certain excesses of cruelty in contemporary cinema, and you were against them. Isn't that a contradiction?

BUÑUEL: It's that these cruelties, and pornography, have come into vogue, they have been trivialized. I was not against pornography when it always took place in small, secret groups, as it used to. But I am against its popularization and the whole vogue of pornography. It's the same with terrorism and the craze for bombing: they throw bombs at anybody: the priest, such-and-such a person's car, the boy next door. Pornographic films, which are created only to placate people and make a lot of money, make me sick.

TURRENT: But since we are already arguing about the dichotomy between reality and the imagination, I ask: in order for imagination to be a factor of human liberation, wouldn't it have to pass into the level of real life?

BUÑUEL: I don't see that it must necessarily be like that. There is an interrelation between the imagination and reality; they are not separated like light and dark. They influence each other mutually, interchanging elements.

COLINA: Are they André Breton's *Communicating Vessels?*[2]

BUÑUEL: Yes. The difference is that while your imagination can allow you to go to infinity, wherever you want to go, in reality, in practical life, you are necessarily blocked by your conscience, legal sanctions, friends, family. There is always some brake that you or society applies. In my imagination I can commit incest, but as a social being, and dispassionately, my moral sense would impede me.

COLINA: Once again I play the devil's advocate. You just said pornography would be all right if it were kept to a small, secret group, the "happy few."

BUÑUEL: The way it used to be in the brothels.

COLINA: But isn't that an elitist idea? The right of the imagination, yes, but only for a minority, in a closed chapel.

BUÑUEL: In a private little hideaway, yes. In former times that was the brothel. The bad thing is when money and publicity come into it. They have abused sex and violence to make more money. I am also against violence as a mere spectacle. Pornography itself can be violence. During the Surrealist period, the director of Studio 28 gave me a pornographic film called *Soeur Vaseline* (Sister Vaseline), a very good title. But there were two very bad reels. A nun and a gardener in an orchard. The nun, holding her breviary, passes by the gardener; he stops hoeing, grabs the nun, and without any transition, both of them begin to "function." At the same time, a window opens and a friar appears; he sees the couple in the garden, takes a whip and beats the gardener, who has his ass in the air, but later he joins the couple and the function ends in a *ménage à trois*. Completely terrible. Once the Surrealists and I imagined taking over a movie theater and giving a surprise screening of the film. Two of us would go up to the projection booth while two others guarded the theater, and I would show the film. We would do it at a time when there would be children present. We wanted to shock the parents and bourgeois morality because the Surrealists and I thought scandal was a weapon. In the end, we didn't do it. In *L'Age d'or*, I asked Gastón Modot to bash a dog's head in. Everyone balked at this: Modot, the cinematographer, the technicians, so finally I convinced Modot just to kick the dog. I thought the scene was necessary, but I don't enjoy tormenting animals.

COLINA: You accept pornography as scandal and as pleasure for a few. I

2 *Les Vases communicants,* by André Breton (Paris: Éditions Gallimard, 1932).

insist that you can be accused of being an elitist.

BUÑUEL: That's possible. Furthermore, even if I were told that there was going to be a free screening of a pornographic film, one from which no one would make any money, I would still be against it.

COLINA: But there's the problem. Why?

BUÑUEL: Because it trivializes eroticism. This question is complicated and should be treated more profoundly. I am not against eroticism, I am only against pornography, which is the physiology of eroticism. I am against pornography because I believe in love. One of André Breton's poems calls love a secret ceremony that should be celebrated in darkness at the bottom of a cave. For me, that is gospel. On the other hand, pornography is love celebrated in a sports stadium or a bullring. I say this much too schematically. I would have to write about this in an essay, which would be beyond my capabilities.

TURRENT: There is no need for imagination in commercial pornography.

BUÑUEL: As eroticism, pornography is negative because it finishes with everything, it leaves nothing to the imagination, there is no mystery. Whereas suggesting eroticism as a possibility — suggesting it, no more — is much better.

COLINA: In *The Brute*, there is a scene that is suggestive and very crude at the same time. When the innocent girl loses her virginity in the arms of the Brute, we don't see the act itself; instead, the camera focuses on a hunk of meat smoking on the brazier. We hear the girl's sobs and the Brute's voice: "The meat is burned!" It seems like a climax to the sex act, the deflowering of the girl.

BUÑUEL: No, the comment is innocent. The Brute has no secondary intention.

TURRENT: At the end, when both the Brute and the landlord are dead, a horrified Paloma — who has caused both deaths — sees a rooster that seems to look at her in judgment.

BUÑUEL: The idea occurred to me when we were filming the scene, and I asked them to bring me a rooster. I have already told you that I put these scenes in without deliberation, and I leave it to the audience to interpret them as they want. Roosters or chickens form part of the many "visions" I have; at times they are compulsive. It is inexplicable, but for me, roosters and chickens are nightmare beings.

TURRENT: *The Brute* is a melodrama. Did you intend it to be?

BUÑUEL: The film is what it is. I don't know if I did or didn't want to make a melodrama. Things emerged. I had a central idea: the oppressive landlord, the tenants who oppose him, the strong man, who could be either a boxer or a butcher. Things get complicated because the Brute falls in love with the daughter of the man he killed, and besides he has had relations with the landowner's lover, who becomes jealous. Melodrama? It's all the same to me. When I decided I was going to make the film, I didn't say to myself, "I am going to make a melodrama."

12: *ADVENTURES OF ROBINSON CRUSOE*

TOMAS PEREZ TURRENT: Before it was proposed to you, had you ever thought about filming *Adventures of Robinson Crusoe?*

LUIS BUÑUEL: No. The book by Defoe that I wanted to film was *Journal of the Plague Year,* because I was interested in the subject. The plague not only brought physical decomposition, but also social and moral decay: it destroyed families, friendship, love, solidarity, civilized values. A man can have the most crazy love for a woman, but if she contracts the plague, her lover doesn't even want to get close to her, however much *amour fou* he may feel. It's terrible. I put the opposite situation in *Nazarín:* the man who kisses his dying lover, who remains alone with her voluntarily. I was also attracted to Jean Giono's book *Le Hussard sur le toit.* Giono thought I could adapt it to Mexico, but that didn't appeal to me: the plague has more force in countries where human life has more value, where social customs are stronger, more in agreement with Christian culture. A plague in Paris or London or Madrid would impress me more: it's my world crumbling around me. I can deal with certain subjects, either trivial or sublime, if they touch me, if they stir some emotion in me, if they either attract or repel me. For example: I find strange everything that doesn't pertain to the Christian world: Egypt, the Aztecs, Indo-Chinese temples. The subject of death interests me because of my Christian education, which is a very strong element in my formation.

JOSE DE LA COLINA: But it doesn't seem to me that you made *Robinson Crusoe* merely as an assignment.

BUÑUEL: No. Even though the novel didn't appeal to me as such, I did find Robinson's story interesting: the shipwreck, his survival on the island, the struggle with nature, his solitude, the appearance of another human being, a savage... That was what caught my attention when I read the novel when I was fifteen years old. Well, it was proposed that I make the film. Hugo Butler, who used the pen name Philip Roll because of problems with Hollywood's blacklist, had written a first adaptation. I added a few elements, or rather I accentuated them — the dialogues and Robinson's discussions with Friday, the conversion of the savage to some civilized customs — and Butler helped with that. Of course it didn't mean simply illustrating the book. Have you read it? It's full of moral reflections and Biblical parallels, for pages and pages.

COLINA: It seems you were interested in other more concrete problems confronting a man in total isolation. For example: the lack of women, of a friend.

BUÑUEL: Yes. There was the problem of the encounter between an old man living in a state of forced celibacy and a young savage. I didn't overstate this, I only touched on it. For example, I touched on these things when I suggested the idea of the woman's dress. Robinson makes a scarecrow using women's clothes he finds in a chest. The wind whips up the clothes as if it were bringing a woman to life. There is a suggestion, but very discreet, of sexual need. Later, after Friday is Robinson's friend, the savage is fascinated by the women's clothes and innocently puts them on. Seeing him, Robinson is shaken and understands this is a danger for him, and he asks Friday to take them off.

COLINA: The relationship between Robinson and Friday evolves over the course of the film: at first it is only a master-servant relationship, but later it becomes something else, a type of comradeship.

BUÑUEL: I was interested in this evolution, but I must clarify that I didn't want to present a discourse on the master-servant or savage-civilization relationship. I didn't follow a *parti-pris,* I didn't want to generalize, or deduce any social theories. An author has two ways of developing a narrative: either he can impose an intellectual or moral direction on it, or he can allow things to arise according to how they happen and how he feels or thinks them. It wouldn't occur to me — though I believe I do think about it at times — to make an anticolonial film, for example. Yes, I could make a film about a man who arrives at Tahiti or Samoa or the Fiji Islands and meets some surprising beings who give him coconut milk to drink and cover him with flowers. I like that, and go on with the narrative, and soon the fact that I am not a colonialist will be noticeable, although I didn't propose to show it. I don't make thesis films, ones that have a specific message.

COLINA: Aren't you cheating, Don Luis? In *Robinson Crusoe*, there is a "message" scene in which Robinson and Friday argue theology and free will.

BUÑUEL: What happened is that I asked myself the question: and now what are they going to talk about in this scene? They have to talk about something so they're not just doing manual tasks all the time. Then it came to me to have them talk about religion. Robinson is Catholic or Protestant, and Friday is a pagan savage. They talk about God and free will as they would talk about anything else. I didn't put in a theological or antitheological discourse because that really wouldn't interest the audience very much. That's for books, not movies.

COLINA: It's difficult to believe that you don't offer a point of view about religious matters in this film. Because at the beginning, Friday takes Robinson to be almost a god: when Friday sees Robinson shoot his gun, he kneels before him and bows, not just as a servant before his master, but as a creature before his god.

BUÑUEL: If I had thought about that before writing and filming it, you would be right. You think like that only after having seen the film. I'm not completely irrational, but I do not make a film as an intellectual argument, or with the predetermined idea as to its meaning. The argument begins with a scene and, if you want, I enter into it in some way. In the end, this may turn out all right; something interesting emerges, which may even be the best part of the film. But originally it was only one dialogue within the action.

COLINA: In the film, Friday says something that all Christians must have asked themselves at some time: if God wants us to be good and pure, why does he send us temptation? Only to test us? Only to punish or reward us?

BUÑUEL: As you both already know, I was a Catholic, but lost my faith at seventeen years of age. I lost it even before reading Darwin. My doubts began with ideas about hell and God's justice.

COLINA: As in the novel, the Bible is very present in the film. When Robinson shouts into the ravine in order to hear the echo of his own voice, he quotes that line about "man short in days and long in sorrow." And, we often see him reading the Bible.

BUÑUEL: That scene appealed to me because Robinson wanted to hear a human voice, even though it was only the echo of his own voice. The Biblical quote then takes on a dramatic interest. To put in more quotes from the Bible would have seemed too much to me.

TURRENT: The film is very narrative and it adheres closely to the facts...

BUÑUEL: Yes, but remember there are also dreams and hallucinations.

TURRENT: That is where I was going, Don Luis. And the dreams and hallucinations introduce a Surrealist vision...

BUÑUEL: Of course, because I have always been faithful to certain principles of my Surrealist period and these have to come into play, even though I was not making a one-hundred-percent Surrealist film. And, after all, Defoe did put dreams and hallucinations in his book. Because dreams appear in Robinson's life or the Pope's or the life of any citizen whatsoever, don't they? By the way, for that very reason, except for two or three films, neorealism doesn't interest me. They film immediate and logical reality. For example, to a neorealist, a glass is an object made of glass that is used to drink water and nothing more. But — depending on the degree of emotion we bring to our contemplation of it — out of simple irrational compulsion and the intervention of the subconscious, the same glass can evoke a runaway horse, a memory of my mother, or whatever. This is not to say that I intended to make a Surrealist *Robinson Crusoe*, a Robinson *à la Buñuel*. I believe that, in general, I adhered to the principal facts of the book.

COLINA: There are some very powerful images in the dreams or hallucinations. Robinson dreams of being punished by his father.

BUÑUEL: His thirst gives him a fever and he dreams he is tied up and placed in water up to his waist, and the bonds keep him from drinking. His father doesn't want to give him anything to drink and even pushes a pitcher away, spilling its contents, and then laughs. I filmed this because that was how I felt it, because it is a very proper fever-induced dream, nothing to do with Buñuelism or Surrealism. What does the dream mean? Ah, that is an enigma for me, too. I don't pretend to solve it.

COLINA: We will accept it as an enigma. There are other enigmas, perhaps less important. And I like it that they aren't resolved. For example: Robinson arrives on the island with a dog and cat...

BUÑUEL: And the cat bears kittens.

COLINA: But where did the male cat come from? Robinson himself asks the question.

BUÑUEL: It's a small mystery that amuses me. But perhaps there is nothing mysterious about it; the cat could have come from the ship already pregnant, or met up with a wild cat on the island.

COLINA: Furthermore, there is a certain "anthropological" theme. At the end, Robinson's voice tells us that the cats became wild and...

BUÑUEL: If they are abandoned to nature, far from mankind, they become wild, just as dogs do. If I left my dog Tristanita in the woods and she survived, she would revert into a wild dog, like a wolf. This can happen even with a small child at a very young age. Even if they are children of ten or eleven years old, they can begin to turn into savages. For this reason I was very interested in William Golding's novel *Lord of the Flies,* which is the exact opposite of Jules Verne's *Deux ans de vacances* (A Long Vacation). Isn't that right? In Verne's book the children live for a long time on an island and continue to feel very civilized, as if they were still living in an English private school.

COLINA: One of the moments I like most in all your films is in *Robinson Crusoe.* After many years, Robinson leaves the island accompanied by Friday and some sailors. When the island is already very far away, we hear the bark of the dog that in fact had died many years before.

BUÑUEL: That is very much in my style: the sound does not correspond to the image. The bark appears there as a memory, as Robinson's sentimental fixation on the island. It came to me, like so many other of these details, during the production. The scene of Robinson's departure seemed a bit flat to me. Then I thought it would be good to put in the bark of the dead dog.

COLINA: And we have already been impressed by the dog's death earlier.

BUÑUEL: That's natural, because the death signified Robinson's complete human isolation. What most interested me about Robinson was his complete human solitude: what does a man who is completely alone think, feel or dream? I'm sure if any one of us was left abandoned on a desert island, he would begin to hear voices. For that reason, there is the scene in which Robinson gets drunk and thinks he hears the voices of his friends, as if he were drinking with them at a tavern. What also happens, as I told you, is that I like to put in sounds that are not justified by the image. Of course, in this case there is an interior justification. The friends' voices provide more contrast to Robinson's solitude.

TURRENT: Yes, you shudder when the voices cease and Robinson finds himself alone in his hut. That scene indicates the importance of the sound track, which is very carefully done.

BUÑUEL: But the sound track was easy. A number of reels with only one character, plus the noise of the sea, the jungle, the birds, and later some more reels with what Friday says, and then the characters who arrive at the end of the story. It is a film with very little dialogue.

TURRENT: But the natural sounds create an obsessive atmosphere. And later the sounds that don't correspond to the image which we talked about: those elements can take on more importance than the dialogues.

BUÑUEL: Certainly on the first occasions when Friday speaks I had to invent an "island" language. When Friday had to say something, I told him he should say any word backwards; for example *Arerbac Ohcnap* (Pancho Cabrera).[1] That would sound like a savage dialect.

TURRENT: It could be said that the film has three very precise segments: Robinson's solitude, the appearance of Friday and the friendship between the two, and finally, the solidarity with other men and the return to civilization.

BUÑUEL: Perceptive of you. The master-servant relation becomes a friendship because it's natural. Two people alone on an island must survive and help each other, it isn't natural for them to maintain our social conventions. Conventions would ease.

TURRENT: When their friendship is established, the island is made livable, a kind of paradise regained.

BUÑUEL: Before it could be a real paradise, it still lacks a few friends and some women. But then some sleazy producer would want a pornographic version, one in which Robinson says to Friday, "Listen, how are the women on your island?" "Well, sir, they're very good." "Ah, then go back and fetch me three."

COLINA: *Robinson Crusoe* is your first color film. Did that cause any problems?

BUÑUEL: Until then, none of the films I had made in Mexico had taken more than three weeks to shoot. This one took three months, because it was the first film on the continent in Eastmancolor[2] and the negative could only be developed in Hollywood. Dancigers told me: "It doesn't matter to me if you film for one week or four months, but use Alex Phillips as the cinematographer." We filmed for a month and a half in Manzanillo because Alex was a very careful professional and there were days when we managed to get only one shot. For example: I would select the site where we would shoot; Alex would measure the lights there and tell me the shadows weren't right for color film. I would tell him to find a similar place without that problem. Alex would then go out exploring

1 Pancho Cabrera, a Mexican producer.

2 Filmographies usually state that *Adventures of Robinson Crusoe* was filmed in Pathécolor. Buñuel insists it was shot in Eastmancolor, the first time this film was used outside of the United States.

while I sat and drank a couple of beers. Very late in the day, Alex would return. He had found a good site, although a bit far away. We would go see it and these comings and goings delayed the production. Sometimes we walked behind Alex through the jungle for an hour to get only one very short shot. At other times, by the time we arrived at the site Alex selected, he suddenly made a face: the place no longer looked the same as before because in an hour the light had changed. I said, "Let's see if we have time to film something else back where we were, and tomorrow we'll come back here at the right time." It was crazy: the film was dependent on Alex...and Alex was dependent on the changes in light. We would wait hours to film one very brief shot of Robinson shooting a squirrel or scratching an ear.

TURRENT: Did you change your conception of the scenes or your direction of the actors because you filmed in color? For example, did you think about a dominant color?

BUÑUEL: No way. I let Alex work it out with his lenses and his filters. At times he consulted me: "What if we use the magenta filter here?" I told him to do what he thought was best. Later in *Cahiers du Cinéma*, an article came out that discussed Buñuel's palette. Buñuel's palette doesn't exist, only Alex Phillips'.

TURRENT: Kyrou said there was a dominant green in the film, owing to the influence of Rousseau. I don't know if he is referring to the writer or the painter.

BUÑUEL: I thought about neither the writer nor the painter, nor about Buñuel's palette, nor any of that. The truth is that in my color films I select the furniture and the costumes, but I do it precisely to eliminate colors, getting rid of a red that is too lively, a technicolor green, etc. I prefer gray curtains, pallid colors, greens that don't call attention to themselves. I leave everything else to the cinematographer, and he does what he wants as long as he doesn't cause me any problems.

TURRENT: It seems that when they made prints, there were some technical problems with the color.

BUÑUEL: First they made thirty prints from the negative and the color was good. Afterwards, Eastmancolor made another positive that didn't correspond to the first negative, and the prints that came out badly were from that.

TURRENT: Adrienne Mancia, from the Museum of Modern Art, told us that a new distributor had obtained some very good prints and had shown the film in New York with a good deal of success.

BUÑUEL: It could be that they were prints made from the original negative.

COLINA: In general, how did *Robinson Crusoe* do commercially?

BUÑUEL: It was a success, although you can't compare it to *Los olvidados*. A photograph in an English magazine showed lines to see *Los olvidados* at a cinema in Plymouth. It broke box-office records there. In Paris it played for several months at the Cinéma Vendôme. It was shown successfully all over the world. And it cost only five hundred thousand pesos — forty thousand dollars.

TURRENT: And how much did *Robinson Crusoe* cost?

BUÑUEL: One million nine hundred thousand pesos.[3]

TURRENT: It was one of the most expensive films ever made at that time in Mexico.

BUÑUEL: I think so, but the expense is understandable: the color laboratory, the shooting schedule, the Spanish and English versions.

3 Approximately one hundred and fifty thousand dollars.

13: *EL* (THIS STRANGE PASSION); VOYEURISM

JOSE DE LA COLINA: I think you put something of your own way of being into the protagonist of *El.*

LUIS BUÑUEL: It may be the film I put the most of myself into. There is something of me in the protagonist.

COLINA: It's as if you had said: this would be me if I were paranoid.

TOMAS PEREZ TURRENT: To me, the protagonist Francisco Galván seems to be someone who is trying to free himself without knowing how. He bears a certain resemblance to the character of Archibaldo in *The Criminal Life of Archibaldo de la Cruz.* The difference is that while Archibaldo "stages" his fantasies and creates simulations, Francisco confuses his obsessions with reality. But both try to escape through the imagination.

BUÑUEL: Archibaldo is more cerebral, colder, more of an "aesthete."

TURRENT: Archibaldo is seen from a distance, while Francisco Galván is "interiorized." I am struck by his radical selfishness, when, for example, he tells his wife in the church tower, "I hate the happiness of stupid people."

BUÑUEL: Yes. I share his feeling when he looks at the people like ants there below him and says, "I would like to be God, to squash them..."

TURRENT: Entomology!

BUÑUEL: (Laughs) And there is another episode I like because something similar happens to many people. Francisco and his wife are on their honeymoon in Guanajuato. In reality, they are just beginning to know each other. Francisco asks her, "What don't you like about me." She replies, "I like everything about you, Francisco, I don't find any defects." Francisco: "But I must have some." She denies this, but in the end, giving in to his insistence, she says, "Well, yes, perhaps at times you are a little...a little unfair." And he jumps up: "Unfair! I am one of the most fair men around!" This type of reaction is very frequent in all of us, isn't it? For

example: a painter asks a connoisseur, "What do you think of my painting?" The connoisseur replies, "It's good, very good." "No, tell me the
truth. I'm not fishing for compliments; I want frank criticism." "But I
think the painting is good." "But something about it is flawed and I want
you to tell me what." Finally the other one dares, "Well, perhaps that sky
is not very well done and looks a bit flat..." And the painter cries, "What
are you saying! I've never painted a better sky in my life!" ... Aren't we all
a little like this? I won't give you any names, but this happened to someone working in the film industry. After a screening, a director asked a
friend, "What did you think of my film?" "Very good, I liked it a lot."
"No, tell me the truth; did you find any defect?" "Well, the ending may
be a little forced..." "The ending? What are you talking about? It's the
best part of the picture!" *(He laughs.)* All that preamble begging for criticism really just hides the desire for another person to tell us we've made a
masterpiece.

COLINA: Yes, there is that in the protagonist of *El*, a desire to be praised,
but perhaps a certain masochism intervenes as well, or the search for an
excuse to fight with someone else...

BUÑUEL: It's possible. We don't know what is at the bottom of paranoia,
and Francisco Galván is a paranoid. Nevertheless, his predominant need
is for others to take him as perfect; he wants to be considered the best of
all men.

COLINA: We have mentioned Archibaldo. I find Francisco more likable
because he lives passionately and is not a hypocrite. He has contradictory
changes, but he always completely surrenders himself, doesn't he?

BUÑUEL: Yes, he is a man who is faithful to his passions and principles.
There is something else I like, because once again I recognize myself there:
it also happens on the honeymoon. He says, "My beloved, I idolize
you...," etc. She says, "Me too, Francisco. How happy we are going to be,
how I love knowing your birthplace..." She smiles pensively and suddenly he says: "What are you thinking about?" "About you, Francisco, and
about our honeymoon." "No. You were thinking about someone else.
Tell me who you were thinking about or I will..." Then, becoming rabid-
ly angry, he leaves her alone and goes off to sleep separately.

COLINA: A jealous person tries to justify his jealousy. At times Francisco
is capable of great lucidity, of great wisdom, but he suffers from a thirst
for the absolute and even for catastrophe...

BUÑUEL: The paranoid can be the most sane and reasonable of men... as long as you don't touch his weak point: the delirium of persecution, which is reflected in his jealousy or belligerence. Then he distrusts his wife and looks for a fight. I knew a man in the military, a man everyone in Madrid thought was perfect. They adored him, saying, "He is a complete gentleman!" Generous, good, affable. He got along well with everyone, except his wife and his family.

TURRENT: I find a similarity between Francisco Galván and Gaston Modot's character in *L'Age d'or*; both go beyond morality.

COLINA: No, it's the reverse. Francisco Galván is completely moral. He has his own moral code and for that reason he looks down on everyone else.

BUÑUEL: I would say that he follows an inner, traditional morality that he received and believes in. He adheres to society's rules, he is an authentically bourgeois gentleman, authentically Catholic. There is no doubt about that. But he has deliriums of persecution: he believes he is being cuckolded, that a legal trap is being put into place to deprive him of what is his, and then, boom! — he is capable of murder.

COLINA: There is an extraordinary scene: Francisco goes into the bedroom where his wife is sleeping, taking with him a rope, a needle and thread, and a razor blade. You could say he is going to practice some ritual. But is he going to sew up his wife's sex organ?

BUÑUEL: Yes, yes. That is something all the critics have seen. While we were shooting that scene, my assistant told me that when the audience saw this enormous rope, the kind used to tie up a ship, they would burst out laughing. And people did laugh at that.

COLINA: I think people laugh at the absurdity of his intentions, and at the fact that he fails.

BUÑUEL: He makes two knots so that if she wakes up he'll only need one tug to have her tied up. But she screams for help and he flees.

COLINA: That conjunction of objects — the rope, needle, razor, etc. — is very Surrealist, even though each has a precise function. But I don't understand the razor blade very well.

BUÑUEL: It could be to cut the thread after having sewn up her sex. Or...perhaps he wants to cut off her clitoris. I don't know. That is him. I would not have cut off her clitoris. Sew her up, that yes. *(Laughter)*

TURRENT: You told us something about a psychiatrist who had interpreted the entire film as a dream.

BUÑUEL: Yes, Dr. Fernando Cesarman. According to him, at the end, Francisco had regained full use of his reason and... Stop! I told him, look how he goes zigzagging off.

TURRENT: I would say the film could be a dream from the moment when Francisco gets up, goes to his butler's room, etc., until the scene when he bursts into full delirium in the church.

BUÑUEL: In that scene, there is a delirious interpretation of reality, but not a dream. Francisco believes that people are laughing at him and the priest is threatening him. But there is no dream.

TURRENT: Since you acknowledge that there is something of you in the character, there's something I noticed that isn't so farfetched: Arturo de Córdova's movements, principally his shoulders, are yours.

BUÑUEL: At times, when I direct actors, I make the gesture I want from them, to save me from having to describe it. The actor can either copy the gesture or make it in his own way.

COLINA: Since he is so stereotyped as an actor, did Arturo de Córdova cause any problems during the filming?

BUÑUEL: He had some objections. That scene where he gets up at night to go to the butler's room seemed bad to him because the butler was in his underwear. He was afraid people would think he was a homosexual. He told me, "We can name some arbitrators who can give their opinion on this — except, of course, if you insist, we will do the scene as it is." I told him, "I don't see anything wrong with this scene. The butler is in his underwear because he was already in bed. Besides, you're not going to declare yourself to him, you're going to cry to him, to say you are unhappy because your wife is cheating on you..." This had a certain logic. The servant has been with him for years and is Francisco's favorite among the help. Remember how the film begins: Francisco sees the butler and the maid playing around and the one he fires is the maid, even though it was the butler who started playing around. Just because of that, does Francisco have homosexual tendencies? I don't think so. Galván is a pure man, a man of platonic loves. As he tells his confessor, he was a virgin when he got married. The wife goes to the confessional to complain: "Father, life with him is hell; he mistreats me..." And the priest replies, "My daughter, this man is good and pure. He is forty years old and has known no other woman than you... It's your fault. You must be more understanding with him...," etc. The priest even tells the wife, "I saw you dancing the other day with the lawyer. You should be more modest."

You remember the incident at the dance: Francisco, very dignified and respectful, dances with a guest. His wife dances in a more friendly manner with the lawyer, because Francisco himself had asked her to (he has business dealings with the lawyer). The priest, who was present at the dance, comments, "You can see people's decency immediately when they dance. Look at Francisco, what a gentleman. On the other hand, the lawyer, how indecent!" Even though the lawyer, of course, dances respectfully.

COLINA: The film is based on a work by Mercedes Pinto that is part novel and part testimony based on her life.

BUÑUEL: An interesting book she had composed from her notes on her life with her husband, Foronda. Some pages could have been passed exactly as they were to the film. For example, once when she was in the garden taking care of the flowers, Foronda arrived and noticed that, far away in a tower, there was a bellringer busy with his own affairs, and he immediately becomes jealous — "Vixen, you are carrying on with that man!" — and he hit her.

COLINA: What did the author think of how you brought the book to the "big screen?"

BUÑUEL: She liked it a lot. That didn't happen when I made *The Criminal Life of Archibaldo de la Cruz* and Usigli protested because of my treatment of his novel.

TURRENT: Do you remember the initial scene in the church with the feet washing ceremony?

BUÑUEL: I remember everything about *El* very well. Francisco is very dignified in that scene with his Knight of the Holy Sacrament armband.

COLINA: I thought the armband was from the Knights of Columbus, which is a Catholic order here in Mexico, composed of laymen.

BUÑUEL: The Knights of the Holy Sacrament also exists here. And Francisco is aiding in the ceremony of the *lavabo*, in which the priest wets and rinses the feet of the children, then kisses them on the instep. The camera follows the movement of Francisco's gaze across a row of feet, and suddenly moves back to take in the feet of Delia Garcés. The woman feels his look and becomes embarrassed, blushing. One feels the fascination that exists between hawk and the dove. There Francisco's passion begins.

COLINA: I think Delia Garcés, with her modest tone and somewhat genteel manner, is very good in the role of the wife. The *macho's* idea of a model wife. She seems capable of putting up with being married to him for the rest of her life.

BUÑUEL: Delia Garcés is Argentine. She had arrived in Mexico with her husband and filmed several things. She was very modest, very sweet, in fact exactly like the wife of the paranoid I had known in Spain.

TURRENT: Francisco is paranoid but he also has sadomasochistic and fetishistic tendencies. Buñuel's famous foot fetish...

BUÑUEL: Yes. There is a scene you both remember: the two of them are sitting at the table eating. He is in a bad mood, he reads the newspaper and doesn't talk to his wife. She is intimidated. Suddenly the newspaper falls to the floor. Francisco bends over to pick it up and sees her feet under the table. When Francisco raises his head, his expression has changed, it has become friendly. He wants to kiss his wife but, since she has her mouth full, she resists. This makes Francisco furious and he orders her from the table... The important thing is that he had become excited by seeing her shoes.

TURRENT: Here his fetish behavior seems to stem from repressed desire. When the erotic imagination censors itself, doesn't it fall into fetishistic behavior?

BUÑUEL: Why only fetishes? It can lead to many other things, even the most terrible. It can end in incest, sodomy, murder... the imagination can permit anything on a mental level, it can go to the very limit. In practice, dealing with possible acts, it can be terrible. I could grab a shotgun and kill both of you right now... Relax, I'm not going to do it.

COLINA: One moment, Don Luis! If you say that, then you had thought about it. And why did you think about it?

BUÑUEL: To give you an example.

COLINA: But, why that example? Why did you articulate it like that? You could have said, "Now De la Colina takes his shotgun and kills us, Pérez Turrent and myself."

BUÑUEL: (Laughs) All right! You've got it! Now it is you who imagines killing us.

COLINA: Let's not tempt the devil with jokes. The important thing is this: at one time or another, all human beings put "onstage," in their mental theater, actions that could fill volumes like those of the Marquis de Sade.

BUÑUEL: Yes, and that is what is admirable about Sade: his way of giving his imagination total freedom, denying it nothing...but on paper, of course. His real life crimes were of little importance. Today, he would deserve some minor fines at most.

COLINA: But is the imagination so innocent? Let's suppose a sleepwalking man gets up and, without realizing it, does what his imagination dictates: kills his cats and then afterwards, his wife.

BUÑUEL: That act has nothing to do with the imagination. I am aware that in real life I won't pass a certain limit. For example: I am sitting here, alone. Jeanne is sleeping in her room. I get up, grab a knife, enter her room, take her by the hair, there, and I slit her throat. Everything has happened in my imagination and I haven't budged.

COLINA: Let's continue with Francisco Galván. On his wedding night, he believes there is a voyeur in the adjoining room at the hotel and he sticks a hatpin through the keyhole to poke out this Peeping Tom's eye. Doesn't this reveal that Galván himself is really a voyeur, who projects his own voyeurism onto someone else?

BUÑUEL: It could be, but I don't think so. Without being himself a voyeur, he knows that such people exist. I've never spied on anyone through a keyhole, but I know I could. Francisco might spy on his wife through a keyhole, but it would be because he has suspicions about her.

COLINA: But will voyeurism always be an aberration?

BUÑUEL: Well, if it remains only that, if it is the only way through which eroticism is channeled, yes, it's an aberration.

COLINA: Can't it be just a way of completely satisfying the imagination through looking.

BUÑUEL: I doubt the voyeur is satisfied by just looking. He must satisfy his desire in some other way. He either masturbates or remains excited.

COLINA: Let's suppose I am looking distractedly out the window in my room, and in the window facing mine I catch sight of a beautiful woman who takes all her clothes off. It's natural that I watch her. And it's natural that I hide behind the curtains to do so, because if she discovers me she will either hide or start screaming.

BUÑUEL: I wouldn't call that voyeurism. Voyeurism would be if you are staying at a hotel, and you go to the door of the room across the hall and spy on a woman through the keyhole.

COLINA: What counts then is premeditation.

BUÑUEL: The obsession.

COLINA: But isn't obsession simply a fantasy that repeats itself?

BUÑUEL: (Laughs) You are a sophist... By the way, there is a voyeurism of the ear and it is better than that of the eye.

COLINA: Do you see yourself as a voyeur?

BUÑUEL: A little. Everyone is.

COLINA: If everyone is, why do you call it an aberration?

BUÑUEL: If it completely substitutes for the erotic act, yes.

COLINA: We will stay with that to define voyeurism. And are the film-maker and the filmgoer voyeurs on a grand scale?

BUÑUEL: So much so that in a "refined" movie theater, the best thing would be to give each spectator his own keyhole so he could watch the film more comfortably.

TURRENT: Did you feel more secure about film technique when you made *El*?

BUÑUEL: Cinematic technique has always interested me. What happens is, I don't know how to improve it. If I watch *El* now, I'm aware of many things I could have done better. But technique preoccupied me before. Now I only use what is necessary to tell a story.

TURRENT: Speaking in terms of technique, I think *El* is the best film you made in Mexico. In that sense, it is the most perfect of your films, with more camera movements, which are nevertheless not noticed.

BUÑUEL: No, it isn't. It's not even comparable to the films I made recently in Paris. There is almost no moment when I use a fixed camera in those films: it goes from one person to another, to an object, to a group, later again to the character, and without the audience noticing it. I made *El* in three weeks, because at that time in Mexico they didn't give you any more time to shoot a film.

COLINA: There appears to be an economy of camera movements in your Mexican films, even including *Nazarín*, which is a more carefully made film.

BUÑUEL: If you see it again, pay attention and you will notice there are very few. The same as in *El*, more or less.

COLINA: Perhaps the feeling that in *El* there are many camera movements comes from the film's dynamism, the mobility of the situations.

BUÑUEL: Yes, it could be that. But my latest films have even more camera movement. For me, it is almost routine now.

TURRENT: The curious thing is that the mobility of the situations in *El* is presented within very closed, very suffocating spaces: the house, the train compartment, the hotel room, the church, the monastery.

BUÑUEL: The sets are in a style I like because my father, who was an *indiano*,[1] as the painter Gironella says, built a house in the style of 1900, a bit

---

1 An "indiano" refers to a Spaniard who went to the New World, made his fortune, and later returned to Spain to retire.

art nouveau. I love that period. Dalí and I were fascinated by art nouveau and Gaudí's architecture.

TURRENT: Was it all built in the studio?

BUÑUEL: Everything: the living room, the stairs, the upper bedrooms. I filmed very few exteriors. The objects have importance. Francisco calls his butler and says: "Straighten that painting, it's crooked." A crooked painting on the wall or a book that sticks out in the bookshelf bothers me.

COLINA: On the other hand, in *The Phantom of Liberty*, Jean Claude Brialy sees two objects symmetrically arranged on the mantel and alters their position.

BUÑUEL: Deliberately breaking the symmetry. It's like Tristana's two plums. My sister would do the same thing. She would see two identical plums and ask: which of the two should I eat first? The question has no importance, but look a bit more closely: why is it that between two plums or two streets that look alike, we decide on one and not the other? There are many things from my own life in my films, like the one I am telling you now.

COLINA: Did *El* cause any problems when it was shown? Because I think the film has a great subversive charge.

BUÑUEL: I have never had problems with censorship.

COLINA: I am not referring to official censorship. Perhaps some religious association or some guardians of good behavior...

BUÑUEL: No, nothing. The only problem was that when it premiered, the film was a failure. If it lasted three weeks, that was only because of Arturo de Córdova, who was popular at the box office. I went to the cinema, which had already begun its afternoon screening, and ran into Dancigers, who was on his way out. Almost crying, he said, "It's terrible: They are all laughing more than at Cantinflas."[2] I waited until the next screening and went in. The public was quiet for a long time, but when Francisco put the needle through the keyhole, five hundred people burst out laughing. And from then on, it was a laugh a minute.

TURRENT: And nevertheless, *El* is now one of your most famous films.

BUÑUEL: Yes. They even use it in psychiatry classes to depict paranoia.

---

2 Cantinflas, stage name of Mexican comic Mario Moreno Reyes, born in 1911 and star of a series of successful comedies. Besides his work in Mexican cinema, Cantinflas appeared in two U.S. films: *Around the World in 80 Days* (1956) and *Pepe* (1960).

14: *ABISMOS DE PASION* (WUTHERING HEIGHTS); *LA ILUSION VIAJA EN TRANVIA* (ILLUSION TRAVELS BY STREETCAR)

ABISMOS DE PASION OR *CUMBRES BORRASCOSAS* (WUTHERING HEIGHTS)

JOSE DE LA COLINA: At the beginning of the 1930s, you wrote an adaptation of *Wuthering Heights* with Pierre Unik.

LUIS BUÑUEL: It wasn't a script, only a narrative outline about twenty pages long that wasn't very detailed. I always admired the novel, which the Surrealists loved for its climate of passion, for *l'amour fou* that destroys everything.

TOMAS PEREZ TURRENT: What prompted you to return to the project here in Mexico and film *Wuthering Heights*?[1]

BUÑUEL: Dancigers called me one day and said, "I would like to make a comedy with Jorge Mistral, Irasema Dilián, and Lilia Prado, all of whom I have under contract." I told him I had written the script of *Wuthering Heights*, but the story was impossible with that cast: they were nothing like the characters. But my desire to film the story I liked so much won out.

TURRENT: In any case, it would have been difficult to find a more adequate cast at that time in Mexican cinema.

BUÑUEL: Difficult, but possible. The problem was the difference between Irasema and Mistral's accents. Lilia Prado, who is very likable, was good in other roles such as the rumba dancer in *Mexican Bus Ride*, but not as a romantic young female lead. Aceves Castañeda was nothing like the type necessary for Irasema's brother.

---

1 Released in Mexico under the title *Abismos de pasión*, or literally "Abysses of Passion."

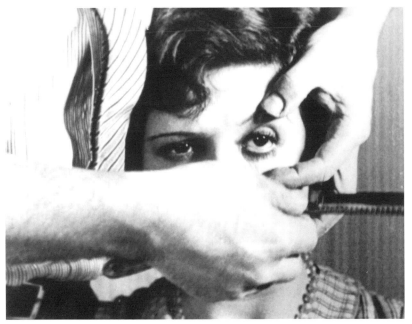

Un Chien andalou (1928–29)

Lya Lys, *L'Age d'or* (1930)

Jorge Negrete and Libertad Lamarque,
Gran Casino (1946)

Fernando Soler, Maruja Grifell, and Gustavo Rojo,
El gran calavera (1949)

From left: Alfonso Mejía, Roberto Cobo, Jorge Pérez, and
Miguel Inclán (on ground), *Los olvidados* (1950)

Fernando Soler and Rosita Quintana, *Susana* (1950)

Pedro Armendáriz and Katy Jurado, *El bruto* (1952)

Fernando Soler (center), *La hija del engaño* (1951)

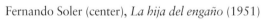

Dan O'Herlihy, *Adventures of Robinson Crusoe* (1952)

Arturo de Córdova, *El* (1952)

Jorge Mistral and Irasema Dilián, *Wuthering Heights* (1953)

Carlos Navarro, Lilia Prado, and Fernando Soto
"Mantequilla," *Illusion Travels by Streetcar* (1953)

Jaime Fernández (standing) and Joaquín Cordero,
El río y la muerte (1954)

Ernesto Alonso and Miroslava, *The Criminal Life
of Archibaldo de la Cruz* (1955)

Georges Marchal and Simone Signoret,
La mort en ce jardin (1956)

Marga López and Francisco Rabal, *Nazarín* (1958)

Buñuel directing *Nazarín* (1958)

From left: Claudio Brook, Kay Meersman (in background),
Zacahary Scott, Bernie Hamilton, Graham Denton,
The Young One (1960)

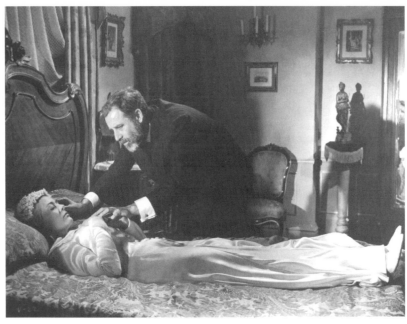

Silvia Pinal and Fernando Rey, *Viridiana* (1961)

The Exterminating Angel (1962)

Jeanne Moreau and Jean Ozenne, *Diary of a Chambermaid* (1963)

Silvia Pinal and Claudio Brook, *Simon of the Desert* (1965)

During the filming of
The Milky Way (1969)

VINI, VIDI, VINCI,
Cartoon by Alberto Isaac

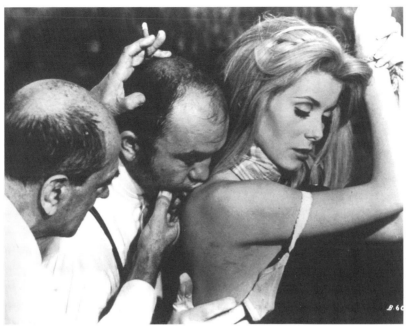

Buñuel directs a scene with Catherine Deneuve,
Belle de jour (1966)

The Milky Way (1969)

Catherine Deneuve, *Tristana* (1970)

Fernando Rey, Jean-Pierre Cassel, and Paul Frankeur,
The Discreet Charm of the Bourgeoisie (1970)

In Los Angeles for the premiere of *The Discreet Charm of the Bourgeoisie*, Buñuel attends a lunch given for him by George Cukor. From left (standing): Robert Mulligan, William Wyler, Cukor, Robert Wise, Jean-Claude Carrière, Serge Silberman, Charles Chaplin, Rafael Buñuel; (seated) Billy Wilder, George Stevens, Buñuel, Alfred Hitchcock, and Rouben Mamoulian. (Names are written in Buñuel's hand.)

Billy Wilder   George Stevens   Buñuel   Hitchcock   Ruben Mamoulian
Robert Mulligan   Charles Chaplin
        William Wyler   (L.A. Times)
                George Cukor   Robert Wise   Carriere   Silberman
                                                        Rafy Buñuel

Adriana Asti plays cards with priests, *The Phantom of Liberty* (1974)

Buñuel with Fernando Rey and Carole Bouquet, *That Obscure Object of Desire* (1977)

TURRENT: The audience's impression is that the music tries to give the film what the actors couldn't. There is a lot of Wagner.

BUÑUEL: It was my fault for not having supervised the music. I have always been very Wagnerian and it seemed to me that *Tristan* would go well with the story. After editing the film, I left for Europe, having indicated that it would be suitable to put in Wagner's music. Dancigers paid too much attention to what I said about Wagner and put music everywhere, even when a character was just drinking a cup of coffee.

TURRENT: It is noteworthy that you filmed in Mexico's tropical zone and nevertheless managed to obtain a dry, austere, and very sterile landscape in the film.

BUÑUEL: We filmed the exteriors at San Francisco Cuadra, an estate close to Taxco. It must have been in March or May — the time of year when the Mexican landscape can get very dry. The interiors, designed by Edward Fitzgerald, were shot in the studio.

TURRENT: Had you seen William Wyler's film[2] based on the same novel?

BUÑUEL: I had seen it years before. If you overlook the sad cast imposed on me by the producer, I think my film is better from the point of view of the novel's spirit.

TURRENT: Your version is less academic and cold.

BUÑUEL: Yes, the critics said that.

COLINA: In Wyler's film you don't feel the damning aspect of this love so much — it's not only opposed by the conventions of the time, but even by God himself, and it ends up destroying the very protagonists.

BUÑUEL: Love and hate within the protagonists at the same time. An eternal conflict.

COLINA: But it's more: it is a cosmic revolt, a blasphemy.

BUÑUEL: It is *l'amour fou,* the love that destroys everything.

COLINA: And Wyler never dared film the final scenes, which you did: the delirium, kissing the dead woman, profaning the grave.

BUÑUEL: In the book it says that Heathcliff roams around Catherine's grave. It is easy to imagine the scene: he descends into the tomb, opens the coffin, and excitedly contemplates Catherine's cadaver. It's not necrophilia, but rather pure love that goes beyond the grave. Later comes the delirium: Catherine goes down the stairs into her crypt, but it's not really her; it's her brother with a rifle, who has come to kill him...

---

2 *Wuthering Heights* (1939), dir. William Wyler, starring Sir Laurence Olivier and Merle Oberon.

COLINA: And elements of Gothic literature: the lugubrious crypt, the ghostly image, the white veil...

BUÑUEL: I have also been an enthusiast of the Gothic novel: those of Radcliffe, *The Monk* by Lewis,[3] *Melmoth* by Maturin.

TURRENT: There is a bestiary: the toad in the fire, the butterflies a character sticks down with pins, the spider that devours a fly.

BUÑUEL: I filmed the scene of the spider and the fly at two o'clock in the morning. The photographer Agustín Jiménez told me, "It's very late, and I'll have to wait until the spider traps the fly." Since I knew spiders' habits very well, I told him, "We won't have to wait long, you'll soon see." We put the camera in front of the spider's hole, and I shouted, "Action!" and threw a fly I had prepared onto the spiderweb — and zip! the spider immediately came out, trapped the insect, and returned to put it in the hole.

COLINA: It is difficult not to see this scene as a kind of symbol for the severity of the characters' relationships.

BUÑUEL: In the film, a boy caresses a drowsy man; to amuse himself, he traps a fly and tosses it onto the spiderweb. It's a kind of "gag" that makes a scene that could have otherwise been monotonous. It came to me while we were filming, on the set, as the actors and technicians were making preparations. An object or part of the set generated the idea...

TURRENT: In general, these details occur to you in relation to animals.

BUÑUEL: Also with any object. Now, for example, as we are drinking coffee, let's suppose that we wish to film this moment, but feel it must be enriched. Suddenly it occurs to me that instead of putting the sugar cube in the cup, you keep it between your fingers and let it soak up the coffee little by little.

COLINA: Yes, that's a common habit among Latinos. It gives more weight to a scene's reality, even though it doesn't especially "mean" anything, like the fact that Viridiana peels an orange for Don Jaime in one long ribbon.

BUÑUEL: That's it. Later you critics write ten-page essays about details like that.

COLINA: For example, which critics? Names, names!

BUÑUEL: Ah, no. Some are friends of mine.

COLINA: And two of them could be Pérez Turrent and myself.

---

3 *The Monk* (Le moine), based on the Gothic novel by Matthew G. Lewis, was adapted as a screenplay by Luis Buñuel and Jean-Claude Carrière. Due to production problems, Buñuel never made the film; it was later directed, using Buñuel's script, by Ado Kyrou in 1972.

BUÑUEL: I'm not saying anything.

COLINA: You are more guarded than usual in this interview, Don Luis. I'm going to try to draw you out and I'm going to do it through the film's content, the aspect of your work about which you are almost always reticent. In *Wuthering Heights* there is total love, *l'amour fou*. It is something very dear to Breton and the Surrealists, you among them, a position that might perhaps seem anachronistic or naive to the younger generation. Are you still faithful to it?

BUÑUEL: The idea continues to move me, though, if you like, at my age, in a theoretical manner.

COLINA: I will give you an imaginary test. You are sitting in front of two buttons: A and B. You must press one of them, but you can choose. If you press button A, the entire world disappears, all humanity except your beloved. If you press B, the world is saved, everyone, but Buñuel's beloved disappears. What would you do?

BUÑUEL: I would leave the buttons alone and have a drink.

COLINA: You don't believe a situation like that could ever happen, or one like it, if on a lesser scale, less cosmic. There is a case that happened in Cuba, during the time of opposition to Batista. Batista's men had captured a woman who was fighting in the underground; they told her, "We have your fiancé in the next cell. If you don't give us the names of your guerrilla contacts, we'll bring you his eyes on a platter." She did not give them names, and they carried out their threat. What do you say to that?

BUÑUEL: Well, I don't know. It is a terrible dilemma: to compromise the lives of many for... I understand the woman who did not give the names.

COLINA: For Catherine's eyes, Heathcliff would have allowed the world to blow into bits (I believe it is Camus who said that). And the Marquis de Sade...

BUÑUEL: Sade would have taken out someone's eyes for pleasure, in theory. But he wouldn't have accepted the reasons of those Batista torturers, or political-revolutionary motives. That would have outraged him.

COLINA: Meaning that if someone's eyes were poked out for sadistic pleasure, as opposed to it being done in the name of revolution, it would be within Sade's moral code.

BUÑUEL: Of course. Sade would never have betrayed his principles.

COLINA: And on the other hand, he would be faithful to his desire. He would consider every desire his right.

BUÑUEL: Yes. Besides, Sade carried out everything in his imagination and only there. Except for two or three occasions...we have already discussed that. Sade opposed the guillotine. He would have likewise opposed the barbarism of the Nazis and they would surely have had him shot.

COLINA: Besides, Sade is not Heathcliff. Sade is not in love with a single being; he seeks out absolute pleasure. Heathcliff can only love Catherine.

BUÑUEL: Yes. Sade is more cerebral, even though his search for absolute pleasure, as you say, was for him a passion that is principally based on hatred of society.

TURRENT: I believe someone told me you wanted to remake the film.

BUÑUEL: To make it better. I would film it with a good cast in England or France. For an ideal cast I would choose Claudia Cardinale for Catherine. I like Cardinale a lot in Visconti's film *Sandra*.[4] I would also have used her in the role of the female devil in *The Monk*. Peter O'Toole would play a duke, a character I created. Omar Shariff offered to play the monk, but I didn't accept him because I was thinking about Francisco Rabal. But, I've always liked the story of *Wuthering Heights*, in which love is also enmity and destruction.

LA ILUSION VIAJA EN TRANVIA (ILLUSION TRAVELS BY STREETCAR)

COLINA: *Illusion Travels by Streetcar* is reminiscent of Italian neorealist films.

BUÑUEL: It's possible, because we see diverse aspects of Mexican social reality along the streetcar's route: the poor neighborhoods, the butchers from the Rastro slaughterhouse, the black marketeers. But I didn't think about Italian cinema; neorealism doesn't appeal to me. I think Mauricio de la Serna and José Revueltas[5] began writing the story and then Luis Alcoriza and I worked on it. The original story was several pages long: a streetcar disappears, has various adventures, and in the end the streetcar reappears at the depot. You two know it's possible to find people carrying boxes of fruit or live turkeys — the most incredible things — on public vehicles in Mexico, or it was at that time, and that's why I thought that workers from Rastro should travel on the streetcar carrying quarters of beef, and sanctimonious old women carrying an image of a saint.

---

4 *Vaghe Stelle dell'Orsa* (1965), dir. Luchino Visconti.
5 José Revueltas (1914-1976), Mexican novelist, short-story writer, dramatist, and essayist, who later worked as a screenwriter.

TURRENT: That disconcerted some European critics. The French critic Luc Moullet found the film very strange.

BUÑUEL: Seeing these things on a streetcar caught people's attention. In Mexico, it's completely believable. Of course, you don't find so many unexpected elements concentrated into only one streetcar trip.

TURRENT: Are the large quarters of beef a reference to *Un chien andalou?*

BUÑUEL: There are no quarters of beef in *Un chien andalou.*

TURRENT: But there is the unexpected presence of meat: the bodies of the donkeys. You also used the Rastro slaughterhouse in *The Brute.*

BUÑUEL: Some things are repeated from one film to another. Why? I don't know. They are coincidences.

TURRENT: I think that in *Illusion Travels by Streetcar* you insert Surrealist elements into a realist context.

BUÑUEL: Of course, but that is precisely what Surrealism did. For example, not everything had to be Surrealist in a painting by a Surrealist painter, only one small detail that logically shouldn't be there.

COLINA: I would say you are making "collages" in *Illusion Travels by Streetcar*, much like the ones Max Ernst did with old prints.

BUÑUEL: Yes. It may look like the prints in *La Femme 100 têtes* to take some sides of beef from a print of the Rastro slaughterhouse or a print of a church with some devout women carrying an image of a saint and paste them onto a print showing the interior of a streetcar. But those are explanations *a posteriori,* even though I find them valid.

COLINA: The *pastorela*[6] that the neighbors perform could also be called a collage.

BUÑUEL: That is also justified by reality. The story takes place during the *posadas*[7] at the end of the year and until only a short time ago, the people of the district performed *pastorelas* during that period. I've been told they still do it in the neighborhood of Coyoacán, not far from my house. Besides, the *pastorela* in the film is authentic. I took it from a selection of *pastorelas* that I found in a book published in Mexico in the nineteenth century.

COLINA: But you don't just pass over the *pastorela.* You pause to film it as a play within a play; you also put your own author's vision into it. I

6 A *pastorela,* or shepherds' play, is a Mexican mystery play traditionally performed during Christmas, and usually combines Biblical stories with bawdy elements.

7 *Posada,* literally "shelter" or "inn," refers to the two weeks preceding Christmas during which time it is believed that Joseph and Mary looked for shelter. In Mexico, the *posadas* are a time of traditional Christmastime parties, also called *posadas.*

think it's a bit unbelievable that the people in a poor Mexican neighborhood would take such liberties when representing God in a *pastorela*.
BUÑUEL: Why? They don't take liberties. They are amateur actors, inexperienced and naive. They want to offer a worthy performance, but it turns out to be humorous because it is naive. "How do you have God descend to earth?" they might have asked. "We put him on a swing and then lower him down." It's completely logical: if God is in heaven, he must come down from on high.
TURRENT: The film is similar to *Mexican Bus Ride*.
BUÑUEL: Because they are both films in which things happen during a trip. But that is the only similarity. There is a tension in *Illusion* because the streetcar is illegally circulating around the city, and the retired inspector could denounce it to the authorities.
COLINA: There is something like an implied threat hanging over the characters and not the free-breathing quasi-optimism of *Mexican Bus Ride*. Furthermore, there is an obnoxious character: the old former employee, who is an informer.
BUÑUEL: No, he is a retired inspector, who hasn't yet resigned himself to not working. He loves his profession and wants to continue feeling useful to the company. In a novel by Galdós there is a similar character, who has retired after thirty years of service and returns constantly to the office to converse with his former colleagues until they finally get bored and kick him out. The same happens with Isunza's character in my film: without his job, life seems empty and he continues to serve the company, even though he's not paid.
COLINA: There is another similarity to *Mexican Bus Ride*. There are two very analogous photographs from the two films: in both of them, Lilia Prado is getting on the bus (later, the streetcar). Her posture is identical: one foot on the step of the vehicle, the skirt at mid-thigh.
BUÑUEL: Yes, the two photos are very similar. I admit that this has to do with something very personal from my youth and that of anyone else of my generation. When women with those long skirts got onto a streetcar, we would watch them to see if they showed any calf. Of course in the two films the skirt is shorter, so Lilia showed us some of her thigh. These are gestures you remember. I no longer spy on girls with miniskirts getting on buses, but if I were fifteen years old, I surely would.
COLINA: I suspect you made both films only to use this image.
BUÑUEL: *(Laughs)* No. My caprices don't go so far.

TURRENT: *Illusion* and *Mexican Bus Ride* are itinerate films. They seem to be intended as metaphors for life, as if they contained all its elements: life, death, work, and love are all represented in these two trips. It is as if representatives of all humanity boarded these vehicles...

BUÑUEL: Everyone who boards the streetcar is justified by the story line. The butchers leave the Rastro slaughterhouse and take the streetcar home, carrying some meat. The devout women get on carrying a saint for those who have faith. One gentleman, when he sees he is not being charged, exclaims, "This is communism!" For him this is absurd, but not for the conductors, who don't dare charge the fare because the trip on the streetcar is illegal. And this has to do with a trait that is particular to the character. I did not intend to put in a political message. I also didn't want to make a commentary about abandoned children in the episode with the orphans...

COLINA: There is something there that is both very Mexican and very Spanish at the same time. One of the orphans sees a woman out the window, obviously a woman of easy virtue who is arranging her stockings in front of everyone, and he says to another child, "Look, there's your mother!" The other boy looks at the woman and is terribly upset... And it seems like an improvised scene.

BUÑUEL: No, it must have been foreseen in the script, because it is difficult to improvise a scene like that. You must have, at least, the actress who is to play the "mamma" present at the film location. On the other hand, yes, there is a reference to a very traditional Spanish insult: *La puta de tu madre!* (Your whore of a mother!)

TURRENT: And very Mexican: *Tu chingada madre!* (Your fucking mother!) In Mexico this insult has very strong roots because the conquistadors *chingaban*[8] the women.

BUÑUEL: I also didn't want to trace the roots of such-and-such a Mexican complex. It's only the crude joke of a child, which affects another very powerfully. It is also funny that all the orphans on the streetcar have the same last name, but I took that from real life. It happens that last names must be assigned to the children registered in orphanages, and it almost always turns out to be the same name.

COLINA: To finish with this film, I insist on saying it contains more

---

8 The verb *chingar* in Mexico is very complex and literally means to "fornicate" or "rape." Almost invariably negative, it can be traced back to the time of the conquest. *"Chinga tu madre!"* literally "Rape your mother!" is the strongest insult given in Mexico.

Surrealism than you admit. The streetcar departs from its itinerary at night, fooling the guards, and its adventures dissipate at daybreak. Permit me to give you the "delirium of an interpretation": the streetcar could be an image of the unconscious, a dream that travels through reality...and later dissolves.

BUÑUEL: The film is called *Illusion Travels by Streetcar*, but I don't like the title at all and I didn't choose it. I admit that, yes, a subconscious mechanism can be reflected in everything, even in more reasonable films, and even though one doesn't intend it purposely...

COLINA: Well, that would be a triumph for Surrealism: the subconscious emerges into the light without the author intending it.

BUÑUEL: Up to a certain point, because Surrealism isn't playing the flute by chance, like the burro in the fable.

15: *EL RIO Y LA MUERTE* (THE RIVER AND DEATH); *ENSAYO DE UN CRIMEN* (THE CRIMINAL LIFE OF ARCHIBALDO DE LA CRUZ)

EL RIO Y LA MUERTE (THE RIVER AND DEATH)

JOSE DE LA COLINA: *The River and Death* is a film that feels as if you didn't enjoy making it.

LUIS BUÑUEL: That's possible. It was a novel with a social message. I didn't choose it. Clasa Films offered it to me through Mauricio de la Serna and the author, Manuel Alvarez Acosta, who refused to sell the rights to the book unless his message was respected. Furthermore, he corrected the adaptation Alcoriza and I wrote. For the first time in my life I directed a thesis film and it bothered my conscience. The message is very arguable, it goes something like this: "If all men went to university, we would have less crime." Imagine that!

TOMAS PEREZ TURRENT: Or rather, education will straighten out the world.

BUÑUEL: University graduates can also have the desire to kill, isn't that right? In any case, we know that cultured men are less violent than uncultured men, because they are more rational, more cultured, and have moral barriers...and more fear of the consequences, so that the impulse to violence is blocked.

TURRENT: But education isn't the basic problem.

BUÑUEL: I don't think it is. The basic problem is economic and social ...But that cannot be confirmed categorically. Look at the violence of today's terrorists, yet many of them come from families with acceptable economic means and have been highly educated.

COLINA: The bad part of the idea of *The River and Death* is how schematic it is: civilization versus barbarism. But — in this film, at least — we don't see a barbarous community. Certain violent acts are a kind of culture. There is a ritual and a code of honor: if a man is murdered, the family must take justice into its own hands and avenge him. It's a moral code, like going to Mass.

BUÑUEL: I agree: it is a bloody moral code, but not precisely barbaric. The film doesn't deal with a savage community, even though the chain of death seems inevitable. What really interested me about the book was the element of the lack of respect for human life. At the very beginning of the film, two godfathers kill each other at a baptism over a trifle, which for them is a question of honor. Later the deaths begin in earnest. I wanted to show an authentic tradition from the Guerrero coast: when someone has been killed, the corpse is taken to a succession of homes of family members and friends, where the people accompanying it have a few drinks. Later, they take the coffin to the door of the house of the killer, who has fled, and the dead man's relatives shout: "Come out so-and-so! Come out and pay for this death!" And a chain reaction of revenges begins between the families.

TURRENT: The subject matter risked becoming one more cliché about the love affair between Mexicans and death. A European critic even cited Posada's *calaveras*.[1]

BUÑUEL: I wasn't thinking of Posada's prints at all. I hate to make "films about art," putting pictorial references into them. There are critics who, if they happen to see a dwarf or beggar in one of my films, bring up Velázquez and Goya. The same critics could also say I am a "cubist" filmmaker because they see a square house in one of my films. It's like that with "Buñuel's symbols." "Here is a pine tree that symbolizes the penis, according to such-and-such a paragraph of Freud..." It's absurd. This facile psychology becomes laughable. Freud opened a marvelous window into man's interior, but Freudian interpretation has been converted into a religion with answers for everything. Perhaps some Freudian sees all the pistols that appear in the film as phallic symbols...

COLINA: There is a joke about that. A man tells one of his dreams to a psychoanalyst. "I saw a tree along the way," the patient says. "Phallic symbol," notes the psychoanalyst. "I took a pistol out of my briefcase..."

---

1 José Guadalupe Posada (1851-1913), Mexican folk artist who illustrated thousands of broadsheets with popular satirical prints, often using animated sketetons, referred to as *calaveras* (skulls).

"Phallic symbol," repeats the psychoanalyst, etc. Finally the man says, "And, facing the beautiful woman, I took out my prick." And, the psychoanalyst exclaims: "I wonder what that could mean?"

BUÑUEL: *(Laughs)* That's good.

TURRENT: A European critic called *The River and Death* a film for Mexico's domestic market.

BUÑUEL: He wasn't wrong. The film went to the Venice Film Festival. Jaime Fernández and some other Mexicans were there that year and they told me what happened during the screening. There was applause when my name appeared in the credits, but when all the deaths began, everyone laughed uproariously, asking that they kill even more. I had predicted that the film would not be understood in Europe and would have preferred to send *Robinson Crusoe,* but the management at Clasa Films sent *The River and Death.* The audience laughed at the scene where Fernández slaps Cordero, who is crippled and in an artificial lung...

TURRENT: That's a good scene because it breaks with the audience's moral conventions.

BUÑUEL: Perhaps the audience thinks that Fernández, brutal as he may be, is dignified and incapable of taking advantage of a defenseless man. But in fact, the slap is more an insult than an act of physical violence.

TURRENT: At the end, the two *machos* of the feuding families are reconciled, scorning the conventions of the clan.

BUÑUEL: Perhaps this ending is a bit forced, a little unbelievable: a "thesis" ending. It would have been better to have shot everyone dead and then, instead of putting "The End," to put, "To Be Continued," or, "More Deaths Next Week."

TURRENT: In this scene, one of the adversaries says, "To hell with the town and the family!" This has a Surrealist spirit.

BUÑUEL: In the very general sense of anticonventionality. Which is to say, it's no longer important to him "what people say"; he is not disposed to follow tradition and the chain of vengence.

COLINA: Could the film be seen as a black comedy?

BUÑUEL: You can see it however you want. But even though there are humorous characteristics, it is not a comedy. Though I was bothered by the constraints of the thesis, I didn't try to make fun of the story. When I embark on making a film, I make it seriously and don't try to give conspiratorial winks at the audience. That seems to me as bad as an actor who improvises to get applause.

ENSAYO DE UN CRIMEN
(THE CRIMINAL LIFE OF ARCHIBALDO DE LA CRUZ)

COLINA: At first, the subject matter of Rodolfo Usigli's novel *Ensayo de un Crimen* (Rehearsal of a Crime) seems to me to be very different from your usual work. Who proposed that you film it?

BUÑUEL: There was an economic crisis in the film industry and the union decided to produce films as a cooperative. The actor Ernesto Alonso told me that we could film Usigli's novel using that system. Some elements of the book interested me: the obsession, the vocation of a frustrated murderer. I began to adapt it with the author, but we suspended work after fifteen days because Usigli would not permit the slightest variation from his text. When he saw the finished film, he lodged a complaint at a union assembly. But I was absolved, because in the credits I had put "Inspired from..." I didn't aim to make an exact transcription of the novel, but a divergent work that used the book as a point of departure from which to develop specific elements in my own way.

COLINA: When the book was published, it was taken as a *roman à clef* that satirized the bourgeoisie.

BUÑUEL: I was not interested in the *roman à clef* aspect because I didn't know the world Usigli described, nor did I believe it would interest the audience. I was interested in the other part: the character's obsession. I understand why Usigli didn't agree with my version. We weren't angry with each other: we parted as friends. Furthermore, I changed the title under which the film was released abroad to *La vida criminal de Archibaldo de la Cruz* (The Criminal Life of Archibaldo de la Cruz).

TURRENT: Who did you finally work with on the adaptation?

BUÑUEL: With my friend Eduardo Ugarte, a Spanish intellectual who had worked with me when I was an associate producer in Spain. He was the son-in-law of Arniches, who wrote *sainetes,* and the brother-in-law of José Bergamín. He died some years ago.

COLINA: The novel has an intellectual and aesthetic tone that does not coincide with your cinematic style.

BUÑUEL: *Belle de jour* didn't interest me at first either. But it was enough for me that the book gave me two or three stimulating images that I could develop in my own manner.

COLINA: It is curious that, in your answer, you associate *The Criminal Life of Archibaldo de la Cruz* with *Belle de jour*. It seems to me, that there is a certain relationship between the main characters of both films, their attempts to bring their fantasies to life, the demands of their desires.

BUÑUEL: I accept that, even though *a posteriori*. Yes: Archibaldo and the *Belle de jour* imagine forbidden things that they try to live out in real life. A major part of their lives is mere imagination.

COLINA: There is also the fixation on sonorous objects: the music box in *The Criminal Life of Archibaldo de la Cruz*, the small carriage bells in *Belle de jour*.

BUÑUEL: It's true. We have auditory obsessions just as we have visual ones. Besides, I believe auditory obsessions address the imagination more than the visual ones.

TURRENT: You said the protagonist of *El* interested you as a clinical case. Did the same happen with Archibaldo?

BUÑUEL: I would think not. Perhaps there was a clinical case in the novel, but I don't think so. As for Archibaldo (that name is different than the one in the novel), I know that he's not a psychopath; he's a man for whom things do not work out, or come out badly. He wants to kill, but either someone beats him to it or the victim dies beforehand. He is a sane enough man, but he wants to fulfill his dream, his obsession, just as other people want to scale the Alps or grow the most exquisite plant. The music box frees his imagination, makes him return to his childhood, to certain pleasant memories relating to someone's death...what do I know? The music box was in the novel but, if I remember correctly, it was not as important.

COLINA: The music box brings to mind the invention of the Marquis de Hervey-Saint-Denys, author of a book about a way to manipulate dreams. Here is how Breton describes the marquis' experiment: "he had a fashionable orchestra leader systematically conduct two specific waltzes. The marquis then danced with two attractive ladies, dedicating one waltz to each woman. Later, through an ingenious apparatus made from a music box and an alarm clock, Hervey managed to make one or the other of the two ladies appear in his dreams, through the muted sound of the two melodies, etc." Let's say that this would be a systemization of Marcel Proust's "madeleine dipped in tea."

BUÑUEL: The marquis' system does not convince me. It's too direct and mechanical. Theoretically it's all right, even ingenious, but I doubt it really works. It's possible that the smell of gas from this cigarette lighter will trigger a dream tonight in which my beloved appears and grants me her favors. On the other hand, it's also possible that the smell of my beloved's lingerie draped over my face while I am sleeping produces not her in my dreams but rather an elephant passing through the jungle. The subconscious has its own laws and its own system of relationships. If you want to manipulate it rationally, it rebels.

TURRENT: Nevertheless, Archibaldo's music box does bear some resemblance to the "madeleine dipped in tea."

BUÑUEL: It could be. The waltz from the music box excites Archibaldo because it's linked to a childhood memory of eroticism and death, the time when he saw his nanny fall dead with her thighs bloodied. I don't think there is such a strong moment in Proust's novel. Furthermore, Archibaldo knows he can manipulate his fantasies when he is awake with the help of the music box. But he doesn't attempt to manipulate his dreams. Dreams are uncontrollable. Their secret has not been discovered. I wish I could direct my dreams according to my desires. Then...I would never wake up.

TURRENT: As with your other Surrealist heroes, the conjunction of eroticism and death is present once more in Archibaldo.

BUÑUEL: It's there from the very beginning: *l'amour, la mort* was already present in *Un chien andalou*. When Batcheff fondles the woman's breasts, we see his face in a terrible rictus, his eyes white and his mouth drooling like a dead body or a dying person. Erotic ecstasy has frequently been compared to the moment of death. This is something we can all feel.

TURRENT: Archibaldo fails as a murderer. He is frustrated, impotent.

BUÑUEL: But he isn't sexually impotent, if that is what you want to say. He's frustrated by certain relationships he has with reality. Almost all my films have this theme: frustration. Bourgeois people who cannot leave a room, people who want to eat and everything impedes them, a man who wants to kill, but his crimes fail. Already in *Un chien andalou*, frustration appears: the man approaches the woman, but his advance is impeded by ropes with objects tied to them. In the scene in the garden in *L'Age d'or*, the lovers cannot even kiss. It is the distance between desire and reality, intent and failure.

TURRENT: But in *The Criminal Life of Archibaldo de la Cruz*, there is also erotic frustration. Archibaldo prepares an entire *mise-en-scène* to receive Lavinia. She arrives, yes, but...accompanied by some tourists.

BUÑUEL: Of course, and that's even worse: to have the desired person so close without being able to fulfill the desire. Nevertheless, the frustration doesn't come from Archibaldo's supposed impotence, but rather from the situation itself, from reality.

COLINA: Archibaldo performs rituals in order to achieve his desire: he has a dummy that is an exact replica of Lavinia made, has it seated in the parlor, etc. And, when he has prepared all this, Lavinia appears in person. It reminds me of the scene in *Un chien andalou* when the woman makes the man appear from the placement of male clothes...

BUÑUEL: Yes, there is a magical invocation in *Un chien andalou*, but not in *The Criminal Life of Archibaldo de la Cruz*. There is only a very believable coincidence, a happy stroke of luck (or an unhappy one because of the frustration we spoke about). What both films have in common is fetishism, and in some way fetishism is a magical invocation...that, I acknowledge. The man who fondles his beloved's shoe is erotically invoking her.

TURRENT: For Archibaldo, the act of murder has a double function: on one hand, erotic possession, and on the other, freedom from childhood repressions. On an imaginary level, murder liberates Archibaldo...

BUÑUEL: My memory of the film is very vague, but it doesn't coincide with what you say. Archibaldo wants to kill, of that there is no doubt. Possibly from a sexual point of view, murder liberates him, but if he were to actually manage to commit murder, you don't know what he would do afterwards. He is a killer. But evidently he also enjoys the frustration, he adores it. He searches for a woman to kill and fails. He intends to kill another and fails again. You could say that by trying again, he desires failure. Does he do this to free himself? Perhaps he does it for exactly the opposite reason. I know this seems obscure. But I'm attracted to a character's obscurity. If you attempt to construct a very rational character, that character won't live. He must have a shadow zone.

COLINA: But Archibaldo himself is very rational. For example, he doesn't suffer from, or enjoy, *l'amour fou*.

BUÑUEL: No, or platonic love either. He feels sexual desire and is an erotic gourmet, who calculates his relationships with women. The character who does feel *l'amour fou* is not him, but the man played by Linares Rivas,[2] Rita Macedo's husband. That man does have this savage love, a love that is agony, a battle with his beloved, and for that reason he kills

---

2 Buñuel is confused in this scene. In the film the police conclude that Patricia (Rita Macedo) committed suicide.

her and then commits suicide. Archibaldo wouldn't commit suicide. He would coldly search for another woman.

TURRENT: Archibaldo wouldn't end up walking in a zigzag, like the protagonist of *El*?

BUÑUEL: Never. Francisco is a moral being, an innocent, while Archibaldo is an aesthete, a criminal.

COLINA: Some critics have seen latent homosexuality in Archibaldo.

BUÑUEL: He could be a homosexual without knowing it, and for that reason he wants to kill women, but I don't see it like that. If he put on his mother's clothes when he was a child, that is fetishism, perhaps Oedipal. Don Jaime in *Viridiana* also puts on women's clothes, but it is to evoke or invoke his dead wife more intensely. You must distinguish between homosexual transvestitism and fetishistic transvestitism, though they may exist together in some people.

COLINA: There aren't any homosexuals in your films.

BUÑUEL: I hadn't noticed that; as a matter of fact, there aren't any... Yes, I think none except for the pederast in *Los olvidados*, but he is an almost ephemeral character. The absence of homosexuals is not due to any prejudice. On the other hand, there are many fetishes in my films. I think that is due to the fact that we are all fetishists, some more, some less.

TURRENT: In *The Criminal Life of Archibaldo de la Cruz*, there are two very recognizable fetishes: the music box and the dummy.

BUÑUEL: The music box was in the novel. I invented the dummy. Perhaps I am a precursor of the consumers of those rubber dolls sold at sex shops.

COLINA: There are other precursors. Ramón Gómez de la Serna had a wax dummy on his floor in Madrid. I have heard that the playwright Ghelderode had a room full of female dummies...

BUÑUEL: Then perhaps I am the precursor of consumers of dolls to rehearse crimes. Maybe one day they will be sold: "Killable dolls, very practical, with perfect imitation blood." By the way, I found out that Berlanga used seven dummies for his film *Life Size,*[3] at a cost of one hundred and fifty thousand dollars. The wax dummy I used in *The Criminal Life of Archibaldo de la Cruz* cost around a hundred dollars and was made using a cast of Miroslava's face. It wasn't very good.

COLINA: It was perfect. There is a production photograph with you posed between Miroslava and the dummy. It's impossible to tell one from the other.

3 *Grandeur Nature* (1973), a French production directed by Spanish filmmaker Luis García Berlanga.

BUÑUEL: Now that I remember, perhaps we used two dummies, and both were burned in the oven.

COLINA: The entire sequence when Miroslava is cremated in effigy is very impressive for two reasons, one of them extra-cinematographic. First, while its being dragged to the oven, the dummy loses a leg. A chance incident during the filming?

BUÑUEL: No. It was deliberate. I've already told you I always look for some detail to enhance a scene. Yes, I improvised that detail during the production.

COLINA: This is the forerunner of Tristana's amputated leg!

BUÑUEL: You said it. And what is the other reason that makes the scene impressive?

COLINA: It is a detail outside the film and after the fact.

BUÑUEL: I know what it is. Some twenty days after the film premiered, Miroslava committed suicide and her cadaver was cremated, as she had stipulated.

COLINA: The ending of *The Criminal Life of Archibaldo de la Cruz* is ironic, or at least ambiguous.

BUÑUEL: I have been criticized a lot for that happy end. But it is a little like the happy end of *Susana*. Archibaldo throws the music box into the lake, goes walking and encounters Lavinia. His first impulse — the criminal instinct — is to kill her, but he repents, takes her arm, and they leave, happy. Now then, the audience can ask itself, what is going to happen to Lavinia? Archibaldo may kill her an hour later, because nothing really indicates that he has changed.

16: *CELA S'APPELLE L'AURORE;*
LA MORT EN CE JARDIN (DEATH IN THE GARDEN)

CELA S'APPELLE L'AURORE

TOMAS PEREZ TURRENT: You once mentioned that *Cela s'appelle l'aurore* is one of your favorite films.

LUIS BUÑUEL: It's a "love-yes-police-no" film and I have good memories of it. My agent in Paris had recommended Emmanuel Robles' novel, and that year, 1954, I was on the jury at the Cannes Film Festival. I liked the book and began to work on the script with Jean Ferry, a Surrealist writer and author of a study of Raymond Roussel.

TURRENT: Ferry was also one of the founders of the College of Pataphysics.[1]

BUÑUEL: Yes, he was a pataphysician. And a curious thing happened to me with him. He wrote a three-page love scene, with kisses and very lyrical phrases. I would have been embarassed to film something like that. Then it came to me to have the protagonist arrive at his lover's house, they speak tenderly, and, since he is tired, he takes off his shoes. While she serves him some soup, he says, "Look in my pocket. I brought you a present." She finds a live turtle in his pocket. Then the man and the woman kiss. And this way I avoided three pages of dialogue that might have been good on paper, but were impossible to film. Ferry wrote to the producer, demanding that his name be removed from the credits because I had converted a sublime scene into another one about shoes, soup, and trivialities. Poor Ferry, he has since died. He had talent, but on that occasion it failed him.

COLINA: We know there was a problem related to Paul Claudel.

BUÑUEL: A scene opens in the office of the police commissioner. On his

---

1 Collège de Pataphysique, founded in 1949 by a group of French writers to explore the new "science" proposed in the writings of Alfred Jarry. As defined by Jarry: "Pataphysics is the science of imaginary solutions."

desk you can see the complete works of Claudel with a portrait of him, and a pair of *menottes* (handcuffs) on top of them. Later, the commissioner takes his gloves from a chest over which hangs a print of Christ by Dalí. That is to say that Dalí and Claudel were poet and painter of the police, though both are excellent, of course.

TURRENT: But at the same time the commissioner was defined as a cultured man, sensitive...

BUÑUEL: He could be. Well, then Claudel's daughter wrote to me more or less in these words: "Monsieur, I have seen the ignoble film where you profane my father's memory. I can do nothing against you legally, but this letter serves to express my contempt." There was also a scene in the film where the police commissioner, while traveling in a car on the island's highway, refers to the landscape and recites some of Claudel's verses. Julien Bertheau, who played the role of the police commissioner, told me, "Buñuel, I prefer not to recite these lines. I acted in *L'Annonciation à Marie,* and am a friend of Claudel's daughter, and it seems to me you are ridiculing him." "But do you think this scene is going to be grotesque?" I asked him. "No. Recite the verses seriously, without ridicule; you are reciting a good poet."

TURRENT: The ridicule would be in the context. And most people know that Claudel was a *bête noir* of the Surrealists.

BUÑUEL: The Surrealist group attacked Claudel for his nationalism, his praise of the police and later of Franco. But I insist that for me he is a good poet...

TURRENT: And the Claudel-Dalí association?

BUÑUEL: Dalí is also a nationalist and a Catholic, in his own way, and supportive of Fascist regimes. The police commissioner could have ideas similar to theirs and enjoy their works. Where is the ridicule in that? For example, as you know, I have a Dalí portrait here in the house, a portrait of me that he painted. Does this perhaps mean that I share Dalí's current ideas? On the other hand, the police commissioner has some good characteristics: he reprimands the policemen when they go too far in an act of repression. There is the scene where he smashes the hand of the old man locked in a chicken coop... But the police commissioner is indignant because the old man has raped a young girl. You can understand his indignation, though, of course, the old man is defenseless.

TURRENT: There were many attacks on the film, particularly one by Eric Rohmer.

BUÑUEL: I called Rohmer a fascist, although not because of that. One day the editor of *Cahiers du Cinéma* introduced me to him. I remembered that Kyrou and Prévert had called Rohmer a fascist and, as a joke, I said to him, "I have the honor of greeting a fascist." Immediately, I added, "Excuse me, I have been told that you are a fascist." He became red as a beet and I took my leave: "Well, then delighted to have met you."

TURRENT: I remember Rohmer's criticism. He said that you felt obliged to break down doors that had already been opened long before and that you had a *petite place* in the history of cinema as a collaborator with Dalí on *L'Age d'or*, and also as a representative of Mexican cinema. And he concluded: "Nothing much."

BUÑUEL: Well, it was amusing.

TURRENT: Some critics said you had attained serenity in *Cela s'appelle l'aurore*. But the film stirred up violent reactions for being very clear in its position.

BUÑUEL: I like the final scene when Marchal refuses to shake hands with the police commissioner and leaves with his lover and three worker friends, his arm over their shoulders, with an accordion heard in the background. That is the only music in the film. I acknowledge that the scene is a bit symbolic.

TURRENT: Unlike your other characters, Marchal is a very definite character, very simple.

BUÑUEL: But not at the beginning. At first, we see him working as a police doctor. His experiences while living on the island, seeing injustice close-up, make him change. When he hides the fugitive worker at the beginning, he does it only out of generosity and friendship, even against the wishes of his wife and father-in-law. Besides, he has already fallen in love with Bosé. But up to that point, he is only a man with good intentions, compassionate, in love. When they kill Gianni, who became a killer out of desperation, a wider feeling of human solidarity begins to stir within the doctor.

TURRENT: But isn't it possible that after this reaction, the doctor could return to a solidarity with his own class?

BUÑUEL: Impossible. I believe a man who is capable of profound indignation at injustice can no longer accept it. For me, it is clear that, at Gianni's death, Marchal has radically changed. At least he no longer works with the police. Nazarín and Viridiana also change their way of seeing and living in the world. They can no longer remain as they were

before. I'm not a determinist; I mean that I don't believe anyone is morally determined forever because he was born in such-and-such a social
class. Being born bourgeois doesn't condemn anyone to think or behave
like a bourgeois for his entire life. Coexistence changes one's manner of
being. Let's put an extreme case: a guard and a prisoner. It's very difficult
for a guard to maintain an intransigent position toward his prisoner day
after day. He has to be incredibly vile not to establish some type of
human relationship with him. But...there are no rules, isn't that right?
Forced coexistence can also degrade human relations. If you and I were
forcibly locked up forever in a room together, we might be very wonderful people, trying to help each other, but we would almost certainly end
up hating each other, losing our tempers over the slightest thing. To you,
the way I scratch my ear would seem unbearable; to me, the way you
comb your hair.

COLINA: That is part of the theme of *The Exterminating Angel*.

BUÑUEL: Yes. But coexistence can have the opposite result: the sense of
solidarity. The doctor in *Cela s'appelle l'aurore* coexists emotionally,
though not physically, with the poor people on the island; and furthermore, love makes him more generous. For that reason he breaks with
convention: he leaves his wife, sick as she is, and he goes off with his
lover. It would be unbearable for him to live any form of deceit.

TURRENT: So what interests you most about a character is his potential
for change.

BUÑUEL: Of course. If not, what interest would a story have? A story has
to do with seeing whether a character becomes better or worse, happy or
miserable... Zachary Scott's character in *The Young One* changes for the
better: he stops being a racist, he really falls in love with the girl, he's no
longer a brutal rapist and selfish person. But on the other hand, Tristana
becomes vindictive and tyrannical, she becomes hardened. Only in cheap
novels are good characters always good and bad ones always bad. They
don't learn anything, life doesn't change them. Look at an example of
change in the character of Gianni Esposito: he is unhappy through most
of the film, incapable of rebelling against the injustice that overwhelms
him. He's like an automaton of misfortune, isn't he? Suddenly, he can no
longer take it, he picks up a revolver, goes to find the boss, and shoots
him in the belly.

COLINA: The crime scene is splendid because it's like a moment in *L'Age
d'or*, but stronger, because it is more justified. And you forget the kitten...

BUÑUEL: That's right, I forgot. What a memory you two have for details.

COLINA: It's more than a detail, it has beauty, mystery. Esposito arrives at the mansion where the party is taking place. A kitten follows him in the garden and Esposito picks it up, pets it, and carries it in his arms. He enters the drawing room and without throwing down the kitten, he takes out his revolver and shoots the boss. A brilliant poetic conjunction, great tenderness and at the same time a great and justified hate.

BUÑUEL: They are gestures that I would make in a similar situation. And I am interested in a situation that allows two simultaneous contrary actions: to kiss and insult at the same time, to caress and kill at the same time, or the opposite. I'm not interested in characters without contradictions because we know everything about them from the first moment.

COLINA: That is what happens to me with the character of Marchal, despite the fact that you say he is capable of change. This character doesn't surprise me, he seems too linear. I find the entire film like that, except for the crime scene in the drawing room, the "bit with the kitten." Understand, Don Luis, the film doesn't displease me in any ideological way, I simply find it predictable, flat.

BUÑUEL: I understand. It's not enough for me either that a film share my ideas in order for me to like it or for it to touch me.

TURRENT: In addition to the scene with the handcuffs and Claudel's book, there is another, even stronger image in the film: a statue of Christ that is used as a telegraph pole.

BUÑUEL: Many people have said, "A Buñuelian detail." Okay, but I'm sorry, sometimes reality inserts its own Buñuelian touches all by itself. When the Americans invaded Africa during the Second World War, they found a monument of Christ and used it to string needed telephone cables. And since the doctor had been in Africa, he has this photograph in his home: Jesus' face hung full of insulators and cables. This is not an invention of mine, nor was the shrine to the Virgin of Guadalupe at the Rastro slaughterhouse in *The Brute*...

LA MORT EN CE JARDIN (DEATH IN THE GARDEN)

BUÑUEL: I almost don't want to talk about *La mort en ce jardin*. The production was torture; there were difficulties from the very beginning. The producer was bothered by censorship and asked me to modify some things. The star of the film, Simone Signoret, felt uncomfortable because Yves Montand was far away from her in Italy and she wanted to join him; she looked for any excuse to return to Europe. When she entered the United States, she deliberately showed a passport with visas showing trips to the Soviet Union and other socialist countries, but the immigration agents — *rara avis* — let her pass. So many things were changed during the production that scenes often had to be rewritten minutes before the camera began rolling, and furthermore Gabriel Arout had to translate the text into French. I suffered a lot with Michele Girardon, the actress who played the deaf girl; she was only working on the film because her parents wanted her to, and, of course, she was completely ignorant of the craft. I had a lot of problems. By the end of the production I had had enough and I didn't even have a hand in the music. I let them put in whatever they wanted.

TURRENT: A writer whom both De la Colina and I admire very much worked on the script: Raymond Queneau.[2]

BUÑUEL: A talented man. He came up with solutions that are exemplary specimens of good film dialogue. He wrote a very intelligent interlude that I couldn't use because of the need for action. In the town, the miners declare a strike and the government sends in its troops against them. The prostitute goes shopping at a store. She asks for various items and a bar of soap. Then a bugle sounds outside announcing the arrival of the soldiers, and the prostitute amends her order: "Six bars of soap!" We understand immediately that she is going to have more professional activity without having to have her say anything vulgar like, "Uh, what work awaits me!" or putting in some ghastly image of a line of soldiers at the brothel door waiting their turn. Queneau was an exceptional writer with a good feel for spoken language. He had been a Surrealist, but when I entered the movement, he had already left. I met him while making this film. As a scriptwriter, he wasn't attracted to overly strong scenes. Me neither. And even though he complied professionally, I don't think he liked the film. After hours of looking for an emergency solution, every time we found one he usually said, *"Mais, je me demande si... "* ("But, I wonder if...")

TURRENT: The film could be seen as a political metaphor.

BUÑUEL: I only intended to film an adventure story that allowed us to observe the behavior of more-or-less civilized characters in a dangerous

2 Raymond Queneau (1903-1976), former member of the Surrealist movement and one of the founding members of the College of Pataphysics. Queneau is one of the most influencial modern writers in France, whose novels and criticism helped shape 20th-century French literature.

situation in the middle of nature. Marchal is the only character who sides with the miners. Also Vanel, in the beginning, but he later has a change of heart. In reality, the film is a little anarchistic.

TURRENT: It shares a certain relationship with *Robinson Crusoe*.

BUÑUEL: Of course: the theme of nature and the way human relationships change, toward either discord or solidarity. Without this solidarity, the characters, who find themselves in danger, would be lost. This is something that doesn't only happen in the jungle. The characters' conflict is similar in *The Exterminating Angel*...and there it happens in a sumptuous salon.

COLINA: The parallel is curious because in *La mort en ce jardin* the characters hold a formal evening salon party in the jungle, while in *The Exterminating Angel* you could say that the law of the jungle is installed in the salon...

BUÑUEL: As always, I am interested in seeing how circumstances will bring about changes in the characters. It's like putting them into a culture medium. You can prove that, when facing a shared situation of danger, very intelligent and civilized people become brutal, like animals. And you can prove the reverse. The experience makes some of them better, and makes others worse.

COLINA: Toward the end, it appears that both the adventurer and the deaf girl have turned out for the better and will begin a new life. This is not the case in *The Exterminating Angel*, where the characters return to their way of life...and remain locked up.

BUÑUEL: That's why I'm telling you that you can't establish rules, theses, or messages. I don't make a cinema of ideas. Of course, there are ideas to which I am faithful, and I could tell you that many of them are the same I had when I was twenty-eight years old, though I have modified some of them because reality has obliged me to. I expose, not impose these ideas. And more than ideas, they are images, feelings. But it frequently happens to me that in developing a story, or during filming, I have barely finished putting in something that seems to have a certain significance when immediately the opposite comes to my imagination.

COLINA: The Buñuel dialectic?

BUÑUEL: No. Nor is it a system and even less a philosophical method. Perhaps it happens that I am embarrassed by emphatic affirmations or categorical negations. I like what Pilate says to Jesus: "What is the truth?" In this, I understand Pilate more than Jesus. I sympathize with those who make an effort to search for the truth; I disagree with those who speak as if they had discovered it.

COLINA: Borges says: "Spaniards talk like people who don't understand doubt."

BUÑUEL: I accept that, but it doesn't apply only to Spaniards.

TURRENT: Returning to what you told us about how characters who change interest you. For example, the priest in *La mort en ce jardin* ends up using the chalice as a drinking glass, and rips a page out of the Bible to light a bonfire.

BUÑUEL: Because the demands of necessity are stronger than the truth of his dogmas. Besides, he does it in a Christian spirit and to help others. The character who changes radically is Vanel, who turns into a madman. This is the other possibility of a situation such as the one in the film.

COLINA: Let's talk a bit more about the salon in the jungle. The situation is this: the characters discover the remains of a fallen plane amid the vegetation and remove provisions from it, champagne, formal evening wear and so, in effect, they turn the jungle into an earthy salon. This is a kind of incantation that allows them to forestall the encroachment of the jungle... But isn't the discovery of the plane too providential?

BUÑUEL: Perhaps, but that didn't matter to me. What attracted me was the idea of turning the jungle into a salon. It's a type of window onto the imagination, wouldn't you say? A character contemplates a postcard of Paris and feels he is on a street or boulevard with neon lights, vehicles passing. Reality without imagination is only half of reality. You know I'm not a neorealist. Furthermore, even during the most terrible situation there can be a moment of respite.

TURRENT: I see the salon in the jungle in another way. During the journey through the jungle, the characters have come together and put aside their personal conflicts in the name of common salvation. They find the plane, the clothing, the jewels...and become madmen once again.

BUÑUEL: These are *a posteriori* considerations. The first thing that attracted my imagination is this *soirée* in the middle of the wilds. If you want, it is like a Surrealist painting, like a Max Ernst collage, like the sides of beef in the streetcar in *Illusion Travels by Streetcar*.

TURRENT: In this sequence, the priest, who had burned a page from the Bible to make a bonfire, and used the chalice to drink water, returns to his code of values. He says that taking the jewels from the dead bodies on the plane is robbery. Or rather, he returns to the idea that private property is sacred.

BUÑUEL: Because his change cannot be absolute. Some of the old ideas remain, struggling with the new ones. For example, I have already told you I gave up being religious when I was an adolescent. But do you think that I no longer retain many elements of my Christian formation in my way of thinking? Among many other things, I can be profoundly moved by a ceremony honoring the Virgin with novices in their white habits and the purity of their appearance.

COLINA: But for reasons we could call poetic rather than religious.

BUÑUEL: It could be for many reasons. Even erotic ones, no? But why this ceremony and not another? For example, some very beautiful houris dancing in a harem don't excite me as much as this ceremony. Which is to say that I have remained a Christian at heart, Catholic. I am not "one of the flock," but how can I deny that I have been marked culturally, spiritually, by the Catholic religion.

TURRENT: Among the characters, there is a young deaf girl. Why a deaf mute?

BUÑUEL: Why not? She could also sing opera with the angels themselves and that could interest me, too. But undoubtedly I was attracted to her being a deaf mute because it introduces an unexpected dimension among the speaking characters and perhaps makes the acting more interesting for the audience: you have to guess what she thinks and feels through her looks, her gestures.

TURRENT: She is the purest character. And, curiously, she is saved, along with the adventurer.

BUÑUEL: She is saved by her innocence, not because she is deaf. And the adventurer is saved by something very different: because he is best qualified for the difficult tests, he is the strongest and the most cold blooded. So the strongest and the weakest survive. Why? I don't know. Nature doesn't act according to human laws: it is blind.

17: NAZARIN

TOMAS PEREZ TURRENT: *Nazarín* marks the first encounter between you, a Spanish filmmaker, and Galdós,[1] the greatest Spanish novelist since Cervantes. One would assume that this encounter had to take place some day, but it was delayed in happening...

LUIS BUÑUEL: I had been intending to film *Nazarín* ever since the days of *The Great Madcap*. I had purchased the rights to it and *Doña Perfecta* from Pérez Galdós' daughter, Doña María. The producer Pancho Cabrera told me he would work on *Nazarín* while I adapted *Doña Perfecta*. A short while later he brought me his adaptation and it was incredibly bad, the worst ever: Nazarín knelt before the Virgin, his eyes rolled, and he exclaimed: "Oh Mother Most Holy, protect us sinners!" etc. I told him it would be better if we filmed *Doña Perfecta;* then, before I began working on it, an article appeared in the newspapers: Roberto Gavaldón was going to direct the film. I asked Cabrera for an explanation and he told me Dolores del Río was going to be the star and she preferred being directed by Gavaldón. "I am very sorry," he said, adding, "but you have already been paid ten thousand pesos, so we are even." But if I had purchased the story, it was because I wanted to direct the film. I appealed to the union and Cabrera had to pay me the rest. The film was eventually directed not by Gavaldón but by Alejandro Galindo. Well, and so *Nazarín* was not made. Later, there was the project to make *Tristana* with Silvia Pinal and Ernesto Alonso in the leading roles, but it never came to anything concrete. In 1957, when Barbachano Ponce proposed I make a film, we considered various possibilities. Again, one of them was Lorca's *The House of Bernarda Alba,* which we rejected, the subject mat-

---

1 Benito Pérez Galdós (1843-1920), Spanish novelist and playwright who wrote both *Nazarín* and *Tristana*. His sweeping series of 46 historical novels titled *Episodios nacionales* chronicled Spanish history from 1805 to the end of the century. This was followed by 21 novels dealing with contemporary Spanish society, exposing moral decay. In 1912, Galdós went blind, but he continued to dictate his works until his death.

ter seemed too Spanish to me and, above all, Federico's theater is all in the language. There was one more project, Alejo Carpentier's *El Acoso* (The Pursuit), which attracted me more as a story to film. I worked hard on the adaptation, but finally discovered I didn't know what to do with it. For me, it would have turned out to be a simple film of nocturnal adventures, similar to an English film in which a man was also pursued at night...

TURRENT: *Odd Man Out*, by Carol Reed, with James Mason.

BUÑUEL: Yes. Finally I decided on Nazarín, who interested me as a human type, as a conflict of spirit, religion, morality, etc. It was a work written eighty or ninety years previously, but it could be situated in Mexico during the period of the dictator Porfirio Díaz and the situation would be much the same. Besides, I could introduce many personal and more contemporary elements about Christianity, charity...

TURRENT: I think you have already dealt with this character; for example, Fr. Lizardi in *La mort en ce jardin*...

BUÑUEL: But there is no possible comparison! Nazarín is always a pure man, while Lazardi is an ordinary priest, human, but not exceptional. Nazarín is a man who is out of the ordinary and I feel a great affection for him.

JOSE DE LA COLINA: In Pérez Galdós' conception, the character is a cross between Christ and Don Quixote.

BUÑUEL: Yes, he is a Quixote of the priesthood; instead of following the example found in tales of knighthood, he follows the Gospels. Instead of having Sancho Panza as a squire, he is accompanied by two women, who are a bit like his "squiresses." At the same time, Beatriz could be Mary Magdalene and Andara could be a female version of Saint Peter. (For example: Peter draws his sword when Christ is taken; Andara hits a guard when Nazarín is taken prisoner.)

COLINA: How long had you been an admirer of Galdós?

BUÑUEL: I'm not a long-time admirer of Galdós. In my youth, my friends and I weren't very interested in Galdós. He seemed antiquated to us and a little too muddled. It was much later, in exile, when I really began to read him and then he interested me. I found elements of what we could even call "Surrealism" in his works: *l'amour fou*, delirious visions, a very intense reality with lyrical moments. *Nazarín* is a novel from his final period and not one of his best, but the story and the character fascinate me, or at least they suggest many things to me, they disturb me.

COLINA: One critic spoke of Goya's influence on the film...

BUÑUEL: Perhaps he said that because of the dwarf Ujo, but Goya wasn't the one who painted dwarfs, it was Velázquez, so it could also be said that I was influenced by Velázquez. But neither Velázquez, nor Goya, nor El Greco, nor the entire Prado Museum... I don't look to the example of painters. It's a cliché: Spanish filmmaker Buñuel: Buñuel influenced by Goya and Velázquez and even by bullfights. Much of Spain has had an influence on my life, but if there is a detail in a film that might be seen as a cultural quotation, I suppress it.

COLINA: But nevertheless, Galdós...

BUÑUEL: Of course, in this case I used a Spanish novelist as a source. But I have also adapted works by Usigli, Defoe, and Mirbeau, without being Usiglian, Defoean or Mirbeauian. Besides, if you look carefully at *Nazarín* as well as at *Tristana*, they are very different as books from what they are as films. At the end of the novel, Nazarín is delirious and believes he is saying Mass; at the end of the film, none of that. I want to say something else: *Nazarín* is not one of Galdós' great novels and neither is *Tristana*. They are not comparable to *Fortunata y Jacinta* or to the *Torquemada* series. When I film a novel, I feel freer if it's not a masterpiece because I don't feel inhibited about changing it and putting in anything I want. In great works there is a grand literary language, and how do you put that on the screen?

COLINA: When all is said and done, is that why you have never filmed works by Valle-Inclán or García Lorca?

BUÑUEL: Valle-Inclán's use of language is extraordinary — his neologisms, his *Valleinclanisms*. He is very literary in the best sense of the word. I'm also not interested in adapting García Lorca to film.

TURRENT: Some critics here have said there is very little of Mexico in *Nazarín*, that such characters do not portray the country...

BUÑUEL: I don't know if this happened with Pancho Cabrera or with Barbachano Ponce, but in the scene where the three neighborhood prostitutes insult Nazarín, they objected, saying it wasn't believable: three Mexican women don't insult a priest, and even less so during the time of Don Porfirio. I knew that, but I didn't aim to make a film portraying that kind of believability, but rather one about an exceptional priest who wants to live in agreement with the spirit and letter of original Christianity.

TURRENT: Can those who see *Nazarín* as a Christian film be right? Are you really a closet Christian?

BUÑUEL: I belong, and very profoundly, to Christian civilization. I'm

Christian by culture, if not by faith. In reference to *Nazarín*, I can tell you that if I were as close to Buddhist culture as I am to Christian culture, I could perhaps have made a Buddhist *Nazarín*. But as I told you before, the Orient doesn't interest me very much. I know *Nazarín* can be seen as a very Christian film, and even a Catholic one. When it was nominated for a Catholic award at Cannes, it received three votes in favor and five against. One day, Federico Amérigo, the production manager for the film, told me I should go to New York because Cardinal so-and-so was going to give me an award for the film. I turned it down. It's neither a Catholic nor an anti-Catholic film. The protagonist does not wish to preach, he doesn't wish to convert anyone. He wants to go into the countryside and live off alms, but he's not a missionary, he doesn't look to make proselytes. Of course, he is motivated by his beliefs, his ideology. What moves me is what happens inside him when his ideology fails, because whenever Nazarín gets involved, even in the best of faith, he only begets conflicts and disasters. There is one episode in the movie, one that doesn't appear in Galdós' book, when Nazarín offers to work for food alone. The other workers come and tell him, "By doing this, you hurt all of us. Get out!" Without knowing it, he is being a scab. The foreman isn't eager to lose such cheap labor and argues with the workers. When Nazarín is already far away on the road, we hear a gunshot. The incident has probably cost someone his life, though the well-meaning Nazarín doesn't realize it.

COLINA: Or rather: for a moment, Nazarín became a proletarian, but doesn't attain a class consciousness.

BUÑUEL: He's not a worker priest. He couldn't be one because of the time period depicted in the story. Besides, I transferred a present-day conflict to the Mexico of Porfirio Díaz. In those times, some road workers would never have thought it was so bad for a man to sell his labor only for something to eat, since they might have done the same.

COLINA: But at that time in Mexico there were already anarchists, union unrest, stirrings of labor unions.

BUÑUEL: Perhaps, but not like now. I think what the dissenting worker tells Nazarín is, above all, a modern attitude. Besides, Nazarín hasn't even thought about unionism, he knows nothing about workers' problems. Of course, he feels social injustice, but he can't explain it in terms of class struggle. The episode shows only how a good man, needing to eat, incites a conflict without wanting to.

COLINA: The episode of the workers could be a kind of apologue, like the dog tied to the cart in *Viridiana*.

BUÑUEL: Very perceptive, even if I don't like the word apologue. If that episode were removed, the film would be more or less the same. With the episode in it, the film is stronger and richer, to my judgment. It shows us how a man so pure and good, with so much love for his fellow creatures, fails in the world as it is.

TURRENT: Nazarín also fails in his Christian attitude...

COLINA: ...To give a particular example, in the town hit by a plague, why doesn't he manage to get the dying woman to commend her soul to God?

BUÑUEL: There comes a time when everything fails for Nazarín. Moreover, he even contradicts himself. He believes in alms, he has proclaimed himself in favor of begging. But at the end, when a poor woman gives him a pineapple, he refuses to accept it. For me, Nazarín fails here because he rejects what has been his life's principle, his own beliefs. And he continues on, weeping.

COLINA: Just a minute, Don Luis, you are forgetting something. At first Nazarín rejects the pineapple, but after going a few steps, he turns around, accepts it, and thanks the woman. After accepting the pineapple, he begins to cry. Thus, his weeping can be interpreted quite differently from the way you interpret it. The woman's generous gesture has moved Nazarín and given him back a little hope.

BUÑUEL: I agree with how you just interpreted the scene, but be careful; I don't try to show that Nazarín has regained his faith in either religion or mankind, or that he has completely lost his faith. What I can tell you is that Nazarín's attitude intrigues me as much as it does you. And it moves me. What will happen to this man after so many experiences? I don't know.

COLINA: We have bumped up against the famous Buñuel ambiguity, Tomás.

BUÑUEL: *(Laughs)* Ambiguity is always present... But, speaking seriously, it's not that I tell myself to put things in my films that can themselves be interpreted in black and white. That would be self-deceptive. What I know is that, in a situation similar to Nazarín's, any man has contradictory reactions. Let's suppose I am Nazarín and inside I am destroyed, overwhelmed by my failure both as a priest and as a man. Someone offers me a pineapple out of pity and my first reaction is to reject it. It has come down to pineapples for me now! Then I take a few steps and reconsider: this poor woman has offered me the only thing she can give; she doesn't see me as either a priest or a criminal, but only an unfortunate man, and I have refused her gesture violently, with a lack of humility. So, I turn around and accept the pineapple. There are no theories or metaphysics in the scene. I would have acted the same way. Nazarín is very close to me.

COLINA: The moment is especially significant because it's the end of the film. And when the word *Fin* (The End) appears, the "i" is in the form of a cross.

BUÑUEL: I don't remember that. But that was done by the people who did the credits for the film, and I had nothing to do with it. What I did put in, because union regulations stipulated that I had to use some music, was the drums of Calanda. And to me it seems right to add them for intuitive reasons, for feeling, and not to give them any particular meaning.

TURRENT: But, whether you like it or not, everything in a film is susceptible to some meaning, because we aren't dealing with a tree or a cloud that left the frame by accident, or with some sounds captured by chance on the microphone. The pineapple, the drums... You had definitively decided they should be there. And not at any moment whatsoever, but rather at the end of the film.

BUÑUEL: I accept that, but it doesn't have anything to do with interpretation in only one sense. I leave the interpretation open to the viewer. Perhaps you'd have to psychoanalyze me to know why we find these details in my film that attract and move me. The bad part — as I think I already told you — is that according to a psychoanalyst, I am nonpsychoanalyzable. Of course, there is no lack of people who, as usual, say the pineapple is an assertion of the phallus.

COLINA: We have one sure bit of information: the Calanda drums. We hear them for the first time in *L'Age d'or* and then again in *Nazarín*, both times in similar situations: they are finales, they are moments of desperation or incertitude.

TURRENT: And we can't help asking whether a "communicating vessel" exists between the protagonists in *L'Age d'or* and *Nazarín*.

BUÑUEL: There is no relation between the characters. In *L'Age d'or*, Modot is a destroyer, a subversive. Nazarín, no. He would be exactly the opposite.

COLINA: What you just said about Modot interests me. I've always interpreted him as a bourgeois prisoner of his class's moral code who suddenly rebels.

BUÑUEL: Modot's character came out of nowhere and even I don't know if he is bourgeois. His character is a bit fantastic, even though he wears a suit and tie. He is a natural Surrealist. He's drawn to love like a moth to a flame, but he destroys everything in his path, not out of clumsiness like Nazarín, but out of rage and perhaps a certain capriciousness. Nothing indicates that he began as a "prisoner of a class's moral code," as you put it.

COLINA: But one supposes that he has a social position, and that he is invested with a humanitarian and very honorable mission.

BUÑUEL: But placed there arbitrarily like a mushroom, that mission is an absurd detail! What I like about the scene where he shows off his titles, the parchment honoring some humanitarian mission, is the absurdity of it. The titles could be counterfeit, he could have stolen them from a government official.

TURRENT: Many critics, myself included, have interpreted this character as De la Colina does: Modot begins to feel like a man who is a prisoner of the conventions of his class and finally he rebels, carried away by the strength of his desire. He dresses and grooms himself in a conventional manner, has some previous dealings with a government official, though he later sends him packing...

BUÑUEL: I don't agree with you two. What's the first thing we see him do in the film? He is rolling around in the mud with his beloved in full view of everyone who has gathered to inaugurate the New City. Which is to say, he begins and ends doing things "in opposition." If some critics, one slim volume, several volumes, or even many psychoanalysts interpret it in another way, I say that is all very well and good, it's their right... But I don't agree.

COLINA: Then do I have the right to give an interpretation of the Calanda drumroll in *Nazarín*?

BUÑUEL: All right, go ahead.

COLINA: The drumming is a firing squad: you shoot the priest Nazarín, but let the man Nazario live.

BUÑUEL: No. Good grief! It's not a firing squad, though for a delirium of interpretation that isn't bad. The church doesn't intend to shoot him. They tell him, "You've left your priesthood in a sorry state. You'll be taken separately from the other prisoners and without your priestly habit." That's all.

TURRENT: There are other priests in the film. One is a very conventional priest, who kicks Nazarín graciously out of his house because he doesn't want any problems. Another is a complete imbecile who accepts without protest the fact that a soldier mistreats some poor peasant.

BUÑUEL: I like that moment because you see Nazarín's quixotic side. An old cart is stalled on the road because the mule that pulls it has sat down. A priest and a soldier wait for the problem to resolve itself and Nazarín offers a hand. A humble Indian passes by in silence and the soldier upbraids him because he hasn't saluted. Nazarín becomes indignant and, very dignified, tells the soldier, "This being, whom you treat like a beast, is a man like you or me and you have no right to treat him so despotically at this or any other time." He says it with authentic indignation but also using a certain rhetoric, no? And the others can't believe what they hear. The priest says, "Leave him alone, colonel. He must be one of those subversive elements that have been keeping the government so busy." Yes, Nazarín is quixotic, but the difference is that Don Quixote is crazy once in a while; Nazarín is always sane. Nor is he a revolutionary, although perhaps one day he could be one, he's so pure and innocent. Perhaps Nazarín ends up believing more in the individual than in God or society. I also believe more in the individual than in society.

TURRENT: In this society or in any imaginable one?

BUÑUEL: In any society whatsoever. At an earlier time, my feelings were directed more toward the collective movement, toward socialism. It was my reaction against organized systems. I sympathized with anything that could have destroyed existing society, which is conventional and unfair. But now I think that when this society is destroyed, another will appear that will end up being the same...but in another way. I don't know if the theory of thesis, antithesis, and synthesis is true or not. Currently, I'm a skeptic, let's say a skeptic with good intentions. I mean I keep my sympathy for those who believe they can make a better society; if I can, I'll help them make this come to pass. For the time being, I may believe that Communism continues to be the most solid pillar of world revolution, but that struggle doesn't really concern me. I can't propose any solutions; I don't know what they could possibly be. I simply try not to betray the convictions of my youth, to do the least possible damage. And I try to make my films morally honest.

COLINA: As someone once said: "If I can't change the world, at least I will try to see that the world doesn't change me."

BUÑUEL: Besides, at my age it would be difficult to change me. I believe that systems change, but men are essentially the same. Hopefully this doesn't sound like one of those "truths" that leave the world shaking, a solemn declaration for television. But...why are we talking about this and not about the films?

COLINA: Because sometimes you close up about your films: "This scene has no deliberate meaning; I put this in because I felt like it; I like this or I don't, I don't know why." And at times, I try to get at you from another direction...even though we may stray from the subject. Sometimes I have the impression that these interviews should be titled: *Assault on The Sphinx Buñuel*. And at times, I even play the devil's advocate with you.

TURRENT: Well let's get back to the subject and return to Nazarín. When he is in jail, the "good thief" says to him: "You do good and I do evil and neither of us is good for anything." Doesn't man's action change the world in any sense?

BUÑUEL: Perhaps he modifies it, yes, but in a positive sense? I don't know, though — forgive me — I would dare to say no. Society goes from bad to worse. Men killed each other before, but not on the scale they do now, which is limitless. In our scientific and technological times, man is still morally like the cavemen. Much worse than in past times, and with a greater charge of sulfur. I don't want to play the prophet, but I believe we are approaching the final catastrophe. If it's not the atomic bomb, it will be the destruction of the environment. Look at how violence is publicized. The excess of information is like a plague. Today, terrorists are more famous than movie stars. In our century, we thought we would finish with dictatorships, but one ends and two more pop up. And smog, and the nightmare of noise and of canned music, and the chaos of our cities. I no longer believe in social progress. I can only believe in a few exceptional individuals of good faith like Nazarín, even though they fail.

COLINA: You have referred to the plague. In *Nazarín*, there is a long sequence about a plague-stricken town. We all remember a terrible image: the girl who cries, dragging a sheet through a narrow street...

BUÑUEL: That image sums up the plague. A scene like that cannot be foreseen in the script. I am filming in an odd, narrow street, almost in ruins. Suddenly an image pops into my mind: a girl approaching, dragging a sheet. It is an irrational image, but it sums up the tragedy. The wrinkled urine-stained sheet. The idea of something that's been trampled underfoot, savaged. The association, of course, came without knowing it. I think I didn't go so far finally as to put vomit and excrement on the sheet. I'm not such a naturalist, I didn't dare. I did make sure, however, that the sheet was very long.

TURRENT: You have said you detest symbols, yet I believe the plague sequence somehow sums up the film. The plague stands for evil. It is impossible to stop it, but within the plague one can give hope and love. BUÑUEL: I accept that. Hope, perhaps not; love, yes. Nazarín leans over a sick woman and tries to help her "settle her accounts" with God so that she will go to heaven. The woman says: "Heaven, no; Juan, Juan!" She cares more about the presence of the man she loves than about the salvation of her soul. The man arrives, kicks the priest and the other women out, and kisses the dying woman on the mouth without fearing contagion. That really moves me: despite everything, this is total love. A love that does not even include hope.

TURRENT: It is reminiscent of the kiss Heathcliff gives Catherine's corpse in *Wuthering Heights*.

BUÑUEL: Yes, the love that takes precedence over everything else. Is that idea too romantic? Maybe, but it still excites me. If you notice, there is a lot of human love in *Nazarín*. That of Beatriz and El Pinto, that of the dwarf for Andara, that of the two women for Nazarín...and that of the dying young woman.

TURRENT: Is the relationship between Andara and the dwarf in Galdós' book?

BUÑUEL: Yes. I also used another of Galdós' tricks: disguising bad words: for example, I had a character exclaim *puño!* (fist) instead of *coño!* (cunt).

TURRENT: That's another of the reasons they say *Nazarín* doesn't paint a true picture of Mexico.

BUÑUEL: I already told you that doesn't matter much to me. It is neither Mexico nor Spain; I portray a possible country in the film. Besides that, you know that in many details — if not in some, then in others — Mexico is very Spanish. It is and it isn't, that makes it more interesting. But the dwarf Ujo's love interests me more, and also what he says: "Everyone calls you a public woman, but I respect you, *puño!*"

COLINA: Ujo is a character who is out of the ordinary within conventional cinematic realism. It is poetically upsetting that this ugly dwarf, who is in love with a prostitute, behaves like a romantic lover. Poe and Hoffmann would have dared this mixture of the sublime and the grotesque, or maybe pioneer filmmakers like Griffith, or perhaps Stroheim... But rarely today do we see a scene like the one in which Ujo follows Andara, who is taken prisoner, and he falls exhausted and you see her in the distance. And when she shouts good-bye to him, he lowers his eyes and lifts his hand to his chest like a romantic lead in an old film... Your work has been associated with the Spanish picaresque tradition, but Ujo isn't a picaresque character. He is completely romantic, like Hugo's Quasimodo. A mixture of gargoyle and angel...or an angelic monster. And Nazarín, of course, seems to be a magnet for marginal characters, those whom society casts aside...

TURRENT: And at the same time he seems to be insensitive to the love that other characters, like Andara and Beatriz, offer him...

BUÑUEL: He is not insensitive and surely he's not impotent either, but for him all of this merges into divine love, in Christian communion. Perhaps, at some moment, the character could feel a carnal inclination for Beatriz and even Andara. Or he could respond to Andara sexually out of pity. But he is chaste by conviction. Besides, that theme would turn it into a different film: the priest and temptation, etc. And it would be ridiculous: "Come here, Andara, let's have a bit of fun together in bed..." Maybe Andara has a purer love for Nazarín than Beatriz. After all, it would be more likely for Andara to lead a nunlike holy life than for Beatriz to do so. Beatriz is horrified and throws a fit when her mother tells her she loves Nazarín "as a man." It's because there is something of that, but she rejects it.

COLINA: There is a very beautiful scene that is very ironic at the same time. Nazarín and the two women are relaxing for the night in the field, sitting on a tree trunk, the two women leaning next to him. A small storm of jealousy breaks out between the women while Nazarín busies himself...with a caterpillar.

BUÑUEL: But he doesn't do it as a way of mocking the women. It's his Franciscan side: "Brother caterpillar." For him, everything is part of the universal love of God for his creatures.

COLINA: It's very clear what a complete Christian Nazarín is, but it isn't the Christianity...of Christ. The only image of Christ in the entire film is the picture Andara sees during her fever: she sees a diabolic Christ who has a burst of laughter. In one of your first Surrealist texts, *A Giraffe*, you had already written: "Christ has a burst of laughter."

BUÑUEL: That was a Surrealist joke. Andara, however, is delirious.

TURRENT: By the way, that image is cut when the film is shown on television here. Delirium or no delirium, it's considered too strong for the Mexican public.

BUÑUEL: I didn't know that because I don't watch television; I can't stand the commercials. Besides, Christ's laugh doesn't necessarily have to be a diabolic detail. Didn't Christ ever have a burst of laughter? In *The Milky Way*, I show him shaving his beard. Why not? I don't believe such details are either diabolic or profane. I don't see why Christ always has to be shown as a solemn, bearded man who walks majestically and only utters phrases for posterity. And on the other hand, the conventional image of Christ can be interesting: there must be a reason why it is the one that has remained in people's memory.

COLINA: Nazarín could be a "demythologized" Christ.

BUÑUEL: He could be, but he is Nazarín.

18: LA FIEVRE MONTE A EL PAO
(LOS AMBICIOSOS); THE YOUNG ONE

LA FIEVRE MONTE A EL PAO (LOS AMBICIOSOS)

TOMAS PEREZ TURRENT: It doesn't seem like you have very good memories of *La fièvre monte à El Pao* (known in Spanish as *Los Ambiciosos* and in English as *Republic of Sin*).

LUIS BUÑUEL: No, and neither did Gérard Philipe. It's the last film he acted in. One day during the filming we dropped our masks. "Why did you agree to make this film?" I asked him. "I don't know," he said. "And you?" "I don't know either," I told him. Neither of us knew why we were working on the film. The role didn't go very well for Gérard; he wasn't the man for that character, that was obvious even in the way he wore his pistol hanging loosely on his belt.

JOSE DE LA COLINA: But how did the project come about?

BUÑUEL: My agent proposed it from Paris. A certain producer wanted to make a film with me and came to see me in Mexico. The truth is that it didn't interest me very much, and I accepted it only because at that time I took everything offered to me, as long as it wasn't humiliating, because I didn't have any money and lived from day to day. I think my lack of interest is apparent. It turned out to be a very routine film, made to get out of my financial predicament.

COLINA: Nevertheless, it could, in principle, have been interesting as a political fable. It seems to me that it tries to show the impossibility of changing society from within an established power structure.

BUÑUEL: There is something of that. Philipe's character is an idealist who wants to end the dictatorship, and to do that, he gets involved in its machinery. But he fails in the end because he gets caught up in the machinery. I should say that in general political films don't interest me.

Objectively, I understand their interest, but I'm not interested in making them, I don't feel they are my terrain.

TURRENT: The protagonist has certain characteristics that bring Nazarín to mind. He is an idealist who doesn't notice anything that goes on around him. He wants to be fair in an unfair system and he does everything wrong. He only makes things worse.

BUÑUEL: The resemblance to Nazarín is only superficial. In the abstract, Ramón Vázquez's character was likeable, humanly and politically agreeable to me, but I ultimately realized he didn't move me. Maybe that's why he dies at the end. I don't remember exactly how.

TURRENT: He consciously chooses death. His positive trait is that he comes to an understanding that all his intentions are worthless. He is in power, but everything remains the same. The only thing he has achieved is to humanize the repression, to help make it tolerable.

BUÑUEL: I barely remember the story line, probably because I didn't want to make the film. Despite everything, of course I tried to make a professional, well-made film, and even to put in interesting details. But there was too much dialogue in the film, situations were resolved with words and I didn't like that, so I managed to enrich the scenes...through certain plagiarisms. I don't know if you noticed the plagiarisms. They are "very respectable," of course, because I took them from works in the public domain.

TURRENT: For example?

BUÑUEL: I've already told you that opera story lines give me ideas for my stories. For *La fièvre*, I stole the ending from *Tosca*. In order to save Philipe's life, María Félix takes her clothes off in front of the tyrant and offers herself to him. It's the same in *Tosca*, and when the tyrant signs the safe-conduct, *Tosca* stabs him. But it doesn't mean anything, because the hero is shot in the end. I have been a fan of Italian opera. I had a wonderful book, which I lost, with the story lines to some four hundred operas. Excellent stories, melodramatic, strong, pure action.

TURRENT: The film's problem isn't only that it's very talky, but that solutions are resolved verbally rather than visually.

BUÑUEL: That's true. And despite everything, I looked for elements that could give life to the scenes. There was a moment when Philipe must declare his love to María Félix. How do you film that without falling into wordiness? It came to me to have María Félix break a glass case and order Philipe to pick up the pieces of glass. She reaffirms her domination over him, no? Philipe then declares his love while picking up the glass like a servant. That contradiction could be interesting, and there are a few small ideas like that in the film — though they may not even be noticed. I felt very sorry when Philipe died shortly after the film was finished and I was the one who had directed him in one of his weakest films. Neither of us could "remove the thorn from our sides" by making something better.

THE YOUNG ONE (LA JOVEN)

COLINA: I think *The Young One* is a "good minor Buñuel film." It's well made, but a little impersonal.

BUÑUEL: You think so? On the contrary, I think it's one of my most personal films.

COLINA: What I wanted to say was that if I didn't know the film was yours, I would have left the cinema saying: "I've seen a good film by an unknown filmmaker." I wouldn't have noticed it was a Buñuel film.

BUÑUEL: It seems to me that is true of *Cela s'appelle l'aurore*, which is more impersonal in its execution. Using the same idea, any director could have made it. As a film, *The Young One* is more mine. There are many details: the cadaver's feet, the spiders, the hens, the impartiality: the film is neither pro-black nor pro-white. I even let the white racist defend himself when he talks with the black man. The racist says to the black man who is tied up, "I feel you suffer because you have blood and you look like me in some ways, but you don't have a soul. You are like an animal." There are no absolutely bad or good characters. The racist gives the black man a cigarette, water to drink, but he can't see him as an equal. This is not due to evilness, but rather to certain social influences. These ideas are mine — even though they aren't brilliant — and I think they are evident in the film.

COLINA: Maybe my impression of the film's impersonality comes from the fact that it is produced like an American movie.

BUÑUEL: The actors are American — except for Claudio Brook — and so are Hugo Butler, who adapted the script, and the producer, though we filmed in Mexico. And of course the subject matter is American.

TURRENT: You hate movies with a message, but *The Young One* could be a film with a clear antiracist message.

BUÑUEL: Racism is one of the problems dealt with in the story, but perhaps it's not the only one. Don't forget, there is also the sexual relationship between the man and a girl, almost a child. Nevertheless, I accept that the problem of racism has a lot of weight in the film. Without trying to send a message, I tried to understand — not defend — the racist characters. There are five characters: Zachary, the girl, the black musician, the Protestant minister, and the violent racist. Zachary is racist; he has been educated to be one, but his treatment of the black man changes as the film progresses. His relationship with the girl makes him more humane and at the end he lets the black man go free. The other racist, Jackson, is an authentic brute, fanatical in his ideas, though he has his own kind of generosity despite this. He could lynch five black men and then turn around and give generously to a beggar. According to him, the black man is an animal, but he can be compassionate to animals. He is a monster...with extenuating circumstances. He sees the black man and says, "What a shame. You have a man's form, but you don't have a soul."

COLINA: The treatment of the black man's character is interesting. Some progressive critics criticized the fact that you portrayed him as too belligerent and, even worse, as a drug addict.

BUÑUEL: The black man doesn't have to be perfect. He can have as many human defects as anyone else. What's wrong with certain thesis films is that, in the case of racism, for example, they portray all black people as saints. I think that is playing with a stacked deck.

TURRENT: The scene where the black man and the racist fight is very good. The black man takes a rifle[1] and is on the point of opening fire on the other man. The lyncher almost provokes him to shoot, but the black man doesn't do it, and for that, the white man feels humiliated. He is offended that a black man has spared his life.

BUÑUEL: Do you know that during the filming, the black man took the fight seriously and really hit the other man? We had to calm him down.

COLINA: The minister also has a racist attitude.

BUÑUEL: The minister is a well-intentioned man within the limits of his ideas. He doesn't think any human being should be mistreated; he acknowledges that the black man has a soul, but when he is going to bed and is given the mattress where the black man slept, he asks to turn it over, because it's stronger than he is: he cannot stand the "smell of niggers." He is the contrast between our morals and our feelings, our purely physical sensibility.

---

1 Pérez Turrent's memory of this scene is faulty. The weapon used in the fight scene is a knife, not a rifle.

TURRENT: The young woman seems to remain outside the problem of racism.

BUÑUEL: She has the innocence of a girl, she's like a little animal. The actress was a nonprofessional and directing her was a nightmare. Zachary Scott's wife, Elsa Ford, who had worked with Faulkner and is a consummate Broadway actress, took the girl aside to teach her how to say, for example: "I don't want any water." When she was in front of the camera, the girl would say it badly again and again. My son Juan Luis, who was my assistant, also went through her scenes with her, with the patience of a saint, and that didn't work out either. The girl was completely useless, but that was justified by the fact that she had never made a film before and, furthermore, it didn't interest her. She was in the film only because her parents wanted her to be there. I think she later made a very important film, which I would like to have seen. During my film, she seemed to be totally allergic to cinema.

TURRENT: Perhaps that helped the character and the film.

BUÑUEL: Perhaps, because she was very natural. In the seduction scene, Zachary Scott told her, "Don't be afraid, nothing will happen to you." He said that more to the actress than to the character because the girl was really afraid, as if the scene were real.

TURRENT: I thought that actress was very good, with an almost animal passivity, in fact. And we all remember the scene where she walks on high heels for the first time.

BUÑUEL: The female walk is one of the things that attracts me most. For example, in *Diary of a Chambermaid*, Jeanne Moreau had to walk in high-buttoned boots. It is a genuine pleasure to watch Jeanne Moreau walk like that, the way she sways sensually on her ankles.

COLINA: I agree, Don Luis. The best scenes in Antonioni's *The Night*[2] are those when we escape from boredom thanks to her walking.

BUÑUEL: But there was already Louis Malle's film *Frenzy*.[3] She also walked very well in that film and for a long time, too.

TURRENT: Malle set her walking and she hasn't stopped yet. *(Laughter)*

COLINA: In *The Young One*, there is a disturbing scene in which an animal devours some hens. I believe it precedes the girl's seduction-rape.

BUÑUEL: The animal is a badger. The scene horrifies me because badgers

2 *La Notte* (1961), dir. Michelangelo Antonioni, starring Jeanne Moreau and Marcello Mastroianni.
3 *Ascenseur pour l'echafaud* (1958), dir. Louis Malle; known in the UK as *Lift to the Gallows*.

kill for the fun of it. They can kill fifteen hens and later suck the blood from only one of them. I tell you that this horrifies me, but it also fascinates me.

COLINA: It's odd how you usually insert some marginal scene with animals in sequences where there is going to be an erotic act. Is this to show a relationship between sadistic cruelty and eroticism?

BUÑUEL: I'll tell you again that this is not premeditated. But give me some examples.

COLINA: In *Los olvidados*, El Jaibo seduces Pedro's mother and then we see some dogs dancing laboriously. In *Viridiana*, when the servant is seduced, a cat pounces on a mouse...

BUÑUEL: I believe the coincidence of those image associations is spontaneous. I didn't intend to illustrate the relationship between eroticism and cruelty. But since that relationship exists, the images you mention rise to the surface. Even though I didn't notice it, thanks be to Zeus.

COLINA: With or without animals, that relationship often appears in your films. How do you explain that?

BUÑUEL: It is the eternal feeling that love and death go hand in hand. For me, there is something terrible about fornication. Considered objectively, copulation seems both laughable and tragic at the same time. It's the thing that most resembles death: the eyes rolled back, the spasms, the drooling. And fornication is diabolical: I always see the devil in it.

TURRENT: Your description of copulation coincides with Batcheff's agonizing images in *Un chien andalou*.

BUÑUEL: And of Modot in *L'Age d'or*. The sexual act is like a form of death. There are many insects and arachnids that die after coitus. The female black widow spider and the praying mantis devour their mates after the nuptials. And the male turtle dies during the love act.

19: THE RETURN TO SPAIN; *VIRIDIANA*

TOMAS PEREZ TURRENT: *Viridiana* is one of your key films, one of the most famous, and it also marks your return to Spain. How did the film come about? Where did the name come from?

LUIS BUÑUEL: The name comes from the Latin *viridium,* a green place. Around 1910, when I was studying with the Jesuits, there was a magazine called *La hormiga de oro* (The Golden Ant), which in one issue recounted the life of St. Viridiana. I don't remember if she was an Italian saint, but she really existed. Here in the Mexico City Museum, there is a portrait of her: she is depicted with a cross, a crown of thorns, and some nails (these objects appear in the film). Well, after *Nazarín,* I think, Gustavo Alatriste — then married to actress Silvia Pinal — told me he wanted to make a film with me: "You have complete freedom to make the film as you want." I had thought of charging the same amount as I had charged until then in Mexico, but Alatriste offered me four times more and wanted us to film in Spain. For me, the conflict began there: should I go to work in Spain? Finally I told myself: if the film is honest, why not make it?

JOSE DE LA COLINA: How did the re-encounter with Spain go?

BUÑUEL: It was moving. I am very sentimental; I live, in great part, through my memories. I rediscovered so many personal images, of childhood, adolescence, youth, it was like when I returned to Paris after the Second World War. I walked around the streets with tears in my eyes.

COLINA: If the twenty-year-old Luis had met Don Luis at seventy, what would have happened?

BUÑUEL: The former would have given the latter a thrashing with my cane. Or perhaps the reverse. Because I hate who I was at twenty. I don't idealize my youth... Besides, I discovered a Spain that was beginning to develop a visible inner tranquility, perhaps even an excessive tranquility. In politics, nothing surprised me: I already knew the situation, though from the outside and at a distance. I immediately contacted the bullfighter Dominguín and the filmmaker Juan Antonio Bardem. Ricardo Muñoz Suay slightly modified the script of *Viridiana*, removing some things the censor wouldn't have accepted. Dominguín took me to talk with the director of the Spanish Film Institute, who told me that the film would be accepted, but only if it had another ending, because it was too terrible for a young novice to end up in a man's bedroom.

COLINA: To sleep with him...

BUÑUEL: Why else? In the original script she knocks on his door, he lets her in, and...the end. The censor found this impossible and I promised him I would change it. So I did, and the new solution satisfied the censor, even though it is even more immoral in my opinion.

TURRENT: It suggests a *ménage à trois.*

BUÑUEL: Viridiana enters the room while her cousin and the maid are playing cards and sits down next to them. The camera begins to move back slowly. The cousin says, "I always knew my cousin Viridiana would end up playing cards with me."

TURRENT: We know where the name came from, but the story?

BUÑUEL: I took a memory from childhood or adolescence as its point of departure. I had a crush on Victoria Eugenia, the Queen of Spain, who was a beautiful blond. Among the things I imagined about her was that I would secretly enter her bedroom, where the queen slept separately from the king, and I would put a narcotic in her glass of milk. The queen drinks the milk, takes her clothes off, and goes to bed. I wait until she is sleeping deeply, I approach her and take her in my arms...etc., etc. The fantasy of a fourteen-year-old schoolboy. What was absurd and marvelous about it were the great differences: socially, age-wise, and other things. A boy from Zaragoza and a queen of English nationality. Though it's the reverse in *Viridiana*, there is also the difference in age. The class differences don't exist, but the fact that she is a novice and he is her uncle does. In any case, great obstacles come into play in both situations, which feed desire even more. I find the idea of having a sleeping woman at my disposal very stimulating. I can do it in my imagination, but in practice it would scare me.

COLINA: You never thought about the story of *Sleeping Beauty?*

BUÑUEL: Never.

COLINA: Because the film has close parallels to that tale. Don Jaime's uncultivated fields could represent the woods: historical time has stopped in both. Viridiana is Sleeping Beauty, of course, but there would be a variation: Don Jaime would be a kind of Sleeping Gentleman. Besides that, there also appears to be an allusion to Spanish history, to the lethargy of the Franco period. "The lands have stood uncultivated for twenty years," Don Jaime says.

BUÑUEL: I could have said fifteen or thirty years. I never thought of making a historical reference. There was the childhood obsession and the addition of the character of Don Jaime who, though he is a selfish landowner, kindles my affection. I identify with him a little bit.

COLINA: The character is a fetishist; he caresses his dead wife's clothes...

BUÑUEL: And he even puts them on. That is also a childhood characteristic of mine. It is fetishistic rather than homosexual transvestitism. As a child, I liked to put on my mother's clothes and sometimes I wore them together with my father's clothes. For example: my father's top hat and my mother's bustle and buttoned boots. My mother noticed that someone had taken her clothes and shouted, "Who made a mess around in here?" I was around six or seven years old. Perhaps for a time I had a taste for fetish transvestitism, or for disguise. I think I have already told you that when I was fourteen, I successfully went out into the street dressed as a priest, wearing the cassock and mantle of an uncle who was a priest... There are other "keys" — as you two say — I can point out to you that pertain to the film's story line. During the entire trip, when I scouted locations for the production, I saw dogs walking behind carts, tied to the axle, and I felt terrible about it. Especially in Alicante. It had such an impact on me that I put it in the film, even though it didn't make much sense, like someone who puts à notation in the margin of a book. Rabal sees a dog tied up that way and asks the cart's driver, "Why don't you carry the dog inside the cart?" The driver responds, "Because inside is for people, not for animals." Later, I learned that they tied the dogs up so they wouldn't run loose and get run over by an automobile. But that could also be prevented by taking the dog inside the cart, couldn't it? Poor animals... Well, finally the episode did end up being integrated into the story, because Rabal criticizes Viridiana's charity: "It's stupid. Why care for twenty beggars when there are millions in the world?" He doesn't notice that he, by buying the dog from the cart owner, has done something similar. There are thousands of dogs in that situation in Spain.

COLINA: Then a parallel is produced between the dog and the beggars.

BUÑUEL: Yes, but it wasn't deliberate on my part. I assure you that it was a coincidence. Rationally, I criticize Viridiana's charity, too, or rather: I am against the Christian type of charity. But, if I see a poor man who moves me, I give him five pesos. If he doesn't move me, if he seems disagreeable to me, I don't give him anything. So it isn't really charity.

COLINA: The film deals with the uselessness of Christian charity?

BUÑUEL: Rather with its counterproductive character, because it produces catastrophes: the beggars make a mess of the house, they brawl among themselves, there is Viridiana's possible rape. Nevertheless, it's not an anticharity film, or anti-anything. I don't think criticizing Christian charity would be an important question in our times. It would be a little ridiculous.

COLINA: Let's say that the theme comes up in passing. I also see a major theme, and one you have dealt with frequently: the separation of reality and desire, or reality and dreaming. We have seen this in your films since *L'Age d'or, El, The Criminal Life of Archibaldo de la Cruz, Nazarín.*

BUÑUEL: It is the abyss that can exist between an idea of the world and what the world really is. In fact, almost all my characters suffer from a disillusionment and later change, for better or for worse. When all is said and done, this is the theme of *Don Quixote*. In a certain sense, Viridiana is a Quixote in skirts. Don Quixote defends the prisoners who are being taken to the galleys and they attack him. Viridiana protects the beggars and they also attack her. Viridiana returns to reality, accepts the world as it is. A crazy dream and finally the return to reason. Don Quixote also returns to reality and accepts being only Alonso Quijano.

TURRENT: So, *Viridiana* would be the continuation of *Nazarín.* Curiously, Rabal, who played Nazarín, plays a character who is exactly the opposite here, a rogue and Don Jaime's immoral son.

BUÑUEL: He is not immoral. He is a very rational man, with a very practical mind, contemptuous of social conventions. He is a positivist who believes in progress from a rational and bourgeois point of view. He is not interested in Viridiana for her inheritance because he already has part of the estate, but rather because he really likes her. Maybe he isn't in love with her, but he does feel an attraction. Since they are from the same social level, and are co-owners of the estate, perhaps they will get married. It's none of my business. Like Pilate, I wash my hands.

COLINA: In reference to the beggars, with this film you return to the Spanish picaresque novel.

BUÑUEL: What can I do? But yes: I have read picaresque novels and many of them have remained in my memory. But in Spain, at least in the time of my youth, you could meet beggars like those you see in the film.

COLINA: The beggars turned out so impressively real that it has been said you used real beggars.

BUÑUEL: No, that is false. They are played by actors, some of whom are even famous in Spain. The only one who was a real beggar is the man who plays the role of the leper. He had been a theater extra, but never an actor. I think he is great. He was from Malaga, had really begged in Madrid, and was poisoned by alcohol. It was impossible to communicate with him during the filming, but I finally managed. In his scenes, the reactions are authentic, he really became indignant or happy.

TURRENT: He could have been a perfect *Simon of the Desert*.

BUÑUEL: Yes, and I would have liked to use him in another film, but the poor fellow died. He was very thin, like an anchorite. He caused problems when he arrived drunk. There was a scene when he was supposed to extend his arm so they could give him some bread and another beggar hits his hand and says, "No, you have leprosy!" Dropping the bread, he was supposed to shout: "'At's a lie! This ain't leprosy!" Well, it was impossible for him to drop the bread, he clutched it the way a drowning man clings to a board. The first day at the studio, he urinated behind the set on a fusebox, causing a short circuit that plunged the set into darkness. The technicians were furious: "Listen, you son of a bitch!" He couldn't understand: "Well, what have I done? Where can a guy piss around here?" *(He laughs.)* In the scene when the cripple tries to rape Viridiana and the leper hits him on the head, Silvia Pinal came to tell me, "Luis, it's impossible. The man stinks." It was true. The poor man had relieved himself in his pants. He had diarrhea, and it was true: he stank. I sent him to the hospital, where he stayed for two days, watched over by my assistant so that he wouldn't drink. He went for three days without drinking, he had been cured of diarrhea, and he returned to the set after three days, well fed, sober, and from then on he worked well. Some months later, Fernando Rey ran into him working as an extra on another film. He said some French tourists had seen him taking sun on a bench; they recognized him, and congratulated him. That was enough to make the good fellow believe that he was famous in Paris. "Don Fernando, can you loan me money to go to Paris?" He thought that once he got there they would immediately contract him to make a film. Poor fellow, he died a year and a half later, drunk... The dwarf was not an actress either, nor at that time was Rabal's daughter who played the girl who jumps rope, and who is now an important actress in Spain.

TURRENT: One of the impressive things about *Viridiana* is the homogeneity and quality of the corps of actors. There are none of the large inconsistencies you notice at times in your Mexican films. Furthermore, they are all Spaniards and that lends more believability to the film. In *Nazarín*, whose action is set in Mexico, there are Spanish actors who don't fit, they are out of place among the authentic Mexican faces.

BUÑUEL: Perhaps you are right. Though they form a mass and are numerous, each of the beggars in *Viridiana*, has his individuality, his truth. The way they speak seems very successful to me. It sounds like very popular Spanish, very alive, no? I get very moved when I hear them talk.

COLINA: After so much time abroad, your return to Spain went well, opening your eyes to these discoveries, and even to particular objects. Like the knife-crucifix, a true object-collage that would have fascinated Duchamp and Ernst.

BUÑUEL: It looks like it was made especially for the film, a Buñuelian joke, doesn't it? But I found it at a store in Albacete while walking around looking for exteriors. I put it in the scene when Rabal examines the objects left by his father. Some people think it was a blasphemous image. Because of *Viridiana*, those little knives were banned in Spain and they no longer make them. I remember a nun in Zaragoza had one of those knife-crucifixes hanging from her rosary that she used to peel apples. A functional and very practical Christ, don't you think? Those objects were sold by the thousands. They were like Mexican curios here. Very popular and very original. Besides, because of the handle, daggers and swords have always evoked the cross.

COLINA: The crucifix-knife draws attention, but it's a marginal detail. There is another object that circulates throughout the entire film and acquires different meanings: the little girl's jump rope. The first time, it is used in orthodox fashion by the girl as a simple jump rope. Later, the rope is used by Don Jaime — who likes to watch the girl jump — to hang himself from a tree. Finally, a beggar ties Viridiana up with the rope to rape her, of course.

TURRENT: No! The beggar has tied up his pants with the rope and Viridiana clings to its handles, which have a phallic shape.

BUÑUEL: There is no intellectual line behind this series of relationships, but doubtlessly there's a subconscious one, related to desire. Don Jaime had noticed the rope when he watched the girl jump. Later, when he goes to commit suicide, unconsciously the first thing he picks up is that rope. The beggar finds the rope by chance and uses it as a belt...

COLINA: In addition to being a fetishist, Don Jaime is a voyeur. He watches the girl jump rope to see her legs.

BUÑUEL: There are erotic fixations. I remember a film by Stroheim, I think it was *The Merry Widow*.[1] A theater, one set, a dancer. The camera picks out three characters in the audience: an older, severe, and dignified man; another man who is deformed and lascivious; and a boy who looks like a dreamer. The three look at different parts of the dancer's body. The older man watches her legs and breasts. The lustful and sadistic man watches her little feet. The boy, the embodiment of pure love, watches her face. It was very good: using different shots to reveal different psychologies. The shot of the dancer's feet remains very fixed in my mind. Perhaps I remembered it subconsciously in the scenes where the girl jumps rope.

TURRENT: What do the ashes that Viridiana puts on Don Jaime's bed signify?

BUÑUEL: It's a somnambulant act by Viridiana. In Catholic tradition, ashes signify death: "From dust thou art and to dust thou shalt return." I don't psychoanalyze my films, but perhaps during her sleepwalking Viridiana is foretelling Don Jaime's imminent death because of her. But if you want a concrete answer, psychoanalyze Viridiana and not me. I've already warned you: a psychoanalyst classified me as "nonpsychoanalyzable."

COLINA: The parody of *The Last Supper* has been much commented upon in every tone from praise to indignation.

BUÑUEL: I don't understand the indignation. The beggars are eating and by chance form the same composition as in Leonardo's painting.

COLINA: One of the beggars says, "I am going to take a photo with a little camera my mother gave me." She hikes up her skirts and "photographs" — with her sex, we suppose — her companions in Leonardo's composition.

BUÑUEL: It is an old joke played by Spanish children. If someone's rear end were sticking out, someone else would shout, "You're taking my pic-

---

1 *The Merry Widow* (1925), dir. Erich von Stroheim. Buñuel refers to the scene in which *première danseuse* Sally O'Hara (Mae Murry) dances and is watched by a trio of admirers: Mirko, Danilo, and the Baron Sadoja.

ture!" The beggar repeats this joke, which is an innocent children's joke.

COLINA: But is it innocent that *you* filmed it?

BUÑUEL: They are Spanish beggars, they are believers, but at the same time they take liberties with religion. That is very Spanish. They have no bad intentions. Besides, they are drunk, having fun. Viridiana had them praying and working all the time. For them, this nocturnal orgy is a liberation. Another thing: some people are upset that you can see the crown of thorns burning in a fireplace. What is blasphemous about that? Old liturgical objects are usually burned...

TURRENT: We now get to the character of Don Jaime. It is obvious that you treat him affectionately. But why does he hang himself?

BUÑUEL: I thought that was clear: because Viridiana will leave him. He is an old man, very alone, and has fallen crazily in love with his niece, who looks so much like his dead wife. Since she leaves him forever and is angry with him, Don Jaime is left without illusions, full of regrets for having intended to possess her...and he commits suicide. He can no longer live in the present, because it shames him, or in the past, because Viridiana no longer reincarnates his dead wife.

COLINA: But there is something intriguing about the moment when he writes his suicide note: he pauses and smiles, as if he were preparing a practical joke.

BUÑUEL: It's an acting nuance that came to me while we were filming. I didn't want to fall into the clichés of scenes like that: an anguished, sweating face, agonized music. At that moment, the smile upsets the convention, it introduces a contradiction that is more interesting. What do we know about how a man who commits suicide thinks? In addition, I confess that I like to surprise the audience. They see him smiling while he writes and then he appears hanging: the surprise is greater and perhaps the emotion also.

COLINA: This smile makes me think Don Jaime is, in fact, playing a dirty trick on Viridiana. By leaving his inheritance to the girl, he makes her leave the convent, he forces her to enter a more concrete reality and to accept the world.

BUÑUEL: And that is what really happens, even though Don Jaime cannot accurately foresee it. Think of the other possibility: when Don Jaime smiles, he thinks something like this: "What a ridiculous old man I am, what stupidities I've committed." He could be laughing at himself. One of the reasons I sympathize with Don Jaime is that — except for when he is most enamored with *Viridiana* — he has a certain sense of humor, a certain irony with himself.

COLINA: The beggars' revolt reminds me of the one that takes place at the end of Galdós' novel *Angel Guerra.*

BUÑUEL: It's possible, but we hadn't thought about it. The story is original, by Julio Alejandro and myself.

TURRENT: Don Jaime's character seems to continue with Don Lope in *Tristana.*

BUÑUEL: No. They are very different. Don Jaime is an old, good-natured soul, humble, capable of falling violently in love, a village nobleman. Don Lope is an old playboy and skirt chaser, somewhat vain. The only similarities are their ages and the fact that both characters are played by Fernando Rey.

TURRENT: Tell us about the scandal that *Viridiana* provoked.

BUÑUEL: We finished filming it shortly before the Cannes Film Festival to which it had been invited. I was still doing the mixing in Paris when the festival began. Two or three days before the competition ended, Juan Luis (my son) arrived at Cannes with the print for the screening. It won the award, and a Dominican priest — the brother of a well-known banker — who was covering the festival for *L'Osservatore Romano,* wrote that *Viridiana* blasphemed Holy Oil, that cinema was morally lost, etc. From *L'Osservatore,* this opinion traveled to Spain, to the episcopacy, the ministers. The director of the Spanish Film Institute, who had accepted the Palme d'Or awarded to the film, was dismissed. The Information Minister resigned, but Franco did not accept his resignation.

COLINA: The truth is that the scandal came from what is referred to as *España negra,* but it also came from those in the so-called *España de las luces.*[2] Exiled Spanish Republicans were indignant that you had agreed to make a film in Franco's Spain. In an article, the journalist Mirabal wrote: "Little Buñuel, the false genius, is already going to Spain to serve Franco a film..." or something like that.

BUÑUEL: He no longer calls me "little Buñuel"; now he calls me Don Luis.

COLINA: In short, the Spaniards in exile were furious with you and considered *Viridiana* a betrayal without even having seen it yet. Then suddenly everyone had to shut up. The cartoonist Alberto Isaac summed up

2 *España negra* refers to the dark side of Spain and also to the supporters of the Franco regime, while *España de las luces* refers to both liberal progressive Spain and the enlightened intellectuals in the exile community.

the episode's denouement very well in a short cartoon: in the first panel we see you arriving in Spain and being received by the Generalísimo with honors; in the second frame you leave Franco a wrapped gift while, from the other side of the sea, a refugee shouts, "Death to the traitor Buñuel!"; in the third and final frame, the package has exploded, leaving Franco battered and the refugee stupefied. The cartoon was titled: *Veni, Vidi, Vinci.*

BUÑUEL: The truth is, I knew *Viridiana* was not a film to the taste of the Franco regime, but I didn't consider it a kind of cinematographic "bomb," as in Isaac's cartoon, nor did I think it would end up being banned for so long in Spain. The Dominican, who was the first to ring the alarm of scandal, was the one who damned *Viridiana*, and he brought the film the kind of publicity that I couldn't have bought for millions of pesetas.

COLINA: The Surrealists were delighted.

BUÑUEL: Of course. More than delighted, Buñuel — the man who is talking with you — was a little perplexed. Some years previously, Breton had told me, "No one is scandalized anymore these days." You can see that that was not completely true in 1961.

COLINA: *Viridiana* seems to be both realistic and romantic at the same time. It's realism is very much at ground level, in fact very much like a picaresque novel, but there is also the romantic *élan,* flashes of the Gothic novel.

BUÑUEL: That's possible, because those are the two currents that correspond to my cultural formation, and, of course, my obsessions appear in the film, which we have already discussed sufficiently.

TURRENT: Even though the film's "writing" is not Surrealist — why there isn't even a dream sequence — I think that *Viridiana* is one of your works that most corresponds to the Surrealist spirit.

BUÑUEL: If by Surrealist writing we mean automatic writing, then of course *Viridiana* is not Surrealist. It has a logical story line, a sequence of events, etc. Julio Alejandro and I gave it a dramatic structure; there is a believability to the characters. Very different from *Un chien andalou,* where we tried to assemble images given to us by the subconscious. But, yes, there is a Surrealist spirit to the film's meaning and to its humor.

20: *EL ANGEL EXTERMINADOR* (THE EXTERMINATING ANGEL)

TOMAS PEREZ TURRENT: *The Exterminating Angel* is always listed as being "based on the play *Los náufragos de la Calle Providencia* (The Castaways of Providence Street), by José Bergamín."

LUIS BUÑUEL: It wasn't at all. The only thing by Bergamín in the entire film is the title. When I went to Madrid to make *Viridiana*, we used to get together regularly at a *peña* that many people went to: bullfighters, writers, film people. One day Bergamín told me he wanted to write a play called *The Exterminating Angel*. The title came from the Bible, from the Apocalypse, but the name was also used by members of a Spanish association, the apostolics of 1828, and also by a group of Mormons, I think. I told him, "That's a magnificent title. If I were walking down the street and saw that title on a marquee, I would go inside to see the show." In the end, Bergamín never wrote the play. Some time later, Alcoriza and I wrote a screenplay called *Los náufragos de la Calle Providencia*. It was based on a story idea that came to me in New York around 1940, along with four or five others, among them one that would later become *Simon of the Desert* and the episode of the "missing" girl that was later included in *Phantom of Liberty*. *Los náufragos de la Calle Providencia* was a long and literary title; I didn't like it. Then I thought of Bergamín's title and wrote him a letter asking for the rights. He answered, telling me he didn't own them since the title was from the Apocalypse.

TURRENT: It would have been difficult at that time to make the film with any producer other than Gustavo Alatriste. No one else would have accepted such a story line.

BUÑUEL: That's true. I might have been able to make it, but with much less freedom. Ideally, of course, it should have been made in England, where a high society really exists. But with Alatriste I had all the freedom in the world. He didn't take anything out, or tell me to put in this or that. In fact he hadn't even seen the script. The only thing I told him was that it was about some people who, for no apparent reason, cannot leave a room. "Go ahead," he told me. "Do what you want." The only reason I didn't go even further was because I censored myself. Today I would make it better.

JOSE DE LA COLINA: In what sense?

BUÑUEL: I would leave the people locked up for a month, to the point where they would resort to cannibalism and fighting to the death, in order to show, perhaps, that aggression is innate.

COLINA: *The Exterminating Angel* would be in each character. . . in all of us.

BUÑUEL: At first I thought the title had a hidden relation to the story, though I didn't know what it was. *A posteriori,* I interpreted it like this: in today's human society, more and more people are less and less in agreement and that is the reason they fight among themselves. But why can't they understand each other? Why can't they get themselves out of this situation? It's the same in the film: why can't they come up with a solution together to get out of the room?

COLINA: This film shares a certain relationship with *The Discreet Charm of the Bourgeoisie...*

BUÑUEL: In a sense they're the same: the characters can't do anything, even though at the beginning they can.

TURRENT: Also we find certain actions being repeated.

BUÑUEL: I think I'm the first to have done that in a film. The shot of the guests entering the luxurious Nobile Mansion and going up the stairs to the main floor is repeated twice, consecutively, with no variation except that the camera is at a high angle in one take and at a low angle in the other. When I finished the editing, Gabriel Figueroa,[1] the cinematographer, rushed up to see me very alarmed: "Listen sir, there's something wrong with the print. A scene is repeated. The editor must have made a mistake." I told him, "But Gabriel, I always do my own editing. Besides, you were my cinematographer and you know that when we repeated the scene, we shot it from another angle. I repeated the scene on purpose..." "Ah, now I see," he said, but he looked really frightened. Later, I saw that

---

1 Gabriel Figueroa, prize-winning Mexican cinematographer, whose distinctive use of atmosphere attracted many leading international directors, including Emilio Fernández, John Ford, and John Huston. Besides *The Exterminating Angel*, Figueroa worked with Buñuel on *Los olvidados, El, La fièvre monte à El Pao, The Young One,* and *Simon of the Desert.*

Ingmar Bergman also repeated a scene in *Persona*.[2] There are two women, a nurse and a patient. The camera is fixed. From the shoulder, the nurse tells a story for a few minutes. She finishes and the shot changes: the one seen from behind is now in front and vice versa, while the story is repeated in exactly the same way.

COLINA: And why the repetition?

BUÑUEL: I felt like it; it has a hypnotic effect. My earlier films also have repetitions, ever since *L'Age d'or*. Only in *The Exterminating Angel* they are constant. After the initial scene in which everyone finds his place at the table, Nobile rises: "Ladies and gentlemen, champagne. Here's to the marvelous evening the diva has given us." Everyone toasts her, then sits down. Nobile rises again: "Ladies and gentlemen, champagne. Here's to the marvelous evening...," etc. There are around twenty repetitions in the film, but some are more noticeable than others.

TURRENT: In the end, the only way to leave the room is to repeat all the actions made just before these people were locked up. It's the key to their prison. So the use of repetition throughout the film was preplanned from the beginning.

BUÑUEL: No, no. It was something that occurred to me while we were filming. Nothing was planned. When I filmed the group entering the house, I wondered, "And what if I do this again? Okay, let's do it. I like it, and it's worth the trouble."

TURRENT: But the film's very structure is based entirely on repetition...

BUÑUEL: Yes, exactly. The film has a circular structure and, of course, the final repetition of the gestures in unison was foreseen. But the repetitions of individual scenes or actions that come in between the beginning and the end, those were improvised during the filming.

COLINA: Incarceration and circular structure are reoccurring motifs in your other films: the excruciating room in *Un chien andalou*, the suffocating salon in *L'Age d'or*, the jungle salon in *La mort en ce jardin*...even the island in *Adventures of Robinson Crusoe*, and the nocturnal streetcar route in *Illusion Travels by Streetcar*. Also, we find a theme of powerlessness: the bandits in *L'Age d'or*, who collapse en route and never make it to the beach; the society people in *The Exterminating Angel* who can't leave the room, and their counterparts in *The Discreet Charm of the Bourgeoisie* who walk down a highway without going anywhere, who can never eat...

2 *Persona* (1966), dir. Ingmar Bergman, starring Bibi Andersson and Liv Ullmann.

BUÑUEL: That's a good observation, though the motifs vary in each case. *Robinson Crusoe* is a good example: he can't leave the island because he lacks sufficient tools to do so. It would have been interesting to have ships arriving every day while, inexplicably, he still can't manage to leave.

TURRENT: Is *The Exterminating Angel* a parable about the human condition?

BUÑUEL: Rather, about the bourgeois condition. It wouldn't be the same if I had used working-class characters, because they would have found a solution to their incarceration. For example, in a working-class neighborhood a man's daughter is christened; he invites fifty friends to a party, and then no one can leave... I believe that in the end they would find a way out. Why? Because workers are more in contact with life's daily difficulties.

COLINA: This story is contained to some degree in the film, since the servants do manage to leave the house. The only one who remains is the butler, because his rank as a servant is closer to that of his masters.

BUÑUEL: A butler is a bourgeois at heart.

TURRENT: If the problem had occurred at a worker's house, the film would be less believable. His alienation is different.

BUÑUEL: Yes. It would deal with an equally serious problem, perhaps, but not something particularly related to being locked in.

TURRENT: When Nobile's guests begin to get dirty, when their masks fall, they forget the rules of etiquette and elegance and turn into beasts. That wouldn't happen among workers...

COLINA: No, please! That's idealizing the working class.

BUÑUEL: I believe that what happens to Nobile's guests is totally independent of the social class to which they belong. With workers or peasants, something very similar would happen, but in a slightly different form. Aggressive behavior isn't exclusively bourgeois or exclusively proletarian. It is innate to the human condition, even though a few, only a few, psychologists or anthropologists deny this. While a worker may hit his wife, someone from the middle or upper-middle class might prefer to torture her psychologically. That's why I say that if it had happened among workers, the drama in *The Exterminating Angel* would be weaker, less interesting; that is why, instead, there is more contrast between the exquisite forms of Nobile's guests and the almost bestial state to which they finally succumb.

COLINA: I wonder if anyone has noticed the similarity between Sartre's *Huis Clos* (No Exit) and *The Exterminating Angel*.

TURRENT: Yes. That is precisely what the critic Michel Esteve does in a very interesting essay.

BUÑUEL: I don't see that parallel. Sartre's play deals with disembodied individuals, souls condemned to hell. They aren't concrete human beings.

COLINA: But both works suggest a similar idea: hell is other people.

BUÑUEL: Although I don't express it in the same way Sartre did, I believe that idea is present in my films, as De la Colina said. The characters in *Un chien andalou* are enclosed in a room where they torment each other; the protagonist of *L'Age d'or* is waging a one-man war against society, and society fights back; the kids in *Los olvidados* fight and kill each other... The characters in *The Exterminating Angel* don't leave because they can't leave, without ever knowing why. In Sartre's play they do know: they are dead and they are in hell. The entire premise is different. My apologies to Sartre, but I think there is more mystery in *The Exterminating Angel*... or if you like, simply more irrationality. I also think there is humor in my film.

COLINA: It seems to me, Don Luis, that *The Discreet Charm of the Bourgeoisie* is little more than a better-acted, better-costumed, and better-decorated version of *The Exterminating Angel*...a more subtle version.

BUÑUEL: The actors in *The Exterminating Angel* should have worn tuxedos as if they were used to wearing them every night.

TURRENT: That's difficult for Mexican actors to do.

BUÑUEL: You notice these details because you live here. Neither in England nor in France, where I thought they would laugh at some scenes, has anyone ever noticed the bad acting. I'm not sure, but perhaps they think those defects are peculiar to Mexican high society. I don't know. I see the defects, too. We used 800-peso tuxedos cut from tropical cloth; the actors would sit down during a rehearsal and when they stood up again their tuxes would be wrinkled. There were no elegant napkins in the dining room with Nobile's initials and coat of arms, just ordinary cloth napkins like you can find in any restaurant. We used one lace napkin because our German makeup person happened to have one in her makeup kit. I put that one napkin in front of each actor during close-ups so that it would look like they all had one.

TURRENT: I think that maybe we are so used to seeing such well-known actors as Loya, Beristáin, Del Campo, Patricia Morán, and Jacqueline Andere in every Mexican melodrama that it's hard for us to believe in them as high society. But basically they were like the Mexican bourgeoisie: parvenus without tradition or nobility, snobs in the worst sense of the word.

BUÑUEL: So there could be a real society dinner much like the one in the film, no?

COLINA: The Angel exterminates...snobs, let's say.

BUÑUEL: Speaking of snobs, I did include one authentic detail that Iris Barry told me about, which happened in New York. She and her husband were invited to a gala, since she was one of the founders of the Museum of Modern Art. There were around twenty guests from the New York aristocracy. A waiter was supposed to bring in a wonderful fountain: a swan sculpted in ice containing about ten pounds of caviar and adorned with pâté de foie gras. The waiter appeared with it at the door, walked a few steps, and *intentionally* tripped, fell on the floor, and spilled everything in front of the delighted guests.

TURRENT: There's another wonderful detail: the large three-doored armoire that serves as a bathroom. One woman uses it and when she leaves, she says she saw a landscape, an abyss, and a falcon.

BUÑUEL: That has intrigued many people. It's a kind of collage, though not a visual one. Actually I put in a memory from my childhood. In Molinos, a small town in the Aragon region and the state of Cuenca, there are steep cliffs up to 100 meters high. At the edge of one of them is a wooden outhouse where the hole offers a view straight down into the abyss. I once saw a falcon circling under me while I relieved myself.

COLINA: There is another detail: Silvia Pinal throws an ashtray at a window and it shatters. On hearing this, two others comment: "What was that?" "Someone broke a window. It must have been a passing Jew."

BUÑUEL: To an anti-Semite, anything, even lightning can be the Jews' fault. In other times, people blamed the Jews for poisoning fountains and rivers, causing plagues. It's an anti-Semitic characteristic that you find in certain sectors of the bourgeoisie.

TURRENT: They try to find reasons for problems that have nothing to do with reality. I believe these people are trapped because they deny the movement of History.

BUÑUEL: That explanation is much too rational; there can be many others.

COLINA: In some way this is reminiscent of the fashionable society reception in *L'Age d'or*. Things happen either in or outside the salon: workers pass by with a cart, the game warden kills his own son, etc. In *The

Exterminating Angel, when at first the people are trapped in the room, nothing enters from outside. But there are also some extraordinary elements, for example, the bear.

BUÑUEL: The story line also dictates that it's not possible to enter Nobile's house. If people could enter, the problem would be partially resolved because the characters could receive fresh food and water, clean clothes...

COLINA: But since these partial saviors couldn't leave, the house would fill with people until it burst.

BUÑUEL: That's true and could be another interesting variant.

COLINA: One that was already filmed by the Marx Brothers in *A Night at the Opera*, when they filled the cabin of an ocean liner.

BUÑUEL: That's right... There's something else I want to mention so you can see how people attribute symbols to me arbitrarily. We were shooting *The Exterminating Angel*; it was about six p.m., and at seven we had to wrap for the day. Nothing occurred to me, but I didn't want to lose an hour of shooting. I told Nobile to sit next to a sheep tied to the piano; I gave him a knife and asked Silvia Pinal to sit near Nobile. Nothing else occurred to me and it was almost seven. The next day I could begin another scene, but we would have to change the lighting and the position. It suddenly occurred to me that Silvia should tie a blindfold around the sheep's eyes and hand Nobile the dagger. And that was that. Completely improvised, without any thought to whether anything was symbolic. A good symbol of nothing. Despite this, several critics gave various interpretations of the scene. The sheep represented Christianity, the knife, blasphemy... I intended none of that, everything was arbitrary. I only tried to evoke some sort of disturbing image.

COLINA: I remember another interpretation of a symbol. One Mexican critic, seeing the scene where the bear goes up the stairs and runs through the upper hallway, wrote that this symbolized "the Soviet threat." On the other hand, a critic from *Positif*, referring to the scene in which Nobile's wife invites her lover to come and see the incunabula, had mistakenly heard "incurable" and commented that the film dealt with someone who is dying and that this dying person is really, of course, the world of high society.

BUÑUEL: I never heard that interpretation. The story of the bear, yes — that the bear was the "Soviet Union holding the bourgeoisie under siege," and thus the film was explained at encyclopedic length.

TURRENT: I know you have your own fantastic zoo, but...how do you explain the bear in the house?

BUÑUEL: I think it's explained within the film. The fall of the servant with the elaborate dish didn't amuse anyone — especially not the character of Antonio Bravo, to whom nothing is humorous. So the lady of the house tells the butler, "These things don't amuse our guests. Leave the bear and the sheep in the garden." Meaning that the animals were to be used as part of another joke. Besides, it's interesting to see a bear walking into a drawing room. When we filmed that scene, I was prepared with a .44 magnum revolver. We closed all the doors. The small salon with the guests in the scene and the camera were all in front of a five-foot barrier. I told Figueroa "Camera!" and they let the bear loose. He suddenly felt like climbing a column and we all ran out, including me with my .44 magnum. If the bear had jumped over the barrier and really threatened us, I would have shot. But I don't like to kill animals, so we all ran out.

COLINA: In the scene with the sheep, why did Nobile wear a bandage on his forehead?

BUÑUEL: It wasn't a bandage, it was a headband that people in Aragón wear called a *cachirulo*. It has a folkloric meaning...but only to someone from Aragón. But then Nobile wore it as if it were a bandage, because he had been hit and wounded.

COLINA: In this scene Nobile seems like the film's Christ.

BUÑUEL: That's because he's kind and suffers less for himself than for his guests, but I don't think he is Christ.

TURRENT: I believe the problem of these characters' incarceration is that essentially they aren't free. Physical imprisonment would then be a complete realization of their moral or spiritual incarceration.

BUÑUEL: Liberty is a phantom. I've thought about that sincerely and I believe it. Freedom is no more than a ghost of mist. Man can seek it out, even believe he has grasped it...and in the end he is left with only fleeting bits of mist in his hands. This is the image by which freedom has always expressed itself for me.

COLINA: You don't see any free men?

BUÑUEL: Yes, there are: *Simon of the Desert*. He is the world's freest man.

COLINA: Why does he reject action?

BUÑUEL: Because he has everything he wants, does whatever he wants without obstacles. There he sits atop his column eating lettuce. Complete freedom.

TURRENT: But what about the protagonist of *L'Age d'or*, who from the beginning, according to you, does what he wants — isn't he free?

BUÑUEL: Relatively. He attempts to be free by destroying prejudices. But since he does so with fury, that in itself shows that he is not free. Like all men, he strives for freedom, but where can you find it? I know that Simon's liberty won't work for everyone, but it works for him.

COLINA: The lovers in *The Exterminating Angel* isolate themselves from the rest, placing themselves outside of social conventions, and end up committing suicide. Is this suicide a type of freedom?

BUÑUEL: The scene of the lovers is a kind of self-plagiarism. In 1933, I published a text called *Une Girafe* (A Giraffe) in the magazine *Le Surréalisme au service de la révolution.*[3] In each of the giraffe's spots there was a different scene. In one of them you hear a man's voice and then a woman's. She begs him and he says, "My little corpse, come here ..." The lights come up and you see a few hens pecking the ground. I also gave the lovers in *The Exterminating Angel* an irrational dialogue. Do you remember it?

TURRENT: "This is where the sea flows in." Afterwards the man's voice says, "Your rictus! Horrible!"

BUÑUEL: It's also a memory of mine from Madrid, from when I studied engineering. There was a seventeen-year-old medical student and a girl of fifteen. Their families were friends and they had everything: both families approved of their marriage and they could see each other whenever they wanted. For no apparent reason whatsoever, they committed suicide together one day at a café in Madrid. Their love was platonic, pure: the girl was a virgin. Why? They must have thought that real love was incompatible with daily life, with the world as it is. "Society is insufferable, unbearable, let's disappear together." It's a poignant act, one that makes you dizzy. Without ever trying to commit suicide, I myself felt like that when I was between thirteen and seventeen years old, when I was in love in the same way. I believe an act like that has no social solution: it will happen in a capitalist society the same as in a Communist one.

TURRENT: Time moves slowly in *The Exterminating Angel*; there is a very subjective sense of time. The more space is compacted, the more time expands.

BUÑUEL: While the characters are shut in and the unease lasts, time is like an eternity. In cinema, time and space are flexible, they are at the ser-

3 *Le Surréalisme au service de la révolution*, No. 6, May 15, 1933.

vice of the filmmaker. In this film, when the characters are locked in, it's as if there were no time. How long were they inside? Ten minutes, ten days, ten years? You don't know. They are in another time altogether. For that reason, actions are repeated: time is not linear.

COLINA: Everything is very physical: hunger, thirst...

BUÑUEL: ...disheveled clothes, sickness, sweat, the stubble on their faces, the garbage that accumulates.

COLINA: It's the intensely materialist side of the film. These characters who produce nothing now run the risk of choking on their own wastes and debris. Everything begins to decompose. The maids and servants — the real productive forces who furnish the consumer class its quality of life — have fled. In a sense, it's a Marxist parable.

BUÑUEL: Well, it may be very Marxist, as you've said, but the fact remains that it has never been shown in the Soviet Union. Of course there can be a Marxist interpretation of the film: bourgeois society no longer has historical impetus, it stagnates within itself, having lost its creative capacity... It could be, without my having thought of it *a priori*.

TURRENT: And the final charge, when the characters are locked up again inside the church? Is this the revolution?

BUÑUEL: No. It's police repression: the mounted police attack the demonstrators. Why? I don't know. It's a scene that returns to my memory. It also appears in *Tristana* and, in a certain form, at the end of *The Phantom of Liberty*. These are memories from Zaragoza, which I've already told you about. Perhaps when the police charge the demonstrators in *The Exterminating Angel*, it has no relation whatsoever to the people locked inside the church; perhaps these are only coincidences. I don't see any other way to present the image but this: the façade of the church, gunshots, screams, the sheep entering the temple. If critics can't come up with a better explanation, they could simply say that I enjoy chaotic situations, that I am an anarchist. *(He laughs.)*

TURRENT: Where does that leave us? Marxist or anarchist?

BUÑUEL: I have to have an anarchistic streak in me because, as you know, if you scratch us, all Spaniards are anarchists. No, I'm joking. Perhaps I'm an anarchistic-nihilist...but also a pacifist. Mentally I'm capable of planting bombs almost anywhere: in a ministry, a factory, a traffic jam, in one of those places where people listen to music blasting away at full volume. At present the only organization I would consider joining is the S.P.C.A. But I would also enjoy being a dictator so I could mete out a few death sentences. Mentally, that is. "What has this boy done?" "Your Majesty, he was caught playing his guitar at decibels that are not permitted." "Well...to the guillotine with him then!"

TURRENT: I've heard you were once going to make another film very much like *The Exterminating Angel*, one in which a group of people are trapped on board a lost ship...

BUÑUEL: I had that story, but it never got close to being actually filmed. A woman friend of Sadoul, who was working for a leftist magazine, sent me a stupendous story idea, which I still have. In it, there is a raft lost at sea with forty-five people on it, a kind of cinematic adaptation of *The Raft of the Medusa*.[4] But it would have been very difficult to make; it was very complicated technically. Hitchcock did something very similar.[5] But it was like an impossible bet...that extremely tight space with so many people piled on top of each other.

TURRENT: Isn't *The Exterminating Angel* a kind of *Raft of the Medusa*?

BUÑUEL: They have nothing to do with each other. There are thousands of situations that could be similar. If you want, we could make a science-fiction film: fifteen astronauts in a rocket ship lost in space. The fundamental difference is that in *The Exterminating Angel* there is absolutely no material circumstance that bars the people from leaving.

COLINA: Have you seen any of the recent disaster films that are currently in vogue?

BUÑUEL: No, I haven't seen any of them but I'd like to. It's quite enjoyable to watch things being destroyed...sequence after sequence of progressive destruction, buildings crumbling and falling, trains and automobiles crashing together, fires...

TURRENT: The problem with contemporary disaster films is that they try to be edifying and don't reach total nihilism. They could be wonderful if they were a form of pure spectacle: a sinking ship, a burning tower. But that is mixed with very conventional characters and situations, with cheap psychology...

BUÑUEL: I know what you mean: the husband and wife who were at odds are brought back together; the unbelieving priest rediscovers his lost faith... Conventional characters. If I were to make that film about a sinking ship, I would get rid of both the priest with the shaken faith and the reconciled married couple, or rather, I would have the priest babbling deliriously and the married couple devouring each other. I would become anguished, I would suffer along with everyone else... Many years ago I

---

4 *Le Radeau de la Méduse*, painting by Théodore Géricault.
5 *Lifeboat* (1944), dir. Alfred Hitchcock.

saw a wonderful film, I think it was called *Cavalcade*.[6] There was a fox-trot at the end, marvelous! It was set in Victorian London...horse-drawn carriages, drawing rooms, all very well done. At the end, the newlyweds board a ship, happy and full of hope. Suddenly, we see one of the ship's life preservers, which reads: *Titanic*. It's fascinating. I haven't seen *The Poseidon Adventure*,[7] but I think it's probably terrible: three days in a ship stuck upside down. Such a situation would horrify me. It's worse than a fire.

COLINA: This pleasure of destruction can be related to the notion of waste and squandering, which Georges Bataille spoke about. These are related to love and eroticism.

BUÑUEL: Eroticism is a diabolic pleasure that is related to death and rotting flesh. I've put some of this in the love scenes of my films.

COLINA: There is a certain uneasiness about watching *The Exterminating Angel*, but one can also feel pleasure. There is a kind of joy in seeing how this society, which has taken centuries to reach such a high level, can completely undo itself within an hour and a half of screen time, literally self-destructing before your very eyes. I hope this doesn't upset you, but *The Exterminating Angel* can also be seen as a comedy.

BUÑUEL: No, that doesn't bother me. It is a type of comedy, yes. But to conclude, I want to tell you that I think the film is a failure. It could be much better, for reasons we have already talked about.

TURRENT: But before finishing, I want to insist a bit on the value of repetition in the film. One supposes that repetitions should close a circle instead of opening it. But in this film it's the other way around.

BUÑUEL: Repetition is an idea of mine, something personal. I repeat myself a lot in my films, when I speak, etc. I don't have to remind you two, my patient interviewers, about that. I am a man of obsessions. As you just said, at the end of the film there is no liberation. It's only momentary. The entire situation of the incarceration will repeat itself infinitely. Everyone reverts to the initial situation; they go back to making the same gestures. They have escaped from the incarceration at Nobiles' house only to be held within the church. And the church will be worse because this time it's not just twenty people, but two hundred. It's like an epidemic that extends outwards to infinity.

6 *Cavalcade* (1933), dir. Frank Lloyd. Oscar-winning adaptation of Noel Coward's play of the same name.
7 *The Poseidon Adventure* (1972), dir. Ronald Neame.

21: *LE JOURNAL D'UNE FEMME DE CHAMBRE* (DIARY OF A CHAMBERMAID)

JOSE DE LA COLINA: Was *Diary of a Chambermaid* an original project of yours?

LUIS BUÑUEL: I was going to film it here in Mexico for Alatriste, with Silvia Pinal in the title role. Silberman asked me to make it for him in France. I proposed Silvia for the lead, but because she is Mexican and the film French, Silberman didn't accept. So as a matter of fact, I did propose the film.

TOMAS PEREZ TURRENT: Did you change the novel very much?

BUÑUEL: The novel is only a point of departure. In it, Célestine works in many houses consecutively. I preferred to concentrate on the episodes that interested me, all within one household. I also added an element from another episode: the old fetishist.

COLINA: I think the novel is like a toned-down de Sade.

BUÑUEL: No, because there are episodes that aren't sexual. A toned-down de Sade would be another of Mirbeau's novels, *Le jardin des supplices* (Torture Garden), which in fact has many sadistic elements.

TURRENT: The script was your first collaboration with Jean-Claude Carrière, with whom you've worked with almost exclusively ever since.

BUÑUEL: Silberman suggested various scriptwriters to me, but none of them seemed appropriate. Then he told me he was going to loan me a young man who had never previously worked in cinema, but who was very intelligent. I accepted. Silberman talked with Carrière and asked him, "Do you drink wine?" Carrière said no. "Well, tell Buñuel you do." When Jean-Claude and I began working, I offered him some wine and he accepted, *enchanté*. He had to drink more than a bottle with me. Now that I remember it, he had done a little work in film: he had made a short with the comic Pierre Etaix.[1]

COLINA: Had you seen the film version Jean Renoir made in Hollywood?[2]

BUÑUEL: No. They offered to screen it for me, but I didn't accept. I preferred to ignore that version while I was making my own.

COLINA: The novel takes place during the *Belle Epoque* (if I'm not mistaken, because I haven't read it). You changed the time period.

BUÑUEL: I love the *Belle Epoque,* but since I didn't want to have the added difficulty of reconstructing the period, I situated the action in the '20s.

TURRENT: There is a particular detail that situates the time period: a demonstration by the French reactionaries in favor of Chiappe.

BUÑUEL: Chiappe was the police prefect who beat leftist demonstrators with clubs. The Camelots du Roi and the Jeunesse Patriotique participate in the demonstration in the film. They shout: "Down with the Republic! Death to the Jews! Long live Chiappe!" It's a memory of my time in Paris and of the '30s, when the right wing attempted to take over the Chambre des Députés. Besides, Chiappe was a *bête noir* of the Surrealists.

COLINA: The film very acidly describes the French rural bourgeoisie. The characters are bourgeois...and morally a bunch of scoundrels.

BUÑUEL: Yes. *(He laughs)* As is, in part Célestine, because she aspires to become bourgeois and doesn't care what means she has to employ. In order to live like a queen, she informs on her lover and marries an old captain from next door.

COLINA: It's notable that Célestine, who has been a passive character throughout the film, only a kind of gaze, enters into the action at the end. She informs on her lover and marries the rich captain. Informing on her lover seems a little gratuitous.

BUÑUEL: It isn't. She wants him to be punished for the little girl's murder. She asks Joseph, "Who killed the girl?" And when she knows it was him, she tells the police. Later, she writes *"Salaud!"* ("Bastard!") on a table with her finger.

COLINA: It's a little disconcerting, because we never see her take a moral position before then. She seems indifferent to everything.

1 Jean-Claude Carrière co-wrote and co-directed two comedy shorts with Pierre Etaix: *Rupture* (1961) and the Oscar-winning *Heureux anniversaire* (Happy Anniversary, 1962).
2 *The Diary of a Chambermaid* (1946), dir. Jean Renoir, starring Paulette Goddard.

BUÑUEL: But not to the girl's murder. She sleeps with Joseph to see if he is the murderer. They talk and he lets it be understood that he did commit the murder.

COLINA: My interpretation is that the fact that he was the killer was more erotically exciting for her.

BUÑUEL: I don't think so.

TURRENT: Did you choose Jeanne Moreau?

BUÑUEL: Yes...well, Silberman had proposed her. We went to eat lunch with her at Saint-Tropez. I knew Moreau only cinematographically through Malle's film. I found her charming and saw that she was very good for the role. Above all, her manner of walking, with that slight swaying of her ankles. That was very good for the scene where the old fetishist asks her to put on some old boots and walk in them. Célestine tells him that if he wants, she can put on some newer ones. "No!" the old man says. "Put these on! These are the most beautiful!" *(He laughs.)*

TURRENT: Again the foot fetish.

BUÑUEL: I can have this obsession, like the one I have for insects, and I suppose they are not going to put me in jail for it. In reality, feet and shoes — either men's or women's — leave me indifferent. I am attracted by foot fetishism as a picturesque and humorous element. Sexual perversion repulses me, but I can be attracted to it intellectually.

COLINA: There is a very strong and very beautiful scene: the snails crawling up the dead girl's legs.

BUÑUEL: I can't explain that image. I must have felt the physical immediacy of the snails, the sensation of humidity and slime...

COLINA: With that image, you feel that nature is already overwhelming the girl, putrefying her so she can dissolve into the natural order...

BUÑUEL: I only see some snails that crawl up the girl's thighs. Now, in the subconscious, perhaps...

COLINA: Don Luis, ...and the anteater?

BUÑUEL: What anteater? There are no anteaters in any of my films.

COLINA: Isn't there an anteater in your subconscious? Could you swear to it? Because you say certain things aren't in your films, but you could have done them subconsciously. Apparently, the subconscious is a very accommodating grab bag.

BUÑUEL: *(Laughs)* Ah, that's good.

TURRENT: Don Luis, this is not to harass you, but let me remind you of some images: the milk on the girl's thighs in *Los olvidados*...

BUÑUEL: And there are also a lot of hens in *Los olvidados*. You aren't going to say that I want to sleep with a chicken.

TURRENT: And in *Susana*, the broken eggs that run down the protagonist's thighs; and in *The Criminal Life of Archibaldo de la Cruz*, the blood on the thighs of Archibaldo's nanny...

BUÑUEL: Who wears black stockings and patent-leather shoes.

COLINA: There you have it. Do you want more evidence?

BUÑUEL: The girl in *Diary* doesn't have patent-leather shoes because she is very poor, but the others, yes, with stockings and garters. And also Silvia Pinal in *Simon of the Desert*.

TURRENT: So we're not just dealing with innocent images.

BUÑUEL: I don't know. More or less. As images, they impose themselves on me and I insert them, but if I began to give them meaning, I would take them out. When you two call my attention to them, I'm astonished, I tell you this sincerely... Today it seems that when you came to the house you had conspired to draw me out.

COLINA: No, but we will... Is the episode of the murdered girl in the book?

BUÑUEL: Yes, and furthermore it's a very important element; it's the book's leitmotif. There weren't any snails, I admit I added those. The shadow of a boar also passed.

TURRENT: Whose meaning you've never pondered.

BUÑUEL: Never.

COLINA: You told us you have never been psychoanalyzed.

BUÑUEL: A psychoanalyst declared me a nonpsychoanalyzable subject. I believe I know myself very well. There is nothing a psychoanalyst could discover in me. Psychoanalysis is really our contemporary substitute for Catholic confession, except there you cleanse your conscience for twenty or thirty minutes. I do that with myself.

TURRENT: And you also have your films. Why psychoanalyze yourself?

BUÑUEL: I release something of myself in my films, but I hate putting in symbols, either literary or invented. Moreover, my images make sense. The murdered girl is left in the woods; the forest is damp and there are snails; they crawl up the girl's legs. Everything is natural.

COLINA: In your orthodox Surrealist films, the images manifest themselves explosively; they don't fuse with the story. Explosive images also appear in your later films, but they are justified by the story line.

BUÑUEL: Now I can no longer begin a film with snails on a character's neck, or ants in his hand. I allow the story to make its own images appear, and many times, if these images are too obviously shocking, I suppress them. Of course visual obsessions appear in one way or another. The ostrich in *The Phantom of Liberty* was a compulsive vision... No, it's not an ostrich; it's an Australian bird.

TURRENT: When you entered the film industry, you were forced to accept a more or less coherent story line.

BUÑUEL: Yes, you must tell a story. At times, I can introduce disturbing elements within the story that suggest a different dimension to things. In my latest films I've returned to being more free.

COLINA: But you've continued to tell a story.

BUÑUEL: *Un chien andalou* and *L'Age d'or* are unrepeatable experiences. I can't keep putting sliced eyes and hands with ants in all my films, but my irrational tendencies remain.

COLINA: *Diary of a Chambermaid* is one of your least disjointed films, least "untidy." As a matter of fact, there is nothing in it that couldn't happen in immediate reality.

BUÑUEL: There is a mixture of intentions. On the one hand, there is the intent to make honorable industry films, films that interest the public, that don't drive them from the cinema. Because I am very conscious that money has been invested in the film and many people have worked on it, and this demands a certain responsibility. On the other hand, there is the subconscious imperative, which attempts to emerge into the light. I make a film for a regular audience and also for friends, for those who will understand such-and-such a reference that is more or less obscure to others. But I try to see that those latter elements don't interrupt the flow of the story I'm telling. For example: in *The Young One*, they put some boots on the dead man. I remember I had to put boots on my father when he died, and I had to cut the leather to get his feet in. Horrible. This is a memory that perhaps only a few friends know about, but, in any case, it enriches the scene, doesn't it? But these are concrete details, not symbols. I realize there's an inevitable tendency to ascribe a symbolic intention to any image. You are reading a novel that goes, "Then so-and-so looked at the candle and fell absorbed into contemplation of the dripping wax." If, while reading that, you happen to be thinking about sex, the association springs immediately to mind: the candle is a phallus, the dripping wax is semen... Stupidities!

TURRENT: Did the Surrealists see *Diary of a Chambermaid*?

BUÑUEL: They had seen other films of mine. That one, I don't know.

Breton was moved to tears by *Viridiana*. On the other hand, it seems he didn't like *The Exterminating Angel*.

COLINA: I would have liked to know Breton's reaction to the scene in *Diary* when Piccoli tries to seduce an ugly, vulgar, and almost hunchbacked maid, telling her, "I believe in *l'amour fou*." It is an unpleasant scene. It could be said that you renounce *l'amour fou* in it...

BUÑUEL: I don't renounce it, I profane it. It's all right to profane. A Christian can profane some element of his religion. I can profane the idea of *l'amour fou*.

COLINA: But who is profaning there, the character or you?

BUÑUEL: The invocation of *l'amour fou* by such an abject character is sheer humor. Apart from that, I'm not a fanatic about the feeling. I don't have any problem profaning it verbally if you two will treat me to a good dinner. An extenuating circumstance: he who profanes, believes. A Catholic takes Communion in the morning, and in the afternoon, when someone steps on his corn, he lets loose a blasphemy: "I shit on...!" It is one thing to renounce and another to profane.

COLINA: But fifty years ago you wouldn't have dared to film a scene like that.

BUÑUEL: That's very different. Then I was a member of the Surrealist group, a group that was very ideologically compact, one in which I was a sectarian. It had to do with shocking people, going against common morality, against "sensible" love. Now I have as much freedom as I want and, if it occurs to me, I can blaspheme against *l'amour fou*. Sometimes, it's vivifying to blaspheme against that which one believes.

TURRENT: But it would have been unimaginable in *L'Age d'or* for an unpleasant character to say, "I believe in *l'amour fou*."

BUÑUEL: Instead, he would have said, "I shit on *l'amour fou*." But you always have to separate what the author of a work thinks from what the character thinks.

22: *SIMON DEL DESIERTO* (SIMON OF THE DESERT)

JOSE DE LA COLINA: At first both the character and the subject matter of *Simon of the Desert* seem outlandish, yet nevertheless the film has a historical basis.

LUIS BUÑUEL: They are found in *The Golden Legend,* a marvelous thirteenth-century hagiography by Jacobus de Voragine, which García Lorca recommended that I read. Federico found the chapter on St. Simeon Stylites delightful; it's about a saint who lived aloft on a column in the middle of the desert. Federico especially prized this description: "Shit flowed down the column like wax drips from candles" (approximate quote). It's an enticing image, isn't it? — because we have the paradigm of spirituality next to the paradigm of realism. During the Middle Ages, painters and writers of holy things didn't hesitate to note the most crude details, they didn't have the aesthetic of the sexton's little religious pictures...which, on the other hand, can be enchanting. That image is etched in my memory...

COLINA: And why isn't it in the film? Self-censorship?

BUÑUEL: No. Let's say, I'm a realistic purist. A man who eats lettuce and only drinks water is like a little bird; he can't possibly excrete very much. And, by the way, I say that somewhere in the film. Furthermore, an ascetic sitting on top of a column wasn't outlandish in those times; it wasn't even exceptional. Many similar cases are documented from the fifth to the fourteenth centuries, particularly in Eastern Europe. The Ukraine, Egypt, Syria, and Turkey all had these so-called Stylites. Some were even women. One of them was on a column for forty-two years and another, during a terrible Syrian winter, was covered with frost for three days: he looked like an ice statue and was taken for dead; he revived when they brought him down and wrapped him up. Extraordinary characters!

COLINA: Isolated characters, like Robinson or, in a certain way, the protagonist of *El*, whom I can easily imagine ending his existence atop a
column.

TURRENT: In a certain way, he is also reminiscent of Nazarín.

BUÑUEL: That's a good observation: both are singular individuals who
are placed at the margin of history, of daily life, and all because of a fixed
idea. I am attracted to people who hold fixed ideas because, as you have
already noted, I myself am one of them. The Marquis de Sade was also
one, though not precisely in the sense of saintliness.

COLINA: There is the possibility that, deep down, Sade wanted to spend
his life behind bars.

BUÑUEL: That we don't know, but it's not an illogical hypothesis.
Despite all its inconveniences, prison gave him a delightful seclusion
where Sade was at liberty to surrender himself to his imagination.
Nazarín wants to be alone with nature and God. In fact, he also secludes
himself, but in a time period when seclusion is not easy. Solitude can be
terrible, but also desirable. I can see this in myself: at times, when I am
alone, I want a friend or two to come visit because I get bored looking at
the tips of my shoes or watching a buzzing fly. But I also like to be alone
with my soul, to daydream, to imagine the imaginable...and the unimaginable. What sense is there in going out into the street to see nothing but
the hoods of cars and to suffer from the noise? Silence is nearly impossible today; it's something precious that is very difficult to find anywhere. For example, if you went to the North Pole to enjoy the silence, I
wouldn't be surprised if an Eskimo immediately appeared on his sled
...with a noisy portable radio. Can you imagine what the silence must
have been like in the Middle Ages? Leaving a town or city, within a few
steps you could find silence, or natural sounds, which are marvelous:
songs of birds, of cicadas, or the murmur of the rain. We have lost this in
our time. There is an infernal instrument that really could have been
invented by the devil or by an enemy of mankind: the electric guitar.
What diabolic times we live in: crowds, smog, promiscuity, radios, etc. I
would happily return to the Middle Ages, as long as it was before the
Great Plague of the fourteenth century.

COLINA: A Middle Ages crammed with elements of the Belle Epoque,
because when Silvia Pinal appears in *Simon* as a seductive demon, she is
wearing a little sailor suit, the kind children wore at the end of the
nineteenth century.

BUÑUEL: With black stockings, fastened with brooches and a garter. These are elements I consider very exciting, much more exciting than complete nudity. During my childhood at the beginning of the century, to see a woman get on a streetcar who showed a bit of her ankle and calf, the leg sheathed in half-shadow and barely visible, was an extraordinary erotic adventure, in the subjective. Too bad you two never experienced it.

COLINA: *Simon of the Desert* is somewhat reminiscent of *The Temptation of St. Anthony*, except with the addition of humor.

BUÑUEL: Yes, there is some black humor...blackish, if you prefer. But only in a few scattered touches, because the character really moves me. I enjoy his sincerity, his lack of interest, his innocence. For example, a monk comes to tell him that the barbarians are coming, talking about various things and among them, the notion of property. "What is property?" Simon asks. "Property is what you own." Simon doesn't understand. "I'll give you an example," the monk says: "Let's suppose that this staff is yours, okay? Now I snatch it away from you." And Simon says, "Very well, keep it." The monk becomes disconcerted: "No, no, you must protest because I took it away from you." Simon: "Why? Keep it." Simon neither knows nor understands what property is. He is even more innocent than a child because children cling to objects. Simon needs nothing more than air, a little water, and lettuce. He is free and would be free even in a jail cell. By the same token, Robinson Crusoe — and here is the difference between the two — is not free because he has a desperate need for company.

TURRENT: With his freedom and lack of feeling for property, his isolation from the establishment, Simon is like an authentic hippy.

BUÑUEL: The hippies could have named him their patron saint and even worn little medals bearing his image. But as you two have seen, the hippies failed in our times. And many of them were also fascinated by noise, rock music, electric guitars, and other demonic things.

TURRENT: The devil takes Simon to the twentieth century and brings him to a noisy discotheque. Why?

BUÑUEL: I don't know. You must remember that the film is not finished: the original story idea included many other things, but the money ran out — the same thing had happened to me before with *Mexican Bus Ride* — and I had to release it as a medium-length film. Simon should have ended up on an even taller column, some twenty meters high, next to the sea, where the hierarchy of the Church would come to see him. I filmed for only eighteen days. Since the story line breaks, I had to look for an ending that didn't have Simon praying atop his column; we had already seen that for much too long. I was interested in seeing Simon's reaction when he returns to the world. But the end result was dubious.

TURRENT: But why does he return to this world, the twentieth century?

BUÑUEL: I don't know.

COLINA: Could it be because of our faithless times?

BUÑUEL: In fact, holiness counts for very little now. But though we are not believers, we can feel that as a loss. A poor Catholic man in the Middle Ages felt that his life, for all its hardships — I think of a woodcutter in the darkest part of the forest — ...he had a feeling that he fulfilled part of a divine order. For this man, the look and will of God was everywhere. He lived with God. He was not like an orphan. Faith gave him a tremendous inner strength. Note that Gilles de Rais — whose life I would love to have filmed except for the problem of reconstructing the time period when he lived — this depraved murderer, was at the same time a devout believer; he had been Joan of Arc's comrade in arms. When his crimes were discovered and he was sentenced to die, he sincerely asked the people to forgive him. And that is what is so extraordinary: many people, including the parents of children whom he had tortured, raped, and killed, cried with him, shared his grief. What enviable times! I entirely share Huysmans' nostalgia in *Là-bas,* an extraordinary novel which tells the story of Gilles de Rais' life.

COLINA: Gilles de Rais and Sade on the one hand, and Simon and Nazarín on the other. The saint and the criminal. These are your two magnetic poles.

BUÑUEL: Yes, they interest me more than the life of an office worker...or that of a great artist.

COLINA: It's curious that in the two films you appear in as an actor, directed by others, you play the parts of a priest (in *In This Town There Are No Thieves)* and of an executioner (in *Time for a Bandit[1]).*

BUÑUEL: But there is no comparison. A priest isn't necessarily a saint; and an executioner...more than anything else he is a petty official. These roles were proposed to me by filmmaker friends and it seemed amusing for me to perform them. I would also have liked to play a Spanish Civil Guard or a Nazi officer. I think my best performance was in the role of the executioner. Saura's idea was that, as an executioner, I apply the *garr-*

---

1 *En este pueblo no hay ladrones* (Mexican, 1964), dir. Alberto Isaac; and *Llanto por un bandido* (Spanish, 1964), dir. Carlos Saura.

ote vil[2] to some members of Spain's real leftist intelligentsia. The censor didn't allow it. Isaac should have been a good actor's director, but he destroyed my acting career. He directed Spanish journalist Octavio Alba, who played the role of the sacristan, very well, and I was upstaged. He left me free without any advice whatsoever, without giving me any gestures; that killed my career as an actor.

TURRENT: Mexican director Arturo Ripstein wanted you to play an inquisitor in *The Holy Office*,[3] but you turned him down.

BUÑUEL: Because I could get used to it, and that would be bad. It's good to feel the delight of being an executioner for a moment, but you can't abuse it.

TURRENT: Despite the difficulties and the interruption of the filming, Simon appears to be one of your freest films.

BUÑUEL: In the beginning, yes, because Gustavo Alatriste, who is a *rara avis* among producers, left me to do what I wanted. I would have liked to give the film a better ending. We had many unforeseen problems. Once, we were already prepared to film under an overcast sky, and when I was just about to shout "Camera!" we suddenly had a clear sky! Figueroa adapted to it, "It doesn't matter, let's go!" I agreed. And so there was no visual continuity: you have a shot with an overcast sky and in the corresponding shot a clear sky, with another light.

TURRENT: But it's all right because you break conventional believability, the "impression of reality." For example, in the scene where we see a coffin slide by itself through the desert, you don't seem to care that we see the ropes that pull it.

BUÑUEL: It was important to me, but there is a moment during filming when it becomes too much and we have to repeat the shots many times, and then I tell myself, "It's finished, let it go as it is." But that doesn't have anything to do with details like the top hat in the kitchen that I wanted to include in *Los olvidados*. There, I wanted to disconcert the viewer for an instant, impose a doubt ("Did you see it? Didn't you see it?"). Here the ropes are seen too much.

COLINA: I like it because it gives the feeling that the devil is someone who doesn't have everything come out well: a bumbler. I also think these over-

2 *Garrote vil,* a horribly painful contraption for applying the death penalty in Spain, which consists of a thick piece of wood and a seat for the victim. A metal collar with a long screw is cranked by the executioner, squeezing the collar against the victim's Adam's apple, effectively breaking his neck and slowly asphyxiating him.

3 *El Santo Oficio* (1973), dir. Arturo Ripstein.

sights help the film. Also the nonagreement of the overcast and clear skies, and the detail that Simon's beard should be down to his feet and it's not.

BUÑUEL: The beard is something else. I'm not interested in giving a definite time to the story. How long has Simon been atop his column? No one knows. It's intentional. Also when we see Simon on the column and later down on the ground, laying in his mother's lap. What has happened? Has he come down from the column? No, he only imagines it. But...doesn't it really look like he has come down? Ah, it doesn't matter. I prefer it to be ambiguous.

COLINA: This brings us to the fantastical part of the film. You have defined yourself many times as a dialectical materialist.

BUÑUEL: And I am. Ever since I lost my faith. And because I have no other choice. Perhaps I don't always want to be.

COLINA: That is where I am going. In the film there is at least one real miracle: a mutilated man suddenly gets both of his hands back.

BUÑUEL: Yes, it's a miracle, but no one present gives it any importance. It's as if miracles were to happen today in Lourdes without anyone paying any attention, as if miracles were considered routine. Not even the man who receives the miracle gives it any importance. What is the first thing he does with his miraculous hands? He slaps his daughter on the head: "Come on, daughter, let's go home!" The man must have thought, "He is a miraculous saint; it's natural that he performed the miracle for me."

TURRENT: But the miracle was performed, and this time it's not an illusion because everyone present witnessed it. Here, a priest could say you are a believer.

BUÑUEL: Today a priest would open an ecclesiastical investigation into a miracle like that. There was a miracle in my town. In the seventeenth century, I believe. A man who had had his leg amputated prayed fervently to the Virgin of Pilar every day; he always lighted candles, and one morning he once again had good use of the leg...which had already been buried. Is it true? For millions of people, yes. Miracles have existed historically. To look in them for a rational, scientific reason is a different matter. But many people have witnessed the dead brought back to life, the blind made to see again... When I recounted my town's miracle to a Dominican, he laughed: "You're going too far, Buñuel." It's that... Let me clarify this: must you exclude everything that is not materialist and provable from a work of imagination? No. There is an element of mystery, of doubt, of ambiguity. I'm always ambiguous. Ambiguity is part of my nature because it breaks with immutable preconceived ideas. Where is Truth? Truth is a myth. I am a materialist; however, that doesn't mean I deny the imagination, fantasy, or even that certain unexplainable things can exist. Rationally, I don't believe a handless man can grow new hands, but I can act as though I believed it, because I'm interested in what comes afterwards. Besides, I am working in cinema, which is a machine that manufactures miracles. Thanks to cinema, we can see an actor who died fifty years ago now, or how a seed germinates and grows into a plant, or how a bullet leaves a gun barrel and strikes an urn, whose fragments settle to the ground with the grace of a dancer. And these miracles don't even surprise us anymore. It's a shame that cinema wasn't invented centuries ago. The most trivial newsreel from the Middle Ages would be marvelous: Joan of Arc's death at the stake, a society ball at the castle of Gilles de Rais, a documentary on the cultivation of beets in those times.

TURRENT: In *Simon of the Desert*, one travels from the Middle Ages to our century on a supersonic plane.

BUÑUEL: I perfected that in *The Milky Way*; where the characters in that film don't even need a plane to travel from one time to another.

COLINA: There is a marvelous novel with a love story that conquers the barriers of time: *Peter Ibettson*, by George du Maurier. The Surrealists liked it a lot. In it, time travel takes place through dreams...

BUÑUEL: Yes, dreams are the first cinema invented by mankind, and they have a greater wealth of possibilities than cinema itself. Not even the richest producer could finance the superproduction of certain dreams. But we always talk about dreams and forget the daydream, the *rêverie*. I think I prefer it to dreams because, as we have already discussed in another interview, you can't direct dreams, but the *rêverie*, yes, up to a certain point.

COLINA: Have you ever dreamed about Christ?

BUÑUEL: I don't know, perhaps I have dreamed about him but I don't remember. Why do you ask?

COLINA: Because there is a curious Buñuelian iconology of Christ. For example, remember the Sade-like Christ in *L'Age d'or*, the Christ telephone pole in *Cela s'appelle l'aurore*, the Christ laughing hysterically in *Nazarín* (which you had already foreshadowed in a Surrealist text), the Christ who shaves his beard in *The Milky Way*. And in *Simon of the Desert*...

BUÑUEL: Christ doesn't appear.

COLINA: In a certain way he does: Silvia Pinal appears wearing a "Nazarene-style" beard with a lamb in her arms.

BUÑUEL: But she's not Christ, she's the Devil, who takes that form to deceive Simon. The trick fails and she casts the lamb to the ground.

TURRENT: Nevertheless, one could discuss an obsession in respect to Christ...

BUÑUEL: I've already acknowledged that: culturally, I'm a Christian. I've prayed two thousand rosaries and I've taken Communion I don't know how many times. This has marked my life. I understand religious emotion and there are certain sensations in my childhood that I would enjoy experiencing again: the May liturgy, the locust trees in full bloom, the image of the Virgin surrounded by lights. These are profound, unforgettable experiences.

TURRENT: There are those who say that "the religious questions" Buñuel brings up in his films have already been resolved.

BUÑUEL: For some people, yes, but not for everybody. And if they are resolved, what do I care? I don't make thesis films, or religious ones, or atheist ones.

COLINA: Your only message could be: "That no one knows?"

BUÑUEL: It could be, but I would cast doubt even on that message.

TOMAS PEREZ TURRENT: You made *Belle de jour* for the Hakim Brothers, who are known as being terrible producers.

LUIS BUÑUEL: My agent in Paris told me that the Hakims wanted me to direct *Belle de jour* and gave me a copy of the book. The story is a bit like a melodrama, and at first I didn't want to make it. In any case, I told them I demanded total freedom. I especially objected to a clause that gave the producers the right to intervene in the final cut to protect their investment. They insisted and we finally came to an agreement, I did the adaptation with Carrière and everything went smoothly. When I finished the film, there was some chance the censor wouldn't allow the film to be released easily. The Hakims told me, "By letting the censors cut one thing, you keep them from cutting even more." There was a scene, one of Christ, that could have been considered disagreeable, and so it was cut.

TURRENT: What was the scene? It appears that Grünewald's Christ was in it.

BUÑUEL: The scene itself was not cut — the episode in *Belle de jour* at the mansion of the necrophiliac, a duke played by Georges Marchal. But it had more value with the painting of the Grünewald Christ, which is the most terrible image of Christ. Do you two know it? It was painted in a ferociously realistic style. This image was important because it prepared the audience for the next scene.

COLINA: At first Catherine Deneuve didn't seem like a Buñuelian actress. Did you choose her?

BUÑUEL: The producers had already chosen her. They introduced us and I had lunch with her. She seemed to me to be a possible type for the character: very beautiful, reserved, and strange. I accepted her. During the filming I noticed she didn't understand me. She complained to someone, "I don't know why I have to do such-and-such a thing." They told her,

"You have to do what Buñuel asks." She didn't want her breasts to be seen and the hairdresser put a strip of fabric around her. She had to appear nude for a moment, putting on a stocking and to keep her breasts from being seen during that movement, she bound them up in a taffeta band. She behaved better in *Tristana* and didn't give me any problems. An excellent actress. So, yes, she had been suggested to me by the producers but I had the freedom to accept her or not. If I don't have that freedom, I don't make a film.

TURRENT: I think she was right for the film in the end. Her beauty is a little asexual, a little abstract, and that makes an interesting contrast to the character.

BUÑUEL: Yes, very good. That's why I later chose her for *Tristana*.

TURRENT: Jean Sorel wouldn't be called a Buñuelian actor either.

BUÑUEL: I don't care that actors be Buñuelian. Besides, I don't know what a Buñuelian actor is. I had never seen Sorel; I met him when we talked about the film. A very likable fellow, very pleasant. On the first day of production, we were in the park: Sorel, Catherine, the two drivers, and the landau, everyone ready to begin shooting. The actors had to repeat a dialogue about conventional love: "I love you... How happy I am with you... I adore you..." An assistant came over to tell me the actors wanted to talk to me. Sorel had crossed out his lines and had written "his" dialogue over them. "What have you done?" I asked him. Very politely, he said, "Excuse me, sir, doesn't this seem ridiculous to you?" "Yes," I told him, "but don't you know what happens afterwards? After this banal dialogue, you begin to beat her with a whip, to drag her through the mud. Just deliver it as it is written." And that's how they said it.

COLINA: Is this double level of reality and imagination in Kessel's novel?

BUÑUEL: No, I added that myself, because that is what stimulated me to film the story. By the end, the real and the imaginary fuse. I myself cannot tell you what is real and what's imaginary in the film. For me they form the same thing. All of the "real" elements happened in the novel: the bourgeois couple, the gangsters, the brothel, but I changed a few things. In the book, the character played by Rabal is a Syrian. I made him Spanish so he could sing flamenco, which he does in a short scene.

TURRENT: Why sing flamenco?

BUÑUEL: Why not? Why are you wearing that color shirt, not another?

COLINA: For me, the film has three levels: Séverine's respectable life with her husband, the life at the brothel, and then her imaginary life. But then, the bordello could belong to her imaginary life.

BUÑUEL: No. We see her in her normal life with her husband. In this normal life she has "indecent" fantasies. Then she really works in a brothel, that is to say she really has a "decent" life and another "indecent" one. More to the point: she asks her husband about brothels and he finds the question odd. That is real. The next day she sees Piccoli at the tennis club and asks him where these "houses" are and he gives her an address. We see her go to the address, but she doesn't dare enter and flees... Everything follows a logical sequence, is real.

COLINA: But since the film balances between reality and imagination, it could be that what happens then — her life at the brothel and her relationship with Marcel (Clementi) — is pure fantasy.

BUÑUEL: No. A woman who would ask her husband what a brothel is couldn't invent the perversions she sees there. For example: a very dignified gynecologist who goes to the brothel to dress up as a butler and humiliate himself in front of a prostitute.

TURRENT: Isn't that a very common perversion?

BUÑUEL: I know it's something that really happened, not to me but to a woman friend of mine, a dancer at Paramount de Paris. The person was a famous obstetrician from Madrid. How could Séverine imagine that there are people like that? The imaginary episodes are different. She is praying at the hour of the Angelus; suddenly she "sees" a herd of bulls and says that these bulls are called Remorse and Final Atonement. It's because she feels the need to atone. But it's nice that the bulls have those names, wouldn't you say?

TURRENT: But I insist that it is unclear whether some episodes are imaginary or not. For example: in that very episode of the gynecologist. Since the man doesn't find her behavior satisfactory, he orders her out of the room and calls in another prostitute. When Séverine leaves the room, she's not wearing a bra. But when she secretly watches what the man does in the room with the other prostitute, Séverine is already wearing one. Would this be a false *raccord* — a break in continuity?

BUÑUEL: No, it cannot be a false *raccord* because during a production there are so many eyes that someone would have warned me. We see the man close the door; then we see her in the other room. There is an unseen moment between the two shots and, during this time, she could have put a bra on.

TURRENT: Another possible false *raccord*: when Séverine goes to the necrophiliac aristocrat's castle, she enters wearing one overcoat and leaves with another one.

BUÑUEL: I don't think so; I would have to see it. Yes, that would have been a false *raccord,* and not even fantasy permits that. Even in a fantasy sequence, I don't film anything whatsoever, because even fantasies, which are not arbitrary, have a form of realism. When Séverine enters in a tiger skin coat and leaves with an ermine one, it could be that she was given the new one for her services, no? A false *raccord* could have occurred in my first films and in those made in Mexico; it's more difficult for that to happen in my French films, which are more carefully made and have higher budgets. It's true that the lack of transition between the real and the imaginary in *Belle de jour* can appear to be a false *raccord,* but for me it isn't. Besides, the episode of the necrophiliac really happens, it's neither a dream nor a daydream. Does it seem like a *réverie* to you? I don't care: I make a film and then set it free. If you two see the film differently from how I made it, that's all right. I would even accept that your vision is better.

TURRENT: Let's go on to another case. In the initial scene, the credit sequence, Séverine and her husband are riding in a landau, the carriage bells are ringing, etc. The camera accompanies them in panorama. Suddenly the vehicle moves in the opposite direction.

BUÑUEL: There is no false *raccord;* it's an ellipsis. The scene, of course, is imaginary. She is imagining that they are riding in a landau and talking of love, that he takes her from the carriage and gives her to the servants, and that they drag her and later whip her, tied to a tree. Then the camera is on her face while we hear his voice off-screen: "What are you thinking about, Séverine?" And we see that they are in their bedroom (this takes place in reality), and she responds, "I'm thinking about you."

COLINA: Since you say that you set your films free, I can also imagine that *Belle de jour* is the story of a prostitute who dreams of being a decent bourgeois.

BUÑUEL: Very good, that is your *Belle de jour.* If you film it, I would like to see it, and later harass you with questions like you two are doing to me.

COLINA: Of course it's useless to ask you what is in the small box that the Asian client shows Séverine.

BUÑUEL: *(He laughs)* I know the little box is upsetting, especially because of the buzzing noise it makes. After seeing the little box, one prostitute rejects the Asian, but Séverine looks inside and accepts what the client proposes. I myself don't know what is in the little box. It must be something extraordinary, something used for an unheard-of perversion. It produced more curiosity than I had expected. Once, Dr. Méndez, head of pharmacology at the Mexican Cardiology Institute, invited me to lunch at his home. The great cardiologist Dr. Chávez had also been invited because he wanted to talk to me. Chávez arrived late, hung up his Spanish-style cape, excused himself for being late... When he was seated, he suddenly asked me, "Listen, Buñuel, what is in the little box?" He surprised me: an eminent scientist, a *savant,* preoccupied with the contents of the little box.

TURRENT: It intrigues all of us, scientists or not.

COLINA: A publicist friend told me the advertising campaign for the film lacked imagination. "I would have organized a competition," he told me, "on the theme: 'Guess what is in the little box and win 5,000 pesos.'"

TURRENT: I have asked several friends about this and we all agreed that there must be some insect in the box. A bumblebee, for example.

BUÑUEL: It could be, because there is the buzzing. Now I ask you: what can you do with a bumblebee?

COLINA: To me, it seems as clear as day: the Asian wants to put the bumblebee into Séverine's sex organ.

BUÑUEL: And the bumblebee would devour her sex: Zzzzzzzzzz! *(Laughs)* It's not a bad little depravity.

TURRENT: Of course, when she sees what one of the brothel's clients is doing, Séverine is suprised that such depravity exists.

BUÑUEL: Because she doesn't notice that she herself is entering another kind of depravity. She separates her erotic fantasies from what she does in reality. I think women don't like fantasies while making love...

TURRENT: This was one of your most popular films in Mexico, perhaps the most popular. There were long lines at the cinemas.

BUÑUEL: And also in Italy and Spain...

TURRENT: That is very revealing, because those are countries where female sexuality has traditionally been repressed, and women made up the majority of the audiences for *Belle de jour.*

BUÑUEL: It seems so, that it attracted women. How do you explain that?

COLINA: Precisely because of this repression. The film demonstrates that all respectable women sometimes want to be whores. Perhaps many prostitutes also went to see the film, feeling that it revindicated them.

BUÑUEL: The psychoanalyst Fernando Cesarman has called me a misogynist; he says that women always end up badly in my films. I don't know.

I don't think I am a misogynist. Perhaps I don't understand women very much. It is also true that I find myself more comfortable in the company of men than women.

TURRENT: In which you are very Spanish, as the saying goes: *La mujer honrada, pata quebrada y en casa.* (The honored wife, with a broken foot and at home.)

COLINA: And at the same time, you could be considered a "woman's director." Consider the titles of your films: *Susana, The Young One, Viridiana, Tristana, Diary of a Chambermaid...*

BUÑUEL: But rarely do I take a woman's point of view. I admit that the world of my films has the theme of desire, and since I'm not a homosexual, desire naturally takes the form of a woman. I'm like Robinson when he sees the scarecrow dressed in women's clothes...

COLINA: In *Belle de jour*, I would venture to say that you recognize yourself a little in the character of Piccoli, who seems to be very much at home at the brothel.

BUÑUEL: He could have something of me yes. I would have liked to be an *habitué* of a brothel where they would treat me as a friend of the house and bestow all kinds of attentions on me. "Don Luis, here is your favorite wine... Don Luis, this... Don Luis, that."

TURRENT: Nevertheless, Piccoli is a negative character. He tells Séverine's husband what she has been up to.

BUÑUEL: That may be an act of pity. He thinks: "This man is paralyzed, adores his wife and feels diminished before her. If I tell him what his wife does, he will hate her and, for him, that could be a type of consolation."

TURRENT: The idea of the landau and the coachmen and Séverine's whipping would seem to respond to some obsession of yours.

BUÑUEL: In fact, that idea comes from *La femme et le pantin,* from the first time I thought of filming it. The image of two *fin-de-siècle* footmen in bowler hats with rosettes and gold buttons on their frock coats whipping a naked woman seems interesting to me.

COLINA: The important thing is that they humiliate and whip a woman who is above them on the social hierarchy.

BUÑUEL: In her imagination, that is more interesting erotically. For this reason, as you can see, she isn't very different from the gynecologist who likes being stepped on by a prostitute.

TURRENT: The film has two endings. After Piccoli's revelation, the husband is freed, he rises from his wheelchair, everything seems back in order... but once again, the small carriage bells ring... Previously, we've seen that they are related to Séverine's erotic fantasies.

BUÑUEL: There are not two endings; only one ambiguous one. I don't understand it. This is my lack of certitude. It's the moment when I don't know what to do, I have various solutions and I can't decide on any one of them. Finally, I end up putting in my own uncertainty. This has happened to me at other times. I can only say that in life there are situations that don't end, that have no solution.

TURRENT: What does Séverine do then? Return to the brothel?

BUÑUEL: Yes and no. It's her problem.

24: *LA VOIE LACTEE* (THE MILKY WAY)

JOSE DE LA COLINA: *The Milky Way* is an unusual film: it's like a long discussion that takes place over centuries.

LUIS BUÑUEL: It came to me long after having reread — here in Mexico — *Historia de los heterodoxos españoles* (History of Spanish Heterodoxies), by Marcelino Menéndez Pelayo, an extraordinary book full of historical facts and more interesting than a novel. Heresies interested me as all nonconformities of the human spirit interest me, whether in religion, culture, or politics. A group creates a doctrine and thousands and thousands of individuals adhere to it. Then dissidents begin to emerge, who believe in everything the religion preaches except for one or two small points. They are punished, expelled from the group, pursued, and sectarian battles develop in which the person whose beliefs differ only slightly is more detested than the declared enemy.

TOMAS PEREZ TURRENT: That can happen with religion, the Communist Party...or even, for example, with the Surrealist movement.

BUÑUEL: The same thing can happen whenever the sectarian spirit appears. Something similar did happen with Surrealism, though Breton didn't torture or burn anyone alive: it was limited to expelling them from the movement. I should clarify here that Breton never expelled me, despite the fact I worked in commercial cinema and have had the weakness to accept awards.

COLINA: Was the film based only on Menéndez Pelayo's book?

BUÑUEL: I did other research. I read books on theology and ecclesiastical history. Carrière gave me a magnificent collection, an eighty-some-volume *History of the Church,* published in France around 1880. Two volumes are dedicated to heresies, and I chose the principal ones, those from the fourth to the ninth centuries and the Protestants. I wanted a certain fictional form and not just a film of sketches, and I thought about two beggars who go on a pilgrimage through time and space and encounter heresies en route.

COLINA: It's a good idea, but not as unexpected as the fact that a *maître d'hôtel* explains the mystery of transubstantiation in a restaurant.

BUÑUEL: To put in two priests arguing dogma would bore me, so I looked for a suitable atmosphere that would create a type of displacement. A *maître d'*, some waiters and a waitress who argue theology would make it more humorous than cardinals and bishops. Besides, the episode is linked to the fact that the beggars had arrived at the restaurant to ask for money.

TURRENT: The beggars' pilgrimage is a connecting thread. In *The Phantom of Liberty*, which also has very diverse episodes, you don't use this thread.

BUÑUEL: It is another option. In *Phantom*, there's not just one theme or story, there are only characters who inhabit a short episode then give up their place to others who do the same in turn. It's a different form of "discontinuous continuity."

TURRENT: It appears that you are tending to discard the idea of a single story that is the same from the beginning to end. This plurality of characters and episodes can also be found in *The Discreet Charm of the Bourgeoisie*.

BUÑUEL: Yes, although in a nonaccentuated manner. While reading a novel or seeing a film, haven't you ever wanted the author to follow another character, another story? I have. For example, if I read *Crime and Punishment*, I may say to myself, "How boring it is to follow Raskolnikov all the time. Now, instead of climbing yet another set of stairs with him, I would like to tell him, 'Good-bye, good night,' and instead follow some boy who goes out to buy bread and has suddenly crossed his path."

COLINA: I think the narrative procedure of *The Milky Way* could be inspired by the Spanish picaresque tradition, or by the Cervantine novel. In *Don Quixote,* above all, the characters stop along the way, meet a shepherd or an itinerate nobleman and, for a chapter or two, Cervantes recounts another novel within the novel. It's a tactic that comes from the Byzantine novel.

BUÑUEL: Yes, I admit that it could come from certain literary works. The epitome of this procedure is *Manuscrito hallado en Zaragoza,*[1] a charm-

1 *Manuscrito hallado en Zaragoza*, an early nineteenth-century novel by Jan Potocki. In 1964, Polish filmmaker Wojciech directed an epic film version: *The Saragossa Manuscript*.

ing book that I love. There are also interpolated stories in *Gil Blas*. Of course, neither of these books does what I do: travel from one time period to another. That does happen in *Peter Ibbetson*, but only in dreams.

TURRENT: Let's give an example for the reader who hasn't seen your film: two pilgrims leave an inn or *auberge* in the present day (where they witnessed a political argument and the crazy priest) and a little while later, on the road, they rest in a forest and encounter Priscillian and his sect.

BUÑUEL: This encounter was provoked by the storm. The pilgrims argue over the existence of God. One of them says if God exists, he should send a lightning bolt...and a bolt strikes. I took this from an adolescent experience of mine, when I went for a ride from Calanda to a farm with some friends. I had already stopped believing in God. One of my friends was Catholic. There was a storm, we saw a lightning bolt strike very close by and I said, "If there is a God, let a lightning bolt strike us." Everyone protested. I remembered this for the storm in the film.

COLINA: I read the script and the appearance of Priscillian precedes the storm.

BUÑUEL: It's possible. The important thing is that I used any detail to travel from one time period to another. For example: two students from another time participate in the scene in which a bishop who had been a heretic is going to be burned; they are going to burn his corpse. One of the Lutherans raises his voice and shouts out a statement that is also heretical. Everyone wants to apprehend the students, who flee. They run away, get to a river, find the clothes of some present-day hunters who are swimming, put the clothes on and suddenly we have them in our times.

COLINA: It's a very ingenious gimmick: instead of using a time machine, simply change clothes.

TURRENT: And without camera tricks: in full view of the camera and using the same location.

BUÑUEL: It means the audience must pay attention to the time travel. This scene precedes the miracle of the rosary, a serious miracle — I think I took it from Gonzalo de Berceo. One of the students is Catholic. He takes the rosary out of his pocket, and explains that it's used to pray to the Virgin. The other one tosses the rosary in the air, shoots, and destroys it. At night the Virgin appears and returns the rosary intact. The Catholic student recounts this to a priest, who in turn recounts another miracle: a nun, tempted by the Devil, leaves the convent and goes off with a man she loves. She travels about for a long time and later, full of repentance, she returns to the convent and discovers that neither the abbess nor the other nuns had noticed her absence, because the Virgin had taken her place during her absence. Another very different miracle. The two pilgrims flee from the inn taking with them a ham and they are detained by the Civil Guard. "And this ham?" "They gave it to us at the inn." "In that case, you can continue on your way." Imagine that? A Civil Guard who captures two scoundrels fleeing at night with a ham and then lets them go at the first excuse! The Civil Guard always comes off well in my films. *(Laughter)*

TURRENT: Christ appears as a character in this film. Even though he has the conventional image of Christ that we know from religious prints, his behavior is not conventional.

BUÑUEL: These are things I imagined when I was ten or eleven years old. I used to imagine Christ running or shaving his beard, I even shocked myself. But surely at some time or other Christ ran or shaved his beard. He doesn't always have to walk so slowly and solemnly; he must have trimmed his beard sometimes because if not it would have reached his feet. I also filmed the scene of the damnation of the fig tree, which is remarkable. Christ becomes angry with a poor tree because it will not give him its fruit. "I damn you and henceforth you will be sterile." And all the leaves fall from the tree. But the special effects made the scene look like a Walt Disney cartoon, so I cut it.

COLINA: Your latest films have a classic fluidity, without having the images appear brusquely, as in your first Surrealist films. The surprising or extraordinary elements occur naturally within the narrative, instead of clashing with it.

TURRENT: And they have a realistic explanation.

BUÑUEL: Are there realistic explanations in *The Milky Way*? I don't think so. There are fantastic elements.

TURRENT: For example: at a country school party, one character hears a volley of rifle fire and asks the man next to him, "What was that?" The man answers, "It's that I just imagined they shot the Pope."

BUÑUEL: There you have it. There is no realistic explanation. How can someone hear gunshots someone else only imagines?

TURRENT: Yes, fantasy invades reality there, but the doubt remains: could there be a rifle range in the vicinity?

BUÑUEL: All right, but I don't show any firing range. I did show the daydream of the Pope's execution, and then the real situation. If they were casual gunshots, it would be incredible that they coincided with the end of the *réverie*.

COLINA: I like it that in some way or another the imagined is made concrete in these scenes. I also like it that the small stories, with their dreams or daydreams, go on interweaving themselves through the diverse characters. The film's story line is like water from a fountain that falls from one bowl into another...

BUÑUEL: That is *The Phantom of Liberty* exactly.

COLINA: It's an entirely new type of construction. You use it again in *The Discreet Charm of the Bourgeoisie* and in *The Phantom of Liberty*...

BUÑUEL: No. In *The Milky Way* and in *The Discreet Charm* there are connecting threads: the two pilgrims or the group of bourgeois characters. In *The Phantom of Liberty*, we no longer find any continuous characters who serve to interconnect the stories. They have their small story and depart so that a new character can enter with a new story. Perhaps, for that reason, the public is disconcerted. *Phantom* was less successful than *The Discreet Charm*.

COLINA: But you also disconcert us a lot in *The Milky Way*. For example: just now you explained that the episode of the stolen ham and the Civil Guards is only a joke. But in an international context, viewers could think it's an allusion to some dogma.

BUÑUEL: That doesn't only happen in the episode of the ham. There are other jokes that people think must have some hidden meaning. They don't miss anything.

COLINA: For example, the episode of the alms. The beggar who has some coins, receives more; the other, who has no money whatsoever, receives nothing.

BUÑUEL: It is a precept from the Gospels: "To him who hath nothing, nothing will be given; to him who hath, more will be added to."[2] This isn't one of my gags, but a quote from the Gospels that almost seems like heresy.

TURRENT: At last you put your admired Marquis de Sade on the screen in this film.

BUÑUEL: Sade wasn't a heretic, but I interpolate him into the story to represent total atheism. Sade has tortured a sweet young woman, she pro-

---

2 *Matthew 13:12:* "For whosoever hath, to him shall be given, and he shall have more abundance: but whosoever hath not, from him shall be taken away even that he hath."

fesses to believe in God and he, sweetly, like a good father, tries to convince her that God is an absurd idea. The girl remains unconvinced. I remembered a girl, the daughter of an atheist friend of mine. When the girl commits a small infraction at the table and the father punishes her and sends her to her room, as she's leaving, the girl shouts, "At least I believe in God, I believe in God, I believe in God!" The girl's revenge is wonderful.

TURRENT: Why is the episode of the crucified nun linked with the theological duel?

BUÑUEL: The Jansenists crucified themselves and they also crucified nuns. They wanted to suffer as Christ did. In my film, a Jesuit arrives and indignantly shouts that this is a filthy sacrifice, a heresy. The things they say while they clash swords come from the texts of real arguments over these matters. Today we understand nothing of the text. I imagined that instead of seeing two men seated, talking and talking, their theological duel could be a real sword fight. I try to come up with visual ideas even for the most abstract themes. If all I did was put verbal arguments in the film, it would be better to write a book...but I am agraphic; I'm allergic to writing.

TURRENT: Besides *Simon of the Desert*, this is another of your films where the devil appears, this time played by Pierre Clementi.

BUÑUEL: The pilgrims hitchhike along a highway. An automobile approaches, they stick out their thumbs and the vehicle doesn't stop. The young pilgrim curses, "I hope you crash!" And offscreen, we hear the automobile crash. The driver is dead and the Devil is in the back seat, smelling a flower. On the radio, we hear a very beautiful text by St. John of the Cross. My friend Father Julián read it and then they asked me to read it. The text says: *"Allí las lágrimas no sirven para nada, el arrepentimiento tampoco..."* ("Tears are useless there, as is regret...")

TURRENT: Why does the Devil sniff a flower?

BUÑUEL: More than the Devil, he is the Angel of Death. The fact that he is smelling a flower has no meaning whatsoever, or perhaps it did have and I no longer remember it now. But does everything have to have a meaning? Be careful: I see you two in danger of becoming like those critics at *Cahiers du Cinéma*.

TURRENT: The episode at the end about the blind men is very ambiguous. We suppose that Christ returns sight to one of the blind men...

BUÑUEL: The way he does it is also in the Gospels. He takes a little bit of dirt, spits on it, touches the blind man's eyes, and the blind man is cured. Where is the ambiguity?

TURRENT: In the fact that the "cured" blind man later says, "A bird just flew by. I recognized it by the sound of its wings."

BUÑUEL: Of course. He could really have seen a bird fly by, but if he couldn't see it previously, how would he know it was a bird? By the sound of its wings.

TURRENT: The other blind man continues to use his cane to be sure of the terrain he walks on, as if he did not see.

BUÑUEL: That could be for various reasons. Perhaps he is still blind, but he didn't want to disappoint Christ. Nevertheless, the most likely reason is that he still has a blind man's reflexes and is not yet accustomed to his new situation. Besides, he doesn't know what a hole or ditch looks like.

COLINA: Christ performs the miracle with dirt and spit. In a poem by García Lorca, he says, "The Virgin cures children with a little saliva from a star."

BUÑUEL: He could have also taken it from the Gospels, to make a poetic extrapolation. What I find odd is that in this miracle, Christ acts like a doctor. When doctors operate, they ask the nurse for a tweezers or some scissors. In the film, Christ says to St. John, "Give me a handful of dirt," and John places the dirt in his hand. Christ could have picked up the dirt himself.

TURRENT: *The Milky Way* was filmed in 1968, the year of the youth rebellion.

BUÑUEL: May 1968 in Paris. I went out to scout for locations for the film and you can't imagine my surprise to find a six-meter-high barricade on the Rue Saint-Jacques.

TURRENT: Perhaps that explains why the anarchists who shoot the Pope look like the rebels of '68.

BUÑUEL: I think a young woman carries a flag. They are very irregularly armed, many of them are young.

COLINA: The theme of the film is very serious, but it has constant jokes.

BUÑUEL: Imagine what it would have been like if it didn't have humorous features. It would have turned out to be unbearable, like a lecture. And yet despite the humor, I know it was a real bore for some people. The film was not made to make money. Silberman knows how to exploit his films and I think he handled this one well. But if I hadn't put in a few picaresque elements and adventures, not even Silberman could have saved it.

COLINA: What did the Catholic church think of it?

BUÑUEL: The entire church, I don't know. I had a long argument over lunch with some Dominican priests; the prior was there and my friend Father Julián. They are inveterate theologians and they didn't like the film, they were bothered a bit. On the other hand, I know the Jesuits liked it. The film the Dominicans liked was *Simon of the Desert*.

COLINA: In this film I notice a serenity, or let's say a lack of passion from you, which continues to grow in the your following films. A kind of serenity, yes.

BUÑUEL: I don't know if what you say is true. It could be. With age one lives everything with more serenity. But I can suddenly become just as enthusiastic or indignant as when I was young. Perhaps I have been getting a bit intellectual, and I tremble just thinking about this.

COLINA: The very Buñuelian laugh has calmed down; it's more like a smile now.

BUÑUEL: There is humor to a greater or lesser degree in all my films, even in *Los olvidados*, which is so grim. There is more humor in the latest films, those I wrote with Carrière, for example. Beginning with the script itself. Let's say I'm waiting for Carrière and it's still an hour before he is to arrive. I drink two martinis and since this stimulates the imagination, things begin to come to me. Later Carrière arrives; he drinks a fake sugared aperitif, and I tell him my jokes. If we both laugh, it's all right. If not, I take the joke out.

TURRENT: Not everyone laughs at *The Milky Way*.

BUÑUEL: It depends on the audience. A naive and fairly uncultured audience will laugh much less than an audience of intellectuals or a group that picks up on some private jokes. The audience is unpredictable. The daughter of Giral, who was first minister during the Spanish Civil War, lives next door to me. She did not have a religious education and doesn't even know how to make the sign of the cross, and yet she liked the film more than *Belle de jour*, which needed less cultural references to be understood. Why? A mystery. At a private screening, I invited some friends: Hernando Viñes and his wife, Carlos Fuentes, Julio Cortázar, etc. When it was over, Fuentes was enthusiastic but Cortázar was very cold. He bid me adieu very politely and left. I asked Fuentes, "What did Cortázar think of the film?" Carlos answered, "He said it was paid for by the Vatican." *(Laughter)* Nevertheless, I was awarded a prize for being an atheist, the *Prix du Chevalier de la Barre,* an atheist writer before Sade. You see what contradictions.

COLINA: You could quote the phrase that has been attributed to various Mexican personalities, including one president: "I am neither an atheist nor a believer, but rather the complete opposite."

(Buñuel laughs.)

25: *TRISTANA;* THE LAWS OF CHANCE

TOMAS PEREZ TURRENT: Since *Tristana* is the most classic of your recent narrative films, it seems like it could have been an old project.

LUIS BUÑUEL: I was going to make it in 1952 with Ernesto Alonso and Silvia Pinal. It is among Galdós' worst novels, of the "I love you, my little pigeon" genre, very kitsch. The only thing that interested me was the detail of the amputated leg. Strangely enough, that also attracted Hitchcock. At a lunch some directors gave for me in Hollywood,[1] Hitchcock, who sat next to me, repeatedly exclaimed: "Ah, Tristana's amputated leg...!" Well, the project didn't go anywhere in the fifties. In 1962, I was going to direct it with Epoca Films in Spain, but the censor did not want Buñuel to film there again. Years passed and I presented the project again. Fraga Iribarne opposed it. I wrote to my friend Rafael Méndez, a Spanish intellectual who was the head of pharmacology at the Mexican Cardiology Institute: "Dear Rafael, your friend Fraga opposes the film." Rafael took a plane — listen to what a friend he is — went to Madrid and spoke to Fraga, who told him, "Tell Buñuel to talk to me." I wanted the interview to take place before witnesses, but Fraga insisted that it must be just the two of us alone. Fraga seemed intelligent and likable, and he wasn't haughty with me. He told me they weren't ready for my films in Spain; I told him that I would film *Tristana* with complete fidelity to the script presented. "Very well," he told me. "You have the green light. Make the film and then we'll see." They didn't cut anything; they didn't bother me at all. One curiosity: the Civil Guards in the film — in Spain, it is of course forbidden to ridicule the Civil Guard, though I didn't intend to do so — are acted by gypsies.

---

1 When Buñuel attended the Los Angeles opening of *The Discreet Charm of the Bourgeoisie* in 1972, director George Cukor invited him to lunch. Also on hand to toaust Buñuel were directors John Ford, Alfred Hitchcock, William Wyler, Billy Wilder, George Stevens, Rouben Mamoulian, Robert Wise, and Robert Mulligan.

JOSE DE LA COLINA: A complete dialectic, because the Civil Guard and the gypsies are traditional enemies.

BUÑUEL: When we were going to film a scene at the plaza in Toledo, the one in which the guards attack the workers, an authentic Civil Guard commander arrived. One of my assistants asked him, "Señor Comandante, are the guards in good formation?" The man said they were and continued on his way. They must have looked like real guards to him.

COLINA: There is a curious scene that is marginal to the story: a rabid dog runs through the narrow streets. A Civil Guard is called; he looks for the dog and later we hear two shots fired.

BUÑUEL: It's only relatively marginal, because thanks to that episode, Tristana meets the painter when she takes refuge in a patio since she is afraid of the dog. In Spanish cinema, a Civil Guard must always hit his target. Yet two shots are heard. Later the guard reappears, putting his pistol into its holster, and justifies the fact that he fired twice. "I had to do it because the first one missed. There was a child close by and the bullet could have ricocheted and hit him."

TURRENT: Tristana has mysterious caprices, such as that of deciding between two streets that are the same...

BUÑUEL: It is a family memory of mine. When I was little, my sister Margarita would put two pieces of bread on the table and ask me, "Luis, which one do you like best?" "Neither," I told her, "they are both the same." She would say, "Then the right one is better." It seems stupid, doesn't it? I find a certain mystery in this. Between identical things, why do we chose one and not the other? And this "stupidity" can change your life. Tristana walks with the maid. They arrive at a crossroads and Tristana says: "Which one do you prefer we take?" The streets are almost identical. The maid says it is all the same to her. Tristana chooses one, walks along it and encounters the dog, goes into the patio and meets the painter. If she had gone down the other street, there wouldn't be a story, or there would be another one that is radically different. This happens again with Fernando Rey. She asks him, "Which of these two columns do you like best?" "Neither," he says, "How stupid." But later, even though it seems stupid to him, he repeats the experience with two chickpeas. He doesn't say anything, but observes them fixedly and "chooses" one of them. Later, I saw that this was repeated in a film with Alain Delon: he goes to serve himself a drink, ponders between two identical glasses and finally chooses the one that he likes.

COLINA: I suppose that it has something to do with chance, which was a fundamental preoccupation of the Surrealists.

BUÑUEL: I won't say this as dogma, but I believe everything in life is a matter of chance. You could make a film showing that Napoleon was born because a Roman scratched his nose at a certain moment centuries before and through a chain of events it led to the birth of Napoleon. Or let's imagine that Hitler is never born. Just think how different the history of our century would be.

COLINA: Give us the story line based on that chance.

BUÑUEL: Very well. Hitler is never born because on a given night his father didn't sleep with his wife. Why didn't he sleep with her? That day at work he had thought about his wife continuously. He leaves work and runs into a friend, the two drink and Mr. Hitler returns home stinking drunk, goes to sleep on the floor and doesn't fornicate with his wife. Why, on precisely that day, does he run into his old friend? He is a man from the country, he has broken his plow and he goes to the city to buy a new one, and there he runs into Mr. Hitler. Why did the plow break? Because it struck a rock. The examples are stupid, but I believe they work. Small details can change your life, even history itself.

TURRENT: But not everything is chance. Though they may arrive a little earlier or later, summer and winter don't happen by chance.

BUÑUEL: I'm talking particularly about human conduct, but nature can give rise to the laws of chance: a storm makes me seek shelter in a shack in the countryside. There's a beautiful shepherdess there and, feeling desire, I rape her. From this rape, Socrates is born. He is my unacknowledged son, but he is also the son of the shepherdess and of the storm. If instead of entering the shack, I go into a cave and there encounter a bear that eats me, Socrates is never born. Let's be less fantastic: why am I here having a drink and talking to you two? I wanted to study music; if I had been a musician, I wouldn't be here. I am here because one day I felt like going to the Vieux Colombier to see a film by Fritz Lang and I became interested in making films. But I also wouldn't be here if I had been in Calanda at the end of the Spanish Civil War. You two would only know of me through Sadoul's book: "Luis Buñuel, ill-fated Spanish filmmaker, director of *Un chien andalou*, *L'Age d'or* and *Las Hurdes*. Shot by Franco's forces as he was beginning a promising film career."

COLINA: Give us an example of chance in Spanish history.

BUÑUEL: Very easy: if King Rodrigo hadn't slept with La Cava (that day she could have woken up with a headache and not felt up to it), Count Julián wouldn't have sought revenge by bringing the Moors to Spain. I would like to dedicate an entire film to the mechanisms of chance, from a political incident today to the caveman, going backwards in time.

TURRENT: What gives a remarkable air of freedom to your most recent films is precisely the fact that what we see on the screen happens as if anything else might have happened.

BUÑUEL: I agree, though it never reaches gratuity or the absurd. Chance occurs often during a production. I have already told you that *Viridiana* was born as haphazardly as this: Alatriste had asked me to make a film and I still didn't have a story. That morning I had passed a very beautiful English woman in the street who reminded me of the queen of Spain who had attracted me so much in my youth and from there the embryo of *Viridiana* arose. If the woman hadn't crossed my path, I wouldn't have thought of the queen and I might have proposed anything else whatsoever to Alatriste instead.

TURRENT: And did you really pass that young woman in the street?

BUÑUEL: I don't think so, but it could happen. Perhaps on that day the young woman was going to the cinema with her boyfriend, who was working late, so she got bored and took a walk, and by chance I passed her. Or maybe the opposite happened: I was detained by tying my shoes on the corner and I didn't see the woman pass by... But we're putting too many examples when one would have been sufficient. Readers of these interviews are going to get bored.

COLINA: I hope they will be very interested in them, Don Luis. They interest me. Why do these small stories come to your mind? Why in every case does Napoleon appear, Socrates, Hitler, a young woman? All of this tells us something about you. What does it tell us? I don't know, but it tells us *something*.

BUÑUEL: But this has to stop, because if not, your book will go on forever.

TURRENT: We will bring the delightful pursuit of chance to an end. Let's return to *Tristana*. As far as I know, this is your first and only film in which the heroine is an amputee. Instead of taking erotic appeal away from the film, this heightens it.

BUÑUEL: Yes, there is a perverse sexual relationship. I say so in *Tristana*. During the Spanish Civil War I used to go to the Café de la Paix, where I met with someone about political issues. I frequently saw two crippled young women, about nineteen or twenty years old, very slender, very pretty and made-up. They passed on their crutches, not hiding the fact that they both were missing a leg. They were prostitutes and never lacked for clients; they were a tremendous success. In the film, I tell the story through the mouth of Don Lope. Catherine Deneuve is not precisely my type of woman, but when she is crippled and made-up, I find her very attractive.

TURRENT: One of the most erotic scenes in the film is the one in which Tristana exhibits herself to the deaf boy. It is a close-up, so we don't see her display her nudity, but the scene has a genuine erotic splendor.

BUÑUEL: I am very discreet and besides I care above all about stimulating the viewer's imagination. To show her breasts would have weakened the scene, no?

TURRENT: Aside from the erotic obsession, there also appears to be a gastronomic obsession in *Tristana*. *Cahiers du Cinéma* noticed this and enumerated the times when food appears. They found sixteen...

BUÑUEL: Do you two see how critics see things that aren't there? I swear there are only three scenes with food.

TURRENT: There are more, that is sure. Even though they aren't complete meals, they are scenes with certain relationships to eating, food, kitchen utensils. The apple that Saturno eats, the *migas de campanero,* the chocolate, the frying pans...

BUÑUEL: Maybe, but you can find many gastronomic references in any film (without speaking of *La Grande Bouffe,*[2] because that's its subject matter: eating acquires Pantagruelian dimensions).

COLINA: What is that about the *migas de campanero?*

BUÑUEL: *Migas* are made with small crusts of bread, garlic, and oil fried in a pan over fire, and they must remain soft. The ones they made at the studio were so hard they looked like bullets. When the bellringer serves them to Tristana, they sound like a hailstorm. So the man calls them *migas de campanero* (bell ringer's crusts). He could just as easily have also called them *migas de artillero* (artillery gunner's crusts), but he is a bell ringer.

COLINA: It is amusing because a woman friend of mine, who had of course seen the film, once told me, "I feel like going to Spain to eat some good *migas de campanero.*" I told her that those *migas* didn't exist, that you had invented them. "Go on!" she told me. "*Migas de campanero* are very well known in Madrid and I ate them numerous times when I was a girl."

2 *La Grande Bouffe* (French-Italian, 1973), dir. Marco Ferreri, about four men who decide to commit suicide by eating themselves to death.

BUÑUEL: I made that up. *Migas de campanero* don't exist.

TURRENT: Don Lope is an unforgettable character, one of your best characters, but very contradictory...or thanks to the fact he is contradictory. He is an idle bourgeois, a playboy, but when a policeman pursues a thief, or an anarchist, he sides with the latter.

BUÑUEL: It's not so much that he takes sides with the anarchist or thief. Rather he sets himself against the police, as he does against the priests. This was already in the novel, and furthermore it's something that happens with certain Spanish gentlemen, at least in my day. He can seduce a poor little orphan girl, taking advantage of his position as her protector, and at the same time become indignant at the abuse of the weak by the strong. At the end he changes, he eats *azucarillos* and hot chocolate with priests, he says hello to the Civil Guard. Age changes all of us.

COLINA: The character resembles Don Jaime in *Viridiana* and, if you don't mind, he's also a little like you.

BUÑUEL: Yes, Don Jaime and Don Lope somewhat resemble each other, but perhaps you exaggerate their resemblance because they are both played by the same actor, Fernando Rey. It is also possible that he is somewhat autobiographical. We have something in common: age.

COLINA: It's touching that at the beginning Don Lope seems only to have taken advantage of Tristana, and yet later he feels love for her, after they cut off her leg.

BUÑUEL: And it gets to the point where he even allows the painter to come back and visit her, the man who had taken her away from him. In a scene I like, when he has just finished buying her some little pastries or some marzipan, he runs into the painter in the street and entreats him to visit Tristana. I don't think I could ever reach that point, but I understand it. And I also understand him when they tell him they have to cut off the young woman's leg. He says, "Poor girl!" Then he becomes indignant because science does these things, but at the same time he thinks, "Now she will be completely mine."

COLINA: Don Lope begins by possessing Tristana and ends up being possessed by her.

BUÑUEL: But possessed in a terrible way, don't you agree? He is totally at her mercy.

TURRENT: Tristana is very passive at first. She lets herself be seduced by Don Lope as if it were perfectly natural, but from the moment her leg is amputated, she changes totally: she turns into a tyrannical puritan.

BUÑUEL: Not so puritanical because she enjoys arousing the deaf mute. A tyrant, yes. She gets even with Don Lope and finally, with total indifference, brings about his death. In the novel they continue living together; he is already very old, and she goes to church all the time. Neither Galdós' novel nor my film deals with women's liberation, or anything like it. In Galdós' time that was inconceivable; it was very rare during the years depicted in the film. I didn't find Galdós' ending to my taste, but I didn't like mine either. To end with Don Lope's death bothered me a lot; it seemed melodramatic, but I couldn't see any other ending but that. She gets her revenge on Don Lope: he has a heart attack and she pretends to call a doctor. Afterwards, she opens the window. Outside it is snowing. It's an ending with a postscript; I don't like it. Maybe that's why I put in a rapid series of retrospective images.

TURRENT: What do you think of Tristana? Does she attract or repel you?

BUÑUEL: In one way or another, she and Don Lope touch my heart. The handsome young man, the painter, interests me much less, practically not at all. He is almost just a pretext so that what happens will happen between Don Lope and Tristana.

COLINA: I can't remember if we see any of the painter's works in the film, but I would bet he is a mediocre artist.

BUÑUEL: I don't know, nor do I care. It's not a film about art. Biographies of artists that have been brought to the screen bore me.

COLINA: Then we won't talk about the "colors of Toledo" in the film...

TURRENT: Nor about "Monsieur Buñuel's palette."

BUÑUEL: So much the better. Down with "Monsieur Buñuel's palette!" I don't know if color film is an advantage. I believe color distorts things more than black and white (in which gray also exists, and that was enough). One thing I can't stand in color films is blood. It's not that I can't stand looking at it, just that it makes me laugh. It always looks fake.

TURRENT: Certain sounds have much importance in your films. The drums of Calanda, the little bells of the landau. In *Tristana*, it's the bells of Toledo.

BUÑUEL: That could come from the belfry in *Là-bas,* but no: they come from my childhood, from the bells that presided over life in my town. We have also talked about that.

COLINA: In one scene, Tristana leans over a recumbent statue and it looks like she is going to kiss it.

BUÑUEL: No. She is fascinated by the image of death. When my friends and I went to Toledo, we always visited this statue of Cardinal Tavera by Berruguete. It's extraordinary: you see the translucent skin, the beginnings of putrefaction. Tristana wouldn't kiss a cadaver, either in person or as a statue, and especially not a cardinal. Although she has a few small defects, she is neither necrophiliac nor sacrilegious. There is a statue that comes to life in *The Phantom of Liberty*, to give not a kiss but a blow.

26: *LE CHARME DISCRET DE LA BOURGEOISIE* (THE DISCREET CHARM OF THE BOURGEOISIE)

TOMAS PEREZ TURRENT: Why are the bourgeoisie charming? And why is their charm discreet?

LUIS BUÑUEL: Why not? I've known bourgeois people who were both charming and discreet. Do you think that everything having to do with the bourgeoisie is bad? No. There are some valuable things about them that are worth conserving.

JOSE DE LA COLINA: Some people find it odd that your own lifestyle can be described as bourgeois.

BUÑUEL: I am bourgeois, but "discreet." But, if I were a bourgeois *comme il faut,* I wouldn't be making films, I'd just be "living off my rents."

TURRENT: There's an ironic or ambiguous scene in the film when one bourgeois says to another, "I'll show you how the lower classes can never be refined." They call in the chauffeur and tell him, "Maurice, we would like you to have a drink with us." Full of thanks, the chauffeur accepts and then tosses the drink down in one gulp without tasting it, without "style." After telling him he can leave, they comment, "Did you see that? That is what shouldn't be done with a dry martini." The ambassador adds, "No political regime can help the masses acquire refinement. You know me and you know I'm no reactionary." Is this you speaking through the mouth of this character?

BUÑUEL: *(He laughs)* No! I find this episode humorous, nothing more. In any case, it proves only the relativity of certain social experiments. Between the bourgeois characters and the chauffeur there is only the difference in habits. Perhaps the ambassador in the film doesn't know how to drink wine from a Spanish wineskin or *porrón* with the consummate art and technique of a worker. Then the worker could just as easily say, "How uncouth the ambassador is! Look, he doesn't even known how to do something as simple as drink wine from a wineskin." But this worker would more likely be considered a peasant for doing that, wouldn't he?

TURRENT: Is the film a ferocious satire of the bourgeoisie?

BUÑUEL: It isn't a satire and it certainly isn't ferocious. I think I made this film in a spirit of good-intentioned humor. I certainly didn't try to make people guffaw from beginning to end. I was very upset that the French poster read: *"On rit comme des fous, comme des fous, comme des fous!"* ("You'll laugh like crazy, like crazy, like crazy!") I was horribly ashamed when I saw the poster with a huge bowler hat on top and this enormous mouth painted over some legs. I could have shot the publicist.

COLINA: Some critics have seen the film as a satire. For example, at various times we see the main characters walking down a road that seems to go nowhere. This has been interpreted as a statement that the bourgeoisie has no historical destiny; it doesn't know where to go. The "discreet charm" would be like the fragrance of a dying flower.

BUÑUEL: I can understand that interpretation because the film ends with the characters walking down the road. Nevertheless, I regret to say there is no message there. In any case, I would be ashamed of myself for deciding to do something like that: "Here I'm going to show you that the bourgeoisie is lost." Besides, I don't believe it's just the bourgeoisie that are on the brink of extinction. In many places, the proletariat is becoming less revolutionary and bit by bit more bourgeois. For example, students now believe they hold the revolution in their hands. In May of '68 in Paris, they certainly behaved in more revolutionary fashion than the workers, who merely looked on indifferently. But there was no revolution in '68 and France has not changed. Besides, in the street, it was exciting to see the walls painted with anarchist, Maoist, and even Surrealist slogans. They seemed to believe the whole social order would change overnight. The attempt at revolution was more romantic than anything else.

TURRENT: Is the revolutionary woman who tries to attack the ambassador an example of this?

BUÑUEL: The woman could be seen as an idealistic revolutionary, but the ambassador is more astute than she is.

COLINA: These scenes bother some leftist viewers I know, who charge that you make fun of young revolutionaries and show far too much sympathy for the ambassador of a "gorilla" republic in Latin America.

BUÑUEL: That's absurd! I have nothing to say to such stupidity. On the other hand, I have no sympathy whatsoever for the ambassador. At the beginning of this episode, he is shown to be very friendly with the revolutionary. He tries to seduce her; he's pleasant with her and says, "I'm going to be generous with you. The door is open, now get out!" The woman leaves and then we see the ambassador lean out the window and make a sign to some police or secret agents who seize her brutally. But I can't always show the ambassador as a melodramatic villain. That would be too...

TURRENT: ...Manichean.

BUÑUEL: I can't divide my characters into absolutely good ones and absolutely evil ones. The ambassador amuses me, yes. I particularly like the scene at the society reception when he is approached and asked about his country, the Republic of Miranda. He is asked very courteously, "Mr. Ambassador, is it true that in your country, the such-and-such volcano erupts every twenty years?" "No, madame, that volcano is not in my country but in another." He meets another guest: "Mr. Ambassador, in your country do they have champagne and caviar like they do here?" "No sir, but we have many other good things." The major says, "Your excellency, it seems there's a lot of administrative corruption in your country." The ambassador has already had enough, but still he forces himself to be nice: "At another time perhaps, but now we are an authentic democracy and corruption no longer exists..." Finally, he reaches the last straw: "I've been told that in your country, people kill each other for the most trivial reasons, and it's impossible to count all the bodies every day." "No, Colonel, you're offending me." "That was not my intention. I read it in a very reliable report." "Colonel, you've insulted the dignity of the Republic of Miranda." "Just between the two of us, I don't give a damn about the Republic of Miranda." The ambassador explodes: "And you can shove your entire army up your a..." The Colonel slaps the ambassador's face; people come between them and there are explanations. At first the ambassador is a bit slow to react, but then he pulls two women aside, takes out a revolver and calls out to the colonel, who turns. Then the ambassador shoots him... *(He laughs.)* I like that scene because all of a sudden the varnish of civilization vanishes completely.

TURRENT: Is the Republic of Miranda based on any particular Latin American country?

BUÑUEL: None in particular. I concocted it out of elements from various countries.

COLINA: Some Mexican viewers think it represents Mexico because in one scene the bourgeois smoke some marijuana.

BUÑUEL: But they smoke it in a European salon, and besides, you can find marijuana anywhere.

COLINA: In *The Discreet Charm,* once again we find the theme of eating...but through its absence. This also seems symbolic: for one reason or another, the bourgeoisie in the film can never eat. It's like the bourgeois characters in *The Exterminating Angel,* who can't leave the house...

BUÑUEL: It's not symbolic, it's just that I'm interested in frustrations. I took a few real anecdotes, either mine or of friends. For example, the episode in which the people go to a restaurant, order dinner and while they're waiting, they begin to notice something strange. In the other room they notice there's a wake going on: the owner of the restaurant has died. That's a real anecdote. There's another scene in which the people finally do eat, or at least they begin to and discover that the chickens are made of rubber and that in reality they are on the set of a play. I think that's a dream someone once told me about.

COLINA: There are dreams in the film, but they are presented in ways that surprise us. They are not presented as dreams but as part of reality. Only later do we discover this confusion.

BUÑUEL: Dreams are a continuation of reality, of waking life. In a film they are only valuable if you don't announce: "This is a dream." Because then the viewer will say: "Ah, this is a dream. Then it's not important." The public is disappointed and the film loses its mystery, its power to disturb people.

COLINA: The most interesting thing is that these dreams don't seem to be locked up in the head of each person. They communicate not only with waking life, but also with characters other than the dreamer... This is very original and poetic.

BUÑUEL: If someone is dreaming, why can't I see what he's dreaming? Why can't I enter the dream and change it? This limitation bothers me. But in a film, I can abolish this limitation altogether.

COLINA: Then the film could also be titled *The Communicating Vessels,* like Breton's book?

BUÑUEL: Only in part, because it deals with more than the problem of dreams. You yourselves have pointed out other themes.

COLINA: The soldier's dream seems very convincing to me. It's one of the few dreams in the history of cinema that capture a genuine oneiric tone, a dreamlike development...

BUÑUEL: I like that sequence best—a soldier approaches the two women in a café and for no reason whatsoever asks them, "Did you have a happy childhood?" It's very much my style. For example, when I see a woman in a café who seems interesting to me — it's not important that she be pretty — and I see that her face reflects an inner serenity, I think: "This woman must have had a happy childhood and it's obvious in everything about her." Why not go up and ask her about it?

TURRENT: Did you do things like that during your Surrealist phase?

BUÑUEL: No. Then I would have asked an aggressive question, a question "against" something. A few of the Surrealists would have asked a question like that, though. Some of them would go into the street "in a state of availability," at random. They might have asked questions like that. But as far as I know, the soldier in the film wasn't a Surrealist...

COLINA: But his behavior is perfectly Surrealist: spontaneously telling his dreams to strangers for no apparent reason...a dream that I suspect is one belonging to Luis Buñuel.

BUÑUEL: Yes. I dreamed, more than once I think, that I was going down a long street at nightfall and I ran into a cousin of mine, who in reality had died. I greeted him and spoke to him. Then I was looking for my mother, calling out to her, "Mother, why are you lost in the shadows?" This was long after my mother's death. Later in the film, when there's the dream of the murdered man with his parents seated on the bed looking like ghosts, the bedroom is an exact reproduction of my parent's bedroom. These are things that return to your memory, and I try to reproduce them as faithfully as possible. At other times, I do it without even realizing it. Later when I see the film I suddenly notice some detail: "Oh, that's one of my memories." Or, "That's something a friend told me." I prefer it when a detail arises unconsciously.

TURRENT: How do you explain the bishop who wants to work as a gardener and later takes the role of an impromptu butler?

BUÑUEL: The idea probably came from the notion of working priests. If there's a priest who works at a factory, then there could be a bishop who shares these ideas and has always wanted to be a gardener. They ask him, "And how much will you charge us?" He answers, "The usual, madam, union wage." *(He laughs.)* I'll tell you something: after the Spanish Civil War when I found myself without a job in New York, I used to ask my American friends if they knew of anyone who needed a butler. "I could take the job," I said. Of course, I said it out of necessity, but also because I would have liked to be a butler.

COLINA: You disconcert me, Don Luis. I can imagine any other sort of job, from boxer (you did box) to... gangster. But a butler! I can't imagine you as a butler. It's too servile.

BUÑUEL: No. A good butler becomes the master's most intimate friend. The work is easy...and you live like a millionaire. When the master goes away on a trip, his entire house is at your disposal, the wines in the wine cellar, the master's best suits. Of course I would be a serious and a very dignified butler. I wouldn't take advantage of the situation.

COLINA: I visited you at Billancourt while you were filming *The Discreet Charm of the Bourgeoisie* and I noticed you used video...

BUÑUEL: It was the first time I used a video system connected to the camera, something I used again later when I made my next two films. It's very easy and precise. You can direct without getting out of your chair. And besides, you can see exactly what will later be projected on the screen, completely planned to the millimeter. I calculate the director has to look through the viewfinder — even if only for a moment — some five hundred times during a normal shoot.

TURRENT: With the video hookup, you become an objective viewer because you are already watching an *image*.

BUÑUEL: I first rehearse the scene without either a camera or a monitor. Then I sit and rehearse with the camera and correct the framing and the movements according to what I see on the small screen. The advantage is that I can see if the camera operator, voluntarily or not, has altered the setup or the camera movement, or if he isn't paying attention and has let a reflector appear in the shot, etc.

TURRENT: We've talked about the fluidity of narration and camera movement in your latest pictures. I also watched you shoot *The Discreet Charm*. I was there when you filmed the scene in which Delphine Seyrig, Paul Frankeur, Fernando Rey, and Bulle Ogier arrive at the house and the maid, Milena Vukotic, receives them. The maid then goes upstairs to announce that the guests have arrived. It was a tracking sequence that involved a very complicated camera movement. Later when you see the film, you don't even notice it.

BUÑUEL: That's the way I work: I've never liked making the technical aspects visible. A long dolly shot or a very complicated arabesque bothers me a lot. The camera must move slowly without the viewer noticing. But I don't overplan these movements; it has something to do with instinct and practice. Arturo Ripstein pointed out a crane movement to me in the same film. Crane shots bother me a lot; you can always see when a crane has been used. There should be no gratuitous camera movements; it's always preferable to take advantage of a character's movement and then follow him to justify using a dolly or a tracking shot.

COLINA: The later films show a tendency to use general shots, long shots and medium shots, but you almost never use close-ups.

BUÑUEL: I hate close-ups, though they are sometimes necessary. Close-ups are often used for easy melodramatic effects.

COLINA: Close-ups privilege a certain character, and in your later films, except for *That Obscure Object of Desire*, there are no "privileged" or main characters.

BUÑUEL: There are many characters, many small stories.

27: *LE FANTOME DE LA LIBERTE* (THE PHANTOM OF LIBERTY)

JOSE DE LA COLINA: Where does the title *The Phantom of Liberty* come from?

LUIS BUÑUEL: From a collaboration between Marx and I. The first line of the Communist Manifesto reads: "A phantom travels over Europe...," etc.[1] For my part, I see liberty as a ghost that we try to grasp... and... we embrace a misty shape that leaves us with only a wisp of vapor in our hands.

TOMAS PEREZ TURRENT: There is another reference. During the theological duel in *The Milky Way*, the Jansenist shouts at the Jesuit: "Free will is nothing more than a simple whim! In any circumstance, I feel that my thoughts and my will are not in my power! And my liberty is only a phantom!"

BUÑUEL: How odd, I didn't remember that. It's the same idea, but in a theological context. Theology is not my specialty, let's pass over it. In Marx, too, the phantom travelling over Europe was that of Communism, and the Bolshevik Revolution made it tangible. In my film, the title came about irrationally, as did the title of *Un chien andalou*, yet nevertheless, I don't think any other titles could be more suited to the spirit of either film.

COLINA: Are you skeptical about liberty?

BUÑUEL: Yes. At certain historical moments, people have even completely rejected the idea of liberty. The shout heard at the beginning of the film, *"Vivan las ca'enas!"* — "Long live chains!" — was really shouted by Spaniards during Napoleon's invasion of the country. They preferred the monarchy's chains to the human rights and liberty the French Revolution offered them.

---

1 In English, the first line of the *Communist Manifesto* is usually translated as, "A spector is haunting Europe..."

TURRENT: The film has a random construction.

BUÑUEL: We have already talked about this. I believe that chance, coincidence, governs our lives. I'm here talking to you because a paternal spermatozoid penetrated the maternal ovum, where it developed. Why did this spermatozoid enter and not another of the thousands that wagged their tails around? — And sorry about the "wagged their tails." Nevertheless, *The Phantom of Liberty* only imitates the mechanisms of chance. It was written in a conscious state; it is neither a dream nor a delirious flow of images.

COLINA: I like the fact that none of the characters seem necessary; they could be these characters or any others. And what we see happening to them happens as if anything else could have happened in the film.

BUÑUEL: They are both gratuitous and necessary at the same time.

COLINA: Somewhere André Breton, quoting someone, said chance is another line that necessity takes or the crossing of two divergent lines of necessity.

BUÑUEL: I think so, but there can also be pure chance, where necessity has nothing to do with it. *(He laughs)* What philosophers we are.

TURRENT: In the construction of the film, each character is the link between his episode and the episodes of other characters. It's what you told us: to follow Raskolnikov up the stairs, to see him pass a boy who is going out for some bread, to leave Raskolnikov and follow the boy, who becomes the main character in the subsequent episode.

BUÑUEL: A single story told through different characters who follow each other in turn. I had already envisioned that in *L'Age d'or* — we begin with the scorpions, follow the bandits, then the founding of the city, then the lovers and the party in the salon, and we end with the characters from *120 Days of Sodom*. The difference is that in *Phantom,* the episodes are more interlinked, they clash less: they flow naturally.

TURRENT: But, I don't recall that the gratuitous sniper — or the "killer-poet," as you call him — is linked to the other characters.

BUÑUEL: Yes, he is. We have seen the episode in which the police commissioner tells the gendarme to shine his shoes. The gendarme goes to a shoeshine boy. I leave the gendarme and follow the new character, who is the sniper. The link may be too subtle, but it does exist.

COLINA: The "nodal" point would be the inn or *auberge,* where various stories intersect, some of them very short: the friars, the sadist and masochist, the young man and his aunt...

BUÑUEL: There are sequences that are somewhat independent of the movement of the film. One of them is about the young man and his aunt. Another one, later on, is about the lost girl who is nevertheless visible. I had previously thought about this episode for *Cuatro misterios* (Four Mysteries), a film I never made. The episode of the young man and his aunt is very concentrated: it would be material enough for a melodrama of an hour and a half, wouldn't it? The fact that various stories intersect at the inn is perhaps a memory of the inn from *Don Quixote,* where the protagonists and other characters arrive and each one tells his story. That's where Don Quixote slashes the wineskins.

TURRENT: The passages from one adventure to another in the film are like doors opening one after the other.

BUÑUEL: A good observation. I think there is a Surrealist painting with a succession of open doors. I didn't think about that either when I wrote *The Milky Way.* But I'm thinking about it now that you have used the metaphor. Yes, each episode gives way to another, each character to another, and thus we could go on continue *ad infinitum.* If we were faithful to its spirit, the film would never end.

COLINA: Or it would close itself into a circle.

BUÑUEL: No, if it closes itself into a circle, it's not liberty, it's death. Completing the vital circle: the end.

COLINA: Without following any particular order, a question occurs to me, Don Luis. Why the lecture on Polynesian traditions at the police academy?

BUÑUEL: It seemed humorous to me because... Look, I've never been to a police academy. So I wondered: what would one of those schools be like? Perhaps the first image to appear — given that the word *school* is usually associated with childhood — is a number of policemen seated at their desks, listening to the teacher, looking at the blackboard, clowning around behind the teacher's back, pulling pranks. The teacher has to talk about something. But what? So I had him talk a little about anthropology. He gives a short lesson on the differences in customs between countries, to show how one country is considered bad, another good, and vice versa. For me, this serves as a prologue to the subsequent scene where some refined people keep up a very genteel conversation while they defecate together, but eat in privacy, alone. It's the inversion of what we do, isn't that right? We defecate alone and in private; we eat with other people. But who can be sure that what is normal and decent won't be precisely the opposite one day. Furthermore, eating is just as repugnant a spectacle: opening your mouth, putting food into it, chewing it, salivating... Why have we made defecation a solitary and secret act? I remember during my military service in 1921, there was a barracks we used as a toilet; it was only a board with holes in a row above a pit. While one soldier went about his business, others waited. At first, it was sickening; but you got used to it and later chatted with your companion. The sequence we're talking about came to me through an association of "thesis and antithesis": defecation in public, eating alone and in secret.

TURRENT: That is to say, a reversal of accepted situations, which is a constant throughout the film.

BUÑUEL: And, if you notice, this also exists in my other films, but less evident, perhaps.

COLINA: I would say that on the subject of excrement, the less said the better, but this film brings it up, and so do your earlier films. We see the female protagonist seated on the toilet in *L'Age d'or*, then an eruption of lava that effectively simulates excrement. The puddle of mud or tar that Jorge Negrete stirs with a branch in *Gran Casino* suggests that this kitsch love scene is — I have to use the word — "pure shit." An enormous three-tiered wardrobe is used as a watercloset in *The Exterminating Angel*.

BUÑUEL: But that use of the wardrobe is only suggested in that film, and furthermore, a character waxes poetic about the situation, talking about how she saw an eagle fly by, saying there was a wind. (We've already discussed this in an earlier interview, when I told you it is associated with a memory of mine.)

COLINA: Not only do the characters defecate during a salon gathering in *The Phantom of Liberty*, but furthermore, excrement is openly discussed in a kind of lecture, this time about the ecology, pollution, etc.

BUÑUEL: I acknowledge that mankind's irrational destruction of nature bothers me a lot. Mankind is slowly committing suicide — or not so slowly: each day it accelerates—producing all kinds of wastes: corporal, industrial, atomic, poisoning the earth, the sea and the air. He destroys the very environment, that which gives him his sustenance. Centuries and centuries of civilization to arrive to this: what a piece of work is man! No other animal would be so stupid. Plagues of locusts are sporadic, they have a limit.

COLINA: You hate statistics, but precise figures are given in the scene of the bathroom salon. I'll summarize what the script says: "What will the world be like in twenty years if the population continues growing at today's proportions. Imagine the quantity of toxic wastes that are dumped into rivers every day. Detergents, insecticides, all the industrial wastes...without forgetting body wastes... It's simple: there are currently close to four billion inhabitants on the earth. In twenty years there will be seven billion. And how much weight in body waste does an individual release every day? Half a pound? Much more? Remember that urine weighs more than water. Including everything, I would say at least three pounds. Multiply that by four billion. It makes...six billion kilos a day. Within twenty years...," etc.

BUÑUEL: Yes, a little of me is talking there. Is it too much talk and too little cinema? I don't care: I had that on my mind and I put it in "at the slightest provocation." I admit that this may be my pedagogic streak. And now, respectable public, a small lesson even though you don't want it. But the situation we see on the screen justifies it. I am more rational than it may seem.

TURRENT: In the episode of the man who secretly gives some postcards to two little girls, and one of them shows them to her parents, there is a reflection on pornography. Again, it's a reversal.

BUÑUEL: It's my delight in surprise, shock, confusion, that stays with me. They are tourist postcards: the Madeleine, the Arc de Triomphe, the Eiffel Tower... The girl's parents are shocked: "It's sickening, repugnant, obscene!" I want to disconcert: the postcards are pornographic and they aren't; the girl disappears and is present. The episode of the postcards may be mocking psychoanalysis. Another episode could be in the film: in a psychoanalyst's consultation room: "What did you dream about last night?" "A cypress tree." "Then you are a pig: how can you have such filthy dreams?" No, it would have been too "funny," and I would have taken it out at the last minute.

COLINA: But you also could have given the counterpart to the postcard scene: a school where the two girls study. Their textbooks are minutely illustrated works by de Sade. The teacher asks one of them to recite the lesson; the girl recites a romance of courtly love, ideal, very chaste, and the teacher indignantly expels her from the classroom.

BUÑUEL: That would be good, but it would be too logical: a geometric inversion of the previous scene. Being so methodical would bore me. I have already recounted how, at one time, some Surrealist friends and I considered taking over a cinema full of children and screening a very daring pornographic film, *Soeur Vaseline*. We didn't do it because we were afraid of the police. No, I wouldn't film the scene you just suggested, not out of fear, but out of shame. I can't imagine filming it in the studio, placing pornographic books in front of the little girls.

COLINA: What Pérez Turrent said about the reversal of situations seems very right to me. Another example: the man you call the "killer-poet," the gratuitous sniper. He shoots at many people, killing them like rabbits, they take him prisoner and condemn him to death...only to take his handcuffs off and set him free. Those in the courtroom ask him for autographs.

BUÑUEL: Absurd, isn't it? But it's only a slight exaggeration of something very real in our times. It happens with terrorism. Some men seize an airplane and threaten to blow it up, using dynamite, with more than a hundred innocent people on board. The authorities negotiate with them and give the terrorists a passport to Libya.

COLINA: André Breton said that in the good old Surrealist days (though he would regret it years later): "The most simple Surrealist act would be to go into the street and shoot indiscriminately into the crowd."

BUÑUEL: Yes, I remember that, but I think the act should be carried out at a literary conference.

COLINA: Breton's friend Jacques Vaché, an immediate precursor of the Surrealists, aimed a revolver at various people in the audience at a theater...[2]

BUÑUEL: I didn't see that. Those are typically Surrealist provocations, but purely theoretical: Vaché committed suicide. Breton...he would never have dared to put that murder into practice. I didn't think about the Surrealists as such for the sniper scene; I thought about a real-life situation I read about in an American newspaper. A fellow climbed the tower of a temple carrying a rifle with a telescopic viewfinder and began to shoot at passersby. In the end, a policeman managed to approach by climbing a cornice and shot the individual. Besides, you can't deny we've all had thoughts about similar actions. "Theoretically," I agree with actions like those, if they are pure, gratuitous. I insist: "theoretically." At an earlier time in my life, I hunted for animals with a rifle. Today I wouldn't kill a fly. What makes me indignant about terrorists, whatever their political affiliation, is that they kill people or threaten to do so, and

2 Jacques Vaché (1895-1919), a friend of André Breton and an officer during World War I, drew his revolver at the premiere of Guillaume Apollinaire's "Surrealist" play *Les mamelles de Tirèsias* (The Breasts of Tiresias), an act often seen as theater criticism in the extreme. Vaché committed suicide by overdosing on opium.

the authorities negotiate with them, they are given enormous coverage in the newspapers, and in some way they become "stars." If I had the power to do so, I would censor these stories from all newspapers and television. There is an excess of information.

COLINA: Another case that could have been in *The Phantom of Liberty*, which also happened in the United States: a woman climbed up on an overpass over a very busy highway. Under her fur coat, she was nude; she opened her coat and exposed herself to the drivers. There was a terrible accident with many wounded and dead because the vehicles crashed, smashing into one another.

BUÑUEL: That would be more pleasing, more elegant, more attractive. A completely gratuitous act.

TURRENT: But it might not be completely gratuitous. She could have been fulfilling some need for publicity, or acting out a sexual hang-up...

BUÑUEL: Perhaps, but, on further examination, the truly gratuitous act doesn't exist: it would always have some irrational obscure motive. The important thing is that it not be committed for some practical purpose. Certainly it's possible that the woman in the coat is sentenced to jail for only a few days for lack of public morality, and is then visited by a Hollywood producer who offers her a contract.

TURRENT: That happened, with insignificant variations: it's the case of the Orson Welles program about the Martian invasion of the earth. He created a terrible panic and caused accidents because drivers were listening to the radio and believed the program was a newscast and not fiction. Then Welles was given a Hollywood contract.[3]

BUÑUEL: It would have been good if Welles hadn't accepted the contract, if he had told the producer, "I did it simply because I felt like doing it." But a radio program presupposes a lot of work. The immediate spontaneous act is better.

COLINA: An association of ideas, regarding the naked woman: in your films, you've generally refused nudity *à poil*. For example, there are nudes in *Un chien andalou*, but you don't see female pubic hair. In *Phantom*, there is full nudity and *à poil*. It's a very beautiful scene: an old woman in bed, the young lover pulls back the sheet and we see the woman's body. Surprisingly, it is a beautiful young body.

3 On Oct. 30, 1938, Orson Welles and the Mercury Theatre's special Halloween dramatization of H.G. Wells' *War of the Worlds* sparked a panic when radio listeners, tuning in late, believed the story was real. The incident brought Welles a certain notoriety, which eventually led to his RKO contract and the production of his masterpiece *Citizen Kane* (1941).

BUÑUEL: You can choose: it's either how the lover sees her... or it's that a true erotic miracle occurs. I clarify that the young man and his aunt are not yet lovers: they are going to be. Ah, I forgot the other possibility: there are women of advanced age who have surprisingly firm and well-formed bodies. I never saw my mother nude, but when she went out in the street at a very advanced age, people would turn around to look at her: she carried herself like a young woman.

TURRENT: There is another nude in *Phantom,* the police commissioner's sister.

BUÑUEL: It's an incomplete nudity. The sister is playing the piano in the parlor. It's a hot day and the police commissioner walks through the house with that laziness of the summer heat. We see only the sister's nude bust. The commissioner's lighter falls under the piano and he bends over to pick it up next to the girl's legs without so much as throwing a glance in their direction. I like this scene a lot. It's ambiguous.

COLINA: If there is no hint of incest, there's at least an idea of promiscuity.

BUÑUEL: Of course. The sister wears black silk stockings and high-heeled shoes. I make this observation so that you two can talk about "Monsieur Buñuel's obsessions."

COLINA: Within the summer relaxation, the moment has the intensity of something that has been lived. Does it come from some memory?

BUÑUEL: I have never had a sister, a lover, or anyone else play the piano nude, in the parlor or anywhere else.

TURRENT: In *The Phantom of Liberty,* we once again find the presence of animals and in a very disturbing manner, certainly...

BUÑUEL: Yes, a rooster and an ostrich appear in Jean-Claude Brialy's dream. No... It's not a dream; a restless sleep, or rather, that zone of consciousness between being asleep and awake. Animals are very vital beings, they make me happy. But they can be very disturbing when presented at a given moment out of context.

COLINA: We see the ostrich again at the end; in fact, the film concludes with him, looking at the audience.

BUÑUEL: To my judgment, it's the best part of the film. The head of that bird, its strange and almost feminine gaze, with its curly eyelashes — they weren't curled; they are like that naturally — and the background sound track: bells tolling, gunshots, shouts. I think it's disturbing.

COLINA: I see that animal's gaze as an expression of astonishment at human lunacy and as a reproach.

BUÑUEL: Perhaps, but I couldn't explain it. It's like the ending of *The Exterminating Angel*, an image that suddenly came into my mind with great strength and without apparent relation to the situation. I felt I had to end *The Phantom of Liberty* with the police charging the workers and students and with this animal's innocent gaze.

TURRENT: A very ambiguous episode, because of the everyday realism with which you present it, concerns the lost girl who is nevertheless present.

BUÑUEL: Another episode without an explanation. If you want to give it one, it can be this: the facility with which we stop seeing precisely that which is always in front of our eyes. It happens to me a lot: I can't find my lighter and wonder, "Where is it?" I look in several places and suddenly discover that it was in full view the entire time. It is so present that sight doesn't register it, and passes right over it. Instead of using a lighter in that episode, I thought the lost "object" should be a little girl. It's more interesting. The little girl tugs on her father's clothes and says, "Papa, here I am..." and the father tells her not to bother him because they are involved in a very serious matter...because this same little girl "is missing." For the adult characters, the little girl is there and she's not there.

TURRENT: Like liberty?

(Buñuel shrugs his shoulders.)

28: *CET OBSCUR OBJET DU DESIR* (THAT OBSCURE OBJECT OF DESIRE)

TOMAS PEREZ TURRENT: What is the "obscure object of desire"? The woman? Her sex organ? Her spirit?

LUIS BUÑUEL: I don't know. I think it could be all three of these things ...or none of them. For the protagonist, the object of desire may really be frustration, which excites his desire more. In Pierre Loüys' novel, it seems to me he says something like "a pale object of desire." I'm more interested in the opposite: an obscure object of desire.

JOSE DE LA COLINA: Dating from the time of its production, the film drew a lot of attention for an original and "absurd" idea: one character played by two actresses, and very different ones at that.

BUÑUEL: You two already know: it was out of necessity. I had originally thought that María Schneider would be good in the role. She's not a dazzling beauty and that would have worked because Fernando Rey's attraction to her would have been even more mysterious. I think she's good in other films, but in mine we didn't understand each other. We had to do one take after another, sometimes even with the easiest, most simple scenes. Finally, I had to tell Silberman, "I made a mistake with this woman. She isn't right for the part." Silberman was very upset and we couldn't come up with a solution. It was serious, because the production had already cost a lot of money. Then it suddenly came to me to say, "We could use two actresses..." Immediately after I said that, it seemed stupid to me. But to Silberman, it seemed magnificent. "No, Silberman, I said that without thinking." "But it seems very good to me, I accept it." So you see how something that seems so mysterious has an explanation.

COLINA: It doesn't have one, Don Luis, because it's logical that you would think of another actress, but not two.

TURRENT: And furthermore, they look nothing at all alike.

BUÑUEL: I don't know why I thought it should be two. It was automatic. I could have said two, three or ten. It makes no sense, but Silberman accepted it. Later, the critics' interpretations came.

COLINA: One critic, Emilio García Riera, told me at the end of the Mexican premiere that he could explain very easily why the protagonist was played by two women, "No one knows the person he loves, it's that person and at the same time, another."

BUÑUEL: García Riera is an intelligent fellow, but to me that seems very bad. The explanation is too logical, and I would have been embarrassed to have thought of it when I was making the film.

TURRENT: Besides, the easy thing would have been to change actresses every time the character changes her mood. But even in that case, the actress can be the same.

BUÑUEL: I've already told you, there is no rational explanation. I find it curious that audiences have accepted the constant change of actresses. At first, I thought, "They'll think they are two different characters." But it wasn't so; they accepted her as one single character. So you see that cinema is like a kind of hypnosis. There is no way you could confuse the two women in real life; they look very different.

TURRENT: It has also been explained in another manner: that woman is "the" woman: she represents all women in the world.

BUÑUEL: That is even worse — a symbol. No, my *trouvaille* is completely arbitrary. If my friend Silberman had told me my idea was stupid, I would have discarded it immediately. I can't explain why I thought of two actresses. In fact, I could have substituted only one of the actresses for Schneider, couldn't I? Either Angela Molina or Carole Bouquet...

COLINA: Another possible explanation: Fernando Rey is really in love with two women but he believes they are only one person.

BUÑUEL: That could perhaps be an interesting film, couldn't it? I think the two of you are only one person, and I don't even notice that you are two, and a series of episodes begins from there. Very good, but it would be another film. Forget about an explanation. There is none.

TURRENT: Did you distribute the scenes to the actresses at random?

BUÑUEL: Not at random. I didn't worry about which scene suited one and which scene suited the other, but I made sure that each had the same number of scenes.

TURRENT: You had tried before to make a film based on this novel by Loüys. I wonder what interested you in it.

BUÑUEL: The idea of a man who wants to sleep with a woman and never manages to. In the book, of course, the man ends up sleeping with her. Then she tells him, "If you want to see me sleep with another man, come to my house tomorrow." The next day he went, and there she was with another man. But I was more interested in the story of an obsession that can never become a reality.

TURRENT: As happens to many of your characters.

BUÑUEL: Yes, I have already told you that I am a man of fixed ideas. Perhaps I am only interested in only one kind of character, only a few situations.

COLINA: Why do we see various terrorist attacks on the margins of this "tale of passion," basically as if they had no importance?

BUÑUEL: That is a totally personal experience. At the time I made the film, I read the newspapers and I read about an attack here, another one there.

COLINA: That interests me because I believe that if you had intended to make a film with terrorism as the central theme, you would have to take into account that terrorism is so frequent today, so banal, that it is hardly noticed. The best film on the subject would show terrorism as something casual, on the sidelines, something off-frame.

BUÑUEL: All right, I accept that. Nowadays you can indeed be at a café talking with a lady friend. An explosion is heard, shouts, a police car's siren, and yet you go on with the conversation very calmly, without even turning around to see what has happened. In fact, that's what happens in my film. Every day the world grows more accustomed to terrorism; it has already become part of daily life, like smog and noise.

COLINA: It seems a bit arbitrary that Fernando Rey enters a train compartment and tells the story of his frustrations with Conchita to some people he doesn't even know.

TURRENT: It's the same as the lieutenant in *The Discreet Charm of the Bourgeoisie* who recounts his childhood to two women he doesn't know.

BUÑUEL: It's the same. I like arbitrary acts. But there is a motivation in *That Obscure Object of Desire*. Some people who are taking the train suddenly see a very respectable bourgeois gentleman throw a bucketful of water on a young woman. Then, to explain his actions, Fernando recounts his story about Conchita. I already know this motivation seems tacked on, but I don't care. So much the better, it can be more amusing.

COLINA: It seems to me that a key scene in the film is the one when

Conchita is in the garden with her lover; Fernando Rey sees them and becomes furious, but he can't do anything because there is a closed grille between them.

BUÑUEL: That was in the book. She says, "My guitar is mine and I can play it how I want."

COLINA: What catches my attention is that Fernando Rey doesn't seem very determined to leap over the obstacle that obstructs his entry in the garden and to punish Conchita and the other man.

BUÑUEL: No, it's that he can't jump over the grille. Not even if he were younger and stronger. Do you think he really enjoys the fact that she's betraying him with another man? No. That's not the film's theme — it's frustration. The same happens when she puts on a tight girdle as a type of chastity belt. He can't unfasten the bonds and she delights in his frustration.

COLINA: What is it that moves Conchita to behave like that with Fernando Rey's character?

BUÑUEL: A sadistic feeling. She takes advantage of him, she knows it's in her best interest to keep him happy, but at the same time she hates him to death, she enjoys tormenting him.

TURRENT: And he has a masochistic tendency?

BUÑUEL: Yes, in that they correspond to each other.

TURRENT: And it creates a very strong bond.

BUÑUEL: Very strong, and when all is said and done, it's the only thing that does exist between them. I don't like the ending, because we see him entering a shopping arcade with her, window shopping like a husband and wife. I should have stated there that the situation remains the same, he still hasn't managed to sleep with her. How do you two interpret it?

TURRENT: I am left with doubt.

COLINA: I thought they had slept together, because in a passageway window we see a woman who is embroidering and there is blood on the cloth mounted on an embroidery hoop. There is the immediate association of the broken hymen...

BUÑUEL: You see? It's badly done; it's not clear. I should have put in some phrases for her, something like, "Go to hell! I haven't slept with you, nor would I even consider it."

COLINA: But if you didn't want to suggest they slept together, why this image of the mended cloth?

BUÑUEL: I don't know, perhaps it seemed to me that we should see a homey scene in the window, a woman who sews tranquilly. What is misleading and was a bad idea of mine is the blood stain. I acknowledge that. A bad idea.

COLINA: It could be interpreted another way. For example, as Fernando Rey's desire to have really penetrated Conchita. The image of the hoop, the needle and thread penetrating the cloth, could crystallize his desire.

BUÑUEL: But that would be too illustrative. I wouldn't use that.

TURRENT: Why does Fernando Rey leave with Conchita carrying a bag that has no justification whatsoever in the scene?

BUÑUEL: It was a gag that came to me. The staff had left a bag with the wooden wedges from the dolly. Suddenly it came to me, for the scene in which Fernando Rey talks with her and says, "Why are you like this with me?" that he pick up the bag and toss it over his shoulder. Afterwards even I wondered: why did I do that? I wanted to take it out and I asked my son, Juan Luis, and Pierre Lary, who had seen the rushes, to tell me if it was bad. They told me that it was better with the bag, so I left it in.

COLINA: Let's go back a little, Don Luis, to the enigma of your titles. Why *Un chien andalou*, *L'Age d'or*, *The Exterminating Angel*, *The Phantom of Liberty*?

BUÑUEL: A title can give a film a richness that stimulates the imagination. The Surrealist painters gave their paintings titles that didn't correspond. For example: a picture showing a woman seated in a garden was titled: *Blessedness Will Come on the Day They Die*. Thus the painting acquired a new meaning which was odd, but not necessarily arbitrary. In my case, if a title suddenly imposes itself in my mind, I immediately decide that it's right. On the other hand, a more rational or deliberate title can seem too literary or explanatory to me, and I discard it.

TURRENT: Nevertheless, you have very precise titles: *Susana*, *El*, *Nazarín*, *Viridiana*, *Simon of the Desert*...

BUÑUEL: In those cases, the film's protagonist generally gave the title, but it can also be given by a region: *Las Hurdes*. I think the best ones are the precise titles or those which at first glance have nothing to do with the film. The worse titles are those with literary or symbolic pretensions. One of the worst is *Abismos de Pasión:*[1] it's cheap melodrama.

TURRENT: If *The Phantom of Liberty* were called anything else, let's say *A Journey Through Charming France*, would the public be aware that you raise the subject of freedom?

1 Literally *Abysses of Passion*, a.k.a. *Wuthering Heights*.

BUÑUEL: I don't know; a test would have to be made. In reality, the film does have something to do with liberty. "Down with liberty," or "Long live liberty." Both things, perhaps. What do you two think?

COLINA: Both things at the same time.

BUÑUEL: I'm not opposed to that interpretation, but I don't subscribe to it either.

TURRENT: But, does it have to do with liberty in social or political terms, or with the freedom to abandon oneself to chance?

BUÑUEL: It could also be — I don't assure this — both things.

COLINA: I think that by joining the two titles, we could have one that embraces all of Buñuel's films: *The Phantom of Liberty: That Obscure Object of Desire.*

BUÑUEL: It's good, even though it is too literary and *a posteriori*.

TURRENT: Do you concern yourself much with the structure of the script?

BUÑUEL: It interests me a lot, though I'm not a structuralist. Above all, I attempt to synthesize, to concentrate a three-minute scene into two minutes. But I don't have fixed norms: during a production I can include some bit that makes the scene last four minutes.

TURRENT: But do you first write a story and then worrry about structuring it?

BUÑUEL: At times the story is already written. This is the case when I am contracted to adapt a book. At other times, in the beginning there is no story, just an image that has some impact on me or a very lively memory. An example is *Viridiana*, but we've already talked enough about that. In general, while already writing the first treatment of a story, I begin thinking about it in terms of visual efficiency. I even have the editing of the shots in mind, particularly while I am filming. I am economical and don't shoot cutaways. The amount of film I shot for *The Phantom of Liberty* must be around eighteen thousand meters, and I have rarely gone beyond that.

TURRENT: Do your scripts have a lot of technical notations?

BUÑUEL: On the contrary, very few. I don't take the script to the studio, I take a sketch of the set, for example, a general idea of where the furniture goes. Once I'm on the set, then I indicate the movements of the actors and camera. I manage to see that the framing is functional and doesn't call attention to itself. When I watch films in which they've wanted to *épater* with the camera, I get up and leave the theater. Technical feats leave me cold.

TURRENT: Do you rehearse the actors a lot? Because filming the way you do implies that there are a lot of rehearsals...

BUÑUEL: In my case, it's the opposite. I only do one run-through before filming it. I also don't like to do a lot of takes. Of course, sometimes it's necessary to repeat a shot, for some detail that came out badly. But if there are too many takes, a moment comes when I finally get fed up and say, "Enough, no more." If you repeat a scene again and again, the actors become mechanical, everything becomes monotonous, without spontaneity.

COLINA: And when you finish the filming?

BUÑUEL: I relax for two days while the editor splices the shots together in order, including the *claques*. When that is ready, I begin selecting the takes and have them take out the clapperboards. I do this work very quickly: I do it in two or three days.

TURRENT: During the filming, do you go to see the rushes, the dailies?

BUÑUEL: Only at the beginning of the production, the first days. After that I rely on what the producer and my assistant tell me.

TURRENT: We've only talked a little about the sound track, the music.

BUÑUEL: I take great care with the sounds, because they can add a dimension that the image alone perhaps doesn't have. At times I'm interested in a noise that has nothing to do with the image and which gives it an enriching contrast. I put in less music with each film. When there is music, it has to be justified, you must be able to see where it comes from: a gramophone or a piano.

COLINA: In your first Mexican films, there is a lot of "commentary" music.

BUÑUEL: Too much. Today I would get rid of it. Music that comments on the action is an easy option. It usually serves to cover up the actors' or the director's mistakes. Sometimes, they've put in music despite me.

COLINA: As for the dialogue...

BUÑUEL: For me, dialogue must also be action. It must be brief and lively, to form part of the progression of the film. *The Milky Way* has a lot of dialogue, but it is inevitable there, because it argues abstract ideas. Despite that, I try to put it within a visual framework, like the elegant restaurant where they debate dogma.

COLINA: To conclude, Don Luis, we will pose two questions that came to us spontaneously.

BUÑUEL: Fine, especially if we conclude with them.

COLINA: If you were not a filmmaker, what would you like to have been?

BUÑUEL: A writer. Or painter... No, because I would have been a very bad painter, I have no talent for it. A writer, yes.

COLINA: A strange response, because you yourself have said that you are "agraphic, allergic to writing."

BUÑUEL: Yes, I am. But theoretically, I would be a writer, because a writer works in magnificent solitude, and if you want to represent, say, Judgment Day, you don't need millions of extras, or to use technical means, etc. Pencil and paper, nothing more. How wonderful! ...And the other question?

TURRENT: What is in the bag that the protagonist carries on his back in *That Obscure Object of Desire*?

BUÑUEL: What do you think it might contain?

COLINA: Everything that the protagonist of *Un chien andalou* pulled on the ropes.

TURRENT: Or his phantoms: that of liberty, those of desire.

BUÑUEL: I see only a man carrying a bag on his back and walking next to a woman, and they move away.

TURRENT: And with that image we can end the book.

BUÑUEL: So it's ended. We can have a drink. What will you have?

1900   Born February 22 in the town of Calanda, in the Aragon province of Teruel. Son of Leonardo Buñuel González and María Portolés Cerezuela, Buñuel is the oldest of seven brothers and sisters.

1903   The Buñuel family moves to Zaragoza.

1908-15   Buñuel studies his *bachillerato* at the Jesuit school Colegio del Salvador, and at the Instituto General y Técnico de Zaragoza.

1915-17   Buñuel finishes his degree at the Instituto de Segunda Enseñanza.

1917-25   Buñuel travels to Madrid and enters the Residencia de Estudiantes, where he meets future Spanish poets and intellectuals who would later be referred to as the "Generation of '27," including Federico García Lorca and Salvador Dalí.

1921   Buñuel does his military service.

1925   He moves to Paris to teach at the Institut International de Cooperation Intellectuelle. He meets a young gymnastics teacher, his future wife, Jeanne Rucar.

1926   In Amsterdam, Buñuel directs Manuel de Falla's *El retablo de Maese Pedro*. At the Cinéma Vieux Colombier he sees Fritz Lang's 1921 film *Der müde Tod (Destiny)*, which sparks his interest in cinema. He works as assistant director on Jean Epstein's film *Mauprat*.

1927   He works as second assistant director on *Siren of the Tropics,* directed by Henri Etiévant and Mario Nalpas, and starring Josephine Baker.

1928   He works as assistant director on *The Fall of the House of Usher,* by Jean Epstein. Buñuel begins writing his first screenplay, *El mundo por diez céntimos*. With a loan from his mother, he directs *Un chien andalou*, which he wrote with Salvador Dalí in six days.

1929   *Un chien andalou* is screened in Paris, where it attracts the attention of the Surrealist group. Buñuel joins the group, which later puts Buñuel on trial over publication of the film's script.

1930   Buñuel directs *L'Age d'or*, whose public screening at the cinema Studio 28 causes a scandal. Armed with stink bombs, a group of right-wing protesters splash ink on the screen, tear up seats, manhandle spectators, and slash paintings by Dalí, Joán Miró, Max Ernst, Man Ray, and Yves Tanguy, on display in the lobby.

1930-31   An MGM European representative, impressed with *L'Age d'or*, offers Buñuel an opportunity to visit Hollywood for six months to learn American film techniques.

1932   Back in Spain, Buñuel makes the documentary *Las Hurdes*. The film is banned for two years by the Republican government.

1933   He marries Jeanne Rucar in Paris.

1933-34   He works dubbing American films into Spanish for Warner Bros. in Madrid. He adapts Emily Brontë's *Wuthering Heights* as a screenplay.

1934   His son, Juan Luis, is born.

1935-36 He works as executive producer for the Spanish production company Filmófono, where Buñuel produces *Don Quintín el amargao, La hija de Juan Simón, ¿Quien me quiere a mí?* and *¡Centinela, alerta!*

1936-37 The Spanish Civil War breaks out and Buñuel works as an attaché at the Spanish Embassy in Paris, where he helps develop film propaganda for the Spanish cause. He supervises the production and editing of the documentary *España 1937/¡España leal en armas!*, directed by Jean-Paul Le Chanois.

1938-39 The Republican government sends Buñuel to Hollywood to supervise films on the Spanish Civil War. The war ends and Buñuel is left unemployed. Birth of his second son, Rafael.

1939-43 Buñuel works at the Museum of Modern Art in New York, where he edits anti-Nazi documentaries for the Office for Coordination of Inter-American Affairs. He resigns when Dalí's autobiography states that he is a Communist.

1944-45 He moves to Hollywood, where he works for Warner Bros. supervising Spanish dubbing.

1946 Buñuel designs an uncredited sequence for Robert Florey's *The Beast With Five Fingers*. En route to Europe, he goes to Mexico where producer Oscar Dancigers offers him the opportunity to direct the musical *Gran Casino*. He decides to stay in Mexico and applies for Mexican citizenship. He works on the Surrealist project *Ilegible, hijo de Flauta*, which is later abandoned.

1949 Buñuel directs *The Great Madcap*. He meets fellow countryman scriptwriter-director Luis Alcoriza. With Alcoriza, Buñuel writes *Si usted no puede, yo sí* (If You Can't, I Can), filmed by Julián Soler in 1950.

1950 Buñuel works on the project *Mi huerfanito, jefe!* (My Little Orphan, Boss!). He directs *Los olvidados*, which puts Buñuel's name back into the international spotlight by winning Best Director at the 1951 Cannes Film Festival, along with the FIPRESCI international critics award.

1951 Buñuel directs *Daughter of Deceit*, *A Woman Without Love*, and *Mexican Bus Ride*, which wins the international critics FIPRESCI award for best avant-garde film at the 1952 Cannes Film Festival.

1952 He directs *The Brute*, *Adventures of Robinson Crusoe*, and *El* (This Strange Passion). *Robinson Crusoe* earns actor Dan O'Herlihy an Oscar nomination when it is exhibited in the United States in 1954.

1953 He directs *Wuthering Heights* and *Illusion Travels by Streetcar*.

1954 He directs *The River and Death*.

1955 He directs *The Criminal Life of Archibaldo de la Cruz* and *Cela s'appelle l'aurore*.

1956 He directs *La mort en ce jardin*.

1957 He adapts Pierre Loüys' novel *La femme et le pantin*, later filmed in 1977 as *That Obscure Object of Desire*. With Alcoriza, he works on the project *Los náufragos de la calle Providencia*, filmed in 1962 as *The Exterminating Angel*.

1958 He directs *Nazarín*, which wins Buñuel a special mention and international jury prize at the 1959 Cannes Film Festival; ironically, the film picks up a National Catholic Film Office award for best foreign-language film in the United States in 1968.

1959 He directs *La fièvre monte à El Pao*.

1960 He directs *The Young One*.

1961 After a quarter century in exile, Buñuel returns to Spain to direct *Viridiana*, which wins the Palme d'Or and the Society of Film Writers award at the 1961 Cannes Film Festival, along with critics' prizes in Paris and Brussels. Although the script was approved by the government, the film is subsequently banned in Spain until after Franco's death, when it is honored by a special belated award at the 1984 Madrid International Film Festival. He meets the *Nuevo Cine* group in Mexico.

1962 Buñuel directs *The Exterminating Angel*, which wins the FIPRESCI International Critics Award at the 1962 Cannes Festival, in addition to prizes in Italy, Paris, and Argentina.

1963 He directs *Diary of a Chambermaid*, his first collaboration with French scriptwriter Jean-Claude Carrière, who was to work with Buñuel on six films in all.

1964 He directs *Simon of the Desert* which, due to lack of funds, has to be released as a short feature. Among other awards, the film picks up five prizes at the 1965 Venice International Film Festival. He works on the unrealized project *Cuatro misterios* (Four Mysteries) for Alatriste, which includes the tale of the lost girl that later appears in *The Phantom of Liberty*. He plays small parts in the films *Llanto por un bandito* and *En este pueblo no hay ladrones*.

1965 With Jean-Claude Carrière, he adapts *The Monk*, by Matthew Gregory Lewis. Although the project is abandoned, the script is filmed by Ado Kyrou in 1972.

1966 He directs *Belle de jour*, which wins the Golden Lion and independent critics award at the Venice Film Festival.

1968 He directs *The Milky Way*.

1969 He directs *Tristana* in Spain.

1972 He directs *The Discreet Charm of the Bourgeoisie*, which wins an Oscar for best foreign-language film. While Buñuel is in Los Angeles for the film's premiere there, George Cukor gives a lunch for him in Hollywood, attended by filmmakers John Ford, Alfred Hitchcock, William Wyler, Billy Wilder, George Stevens, Rouben Mamoulian, Robert Wise, and Robert Mulligan.

1974 He directs *The Phantom of Liberty*.

1977 He directs *That Obscure Object of Desire*.

1979 With Jean-Claude Carrière, Buñuel begins working on an original film project titled *Une cérémonie somptueuse*, which is later abandoned.

1982 He publishes his autobiography *My Last Sigh*, written with Jean-Claude Carrière. Buñuel publishes his collected literary works, *Obra literaria,* in Spain, introduced and annotated by Agustín Sánchez Vidal.

1983 Buñuel dies on July 29 in Mexico City.

1984 Max Aub publishes *Conversaciones con Buñuel* in Madrid.

1986 José de la Colina and Tomás Pérez Turrent publish *Prohibido asomarse al interior* (Objects of Desire: Conversations with Luis Buñuel) in Mexico City.

1990 Buñuel's wife, Jeanne Rucar de Buñuel, publishes her memoirs of her life with Buñuel, *Memorias de una mujer sin piano* (Memories of a Woman Without a Piano), which she wrote with Marisol Martín del Campo.

Below is a list of all completed films on which Buñuel worked either as a director, assistant director, producer, scriptwriter, editor, or actor. The year given is that of the film's release. Synopses are supplied only for the thirty-two films Buñuel directed which are discussed in this book.

Mauprat (1926)
Production Company: Films Jean Epstein (France)
Director: Jean Epstein
Assistant Director: Luis Buñuel
Screenplay: Jean Epstein, based on the novel by George Sand
Cinematography: Albert Duverger
Art Direction: Pierre Kéfer
Cast: Sandra Milowanoff, Maurice Schutz, Nino Constantini, René Ferte, Alex Allin, Bondireff, Jean Thiery, Halma, Lina Doré, Luis Buñuel (extra as a gendarme).
2000 meters (6563 feet). Silent. Black and white.

La sirène des tropiques/Siren of the Tropics (1927)
Production Company: Centrale Cinématographique (France)
Director: Henri Etiévant, Mario Nalpas
Assistant Director: Luis Buñuel
Screenplay: Maurice Dekobra
Cinematography: Albert Duverger, Paul Coteret, Hannebains
Art Direction: Jacques Natanson
Cast: Josephine Baker, Régina Dalthy, Pierre Batcheff, Janine Borelli, Colette Borelli, Régina Thomas, Georges Melchior.
2060 meters. Silent. Black and white.

La chute de la maison Usher/The Fall of the House of Usher (1928)
Production Company: Films Jean Epstein (France)
Director: Jean Epstein
Assistant Director: Luis Buñuel
Screenplay: Jean Epstein, based on *The Fall of the House of Usher, The Oval Portrait,* and *Beatrix,* by Edgar Allan Poe
Cinematography: Georges Lucas, Herbert
Art Direction: Pierre Kéfer
Cast: Jean Debucourt, Marguerite Denis-Gance, Charles Lamy, Pierre Hot, Fournez-Goffart, Halma, Luc Dartagnan, Pierre Kéfer.
1500 meters (4923 feet). Silent. Black and white.

Un chien andalou/An Andalusian Dog (1928-29)
Production Company: Luis Buñuel (France)
Director: Luis Buñuel
Screenplay: Luis Buñuel, Salvador Dalí
Cinematography: Albert Duverger
Editor: Luis Buñuel
Music: Passages from *Tristan and Isolde,* by Richard Wagner, and Argentine tangos (incorporated into a sound track in 1960)
Art Direction: Schilzneck
Cast: Pierre Batcheff (young man), Simone Mareuil (young woman), Xaume de Miravilles, Luis Buñuel, Salvador Dalí.
17 minutes. 430 meters. Black and white.
Synopsis: Once upon a time: A man (Luis Buñuel) slices the eyeball of a young woman (Simone Mareuil). A cloud passes over the moon. Eight years later: A cyclist (Pierre Batcheff) accidentally falls in the street. A young woman helps him and kisses him. The cyclist is reborn in a room and sexually pursues the young woman. From the window, the two contemplate a strange scene in the street below: in the middle of a crowd, an apparent hermaphrodite plays with an amputated hand and is then run over by an automobile. The cyclist fondles the woman, pursues her around the room, pulling diverse objects that are attached to two ropes (a piano, dead mules, etc.). Sixteen years earlier: A double appears and imposes scholastic punishments on the man. The cyclist shoots his double, who dies caressing a woman's torso. The young woman stares at a death's-head moth. The cyclist, reborn again, pursues the woman anew. She leaves the room and is at the beach, where she frolics happily with another young man. In springtime: The young woman and her new companion appear buried to the waist in the sand, devoured by insects under a powerful sun.

L'Age d'or/The Golden Age (1930)
Production Company: Le Vicomte de Noailles (France)
Director: Luis Buñuel
Screenplay: Luis Buñuel, with Salvador Dalí
Cinematography: Albert Duverger
Editor: Luis Buñuel
Music: Georges Von Parys, Mozart, Beethoven, Debussy, Mendelssohn, Wagner, drums of Calanda, a *pasodoble*
Art Direction: Schilzneck
Cast: Gaston Modot (man), Lya Lys (woman), Max Ernst (bandit chief), Pierre Prévert (Peman, bandit), Jacques B. Brunius, Caridad de Laberdesque, Pancho Cosío, Valentine Hugo, Marie Berthe Ernst, Simone Cottance, Paul Eluard, Manuel Angeles Ortiz, Juan Esplandio, Pedro Flores, Juan Castañe, Joaquín Roa, Pruna, Xaume de Miravilles, Lionel Salem, Liorens Artryas, José Artigas, Mme. Noizet, Duchange, Ibáñez.
63 minutes. Black and white.
Synopsis: Documentary prologue on the habits of scorpions. A bandit discovers a group of archbishops (the Mallorcans) saying Mass on the rocks, and he calls his band to attack, but they collapse one by one en route. The Mallorcans are now skeletons strewn around the rocks. A high society delegation arrives at the coast to found Imperial Rome on the remains of the Mallorcans. While they are placing the first stone, there is a scandal: a few steps away a man and a woman are rolling around in the mud, attempting to make love. They are separated and the man (Gaston Modot) is arrested. En route to jail, he thinks about the woman while exhibiting antisocial behavior, finally showing the policemen a diploma that was sup-

posedly conferred upon him for a goodwill mission. Taking advantage of the police confusion, he manages to escape. A formal party at the aristocratic home belonging to the parents of the young woman (Lya Lys), who also thinks about the man. The protagonist enters and continues his outrageous behavior while disturbing incidents take place around them: the servants' quarters burn, a game warden shoots and kills his own son, some peasants drive a wagon through the drawing room, etc. The lovers try to make love in the garden, but various circumstances impede them. Furious, the protagonist insults a government minister, who commits suicide, then plunders the mansion, throwing various items out of the window: a pine tree, a giraffe, a plow, feathers from a pillow, a bishop. At the same time, four characters from the Marquis de Sade's book *120 Days of Sodom* leave the Château de Selliny, appearing to have emerged from an orgy. One of them, the Count of Blangis, who looks like Christ, re-enters the castle with a wounded girl and a shout is heard. When the count re-emerges, his beard has been shaven. A Spanish *pasodoble* is heard while the wind rustles heads of hair that have been nailed to a cross.

Las Hurdes (Tierra sin pan)/Land Without Bread/Unpromised Land (1932)
Production Company: Ramón Acín (Spain)
Director: Luis Buñuel
Screenplay: Luis Buñuel, based on a book by Maurice Legendre
Cinematography: Eli Lotar
Editor: Luis Buñuel
Commentary: Text by Luis Buñuel, Pierre Unik, read by Abel Jacquin
Music: Brahms Fourth Symphony (text and music sound track were added in 1937, when the film was distributed by Pierre Braunberger)
27 minutes. Black and white.
Synopsis: A travelogue about one of the most backward regions of Spain. There are no songs, the people have never eaten bread, the houses have neither windows nor chimneys. Malnutrition and unhealthy living conditions cause malaria, goiters, cretinism, dwarfism. Young people emigrate in search of work; women grow old prematurely. An old woman strolls through the streets at night ringing a bell and calling out to remind everyone that all men are mortal. The teacher instructs children to respect private property. A donkey dies on the road and is devoured by wasps. The corpse of a child in a coffin is carried across a river. The filmmakers return to Madrid.

Don Quintín el amargao (1935)
Production Company: Ricardo Urgoiti, Filmófono (Spain)
Executive Producer: Luis Buñuel
Director: Luis Marquina
Assistant Director: José Martín, Francisco Lejuela
Screenplay: Eduardo Ugarte, Luis Buñuel, based on the play by Carlos Arniches and José Estremera
Cinematography: José María Beltrán
Editor: Eduardo G. Maroto, Luis Buñuel
Music: Jacinto Guerrero, Fernando Remacha
Sound: León Lucas de Lapeña
Art Direction: Mariano Espinosa
Sets: José María Torres
Cast: Ana María Custodio (Teresa), Alfonso Muñoz (Don Quintín), Luisita Esteso (Felisa), Fernando Granada (Paco), Luis Heredia (Angelito), Isabel Noguera (Margot), Porfiria

Sánchez (María), José Alfayate (Sefini), Manuel Arbo, Erna Rosal, Consuelo Nievea, José Marco Davo, María Amaya, Jacinto Higueras, Isabelita Urcola, Manuel Vico.
85 minutes. Black and white.

La hija de Juan Simón (1935)
Production Company: Ricardo Urgoiti, Filmófono (Spain)
Executive Producer: Luis Buñuel
Directors: Nemesio M. Sobrevila, Eduardo Ugarte, José Luis Sáenz de Heredia, Luis Buñuel (uncredited)
Assistant Director: Honorio Martínez
Screenplay: Nemesio M. Sobrevila, Eduardo Ugarte, Luis Buñuel, based on the play by Sobrevila
Cinematography: José María Beltrán
Editor: Eduardo G. Maroto
Music: Fernando Remacha, Daniel Montorio, lyrics by Mauricio Torres
Sound: Antonio Fernando Roces
Art Direction: Nemesio M. Sobrevila, Mariano Espinosa
Cast: Angel Sampedro "Angelillo," Pilar Muñoz (Carmen), Carmen Amaya (Soledad), Manuel Arbo (Juan Simón), Ena Sedeno (Angustias), Porfiria Sánchez (La Roja), Candida Losada (Trini), Emilio Portes (Don Severo), Julian Pérez de Avila (Carlos), Fernando Freire de Andrade (Don Paco), Pablo Hidalgo (Curro), Angelito Sampedro, Baby Deny.
95 minutes. Black and white.

¿Quien me quiere a mí? (1936)
Production Company: Ricardo Urgoiti, Filmófono (Spain)
Executive Producer: Luis Buñuel
Director: José Luis Sáenz de Heredia
Screenplay: Eduardo Ugarte, Luis Buñuel, based on a story by Enrique Horta
Cinematography: José María Beltrán
Editor: Luis Buñuel
Music: Fernando Remacha, Juan Telería
Sound: León Lucas de la Peña
Art Direction: Mariano Espinosa
Cast: Lina Yegros (Marta Velez), José Baviera (Alfredo Flores), Mari-Tere, José María Linares Rivas (Eduardo), Fernando Frerre de Andrede (El Aguila), Luis de Heredia (El Lentes), Carlos del Pozo (Don Ramón), Manuel Arbo (Cintohio Reyes), Emilio Portes (Editor), Raúl Cancio (drug addict), Pablo Hidalgo, Juan de las Heras, Luis Ardenillo, Francisco René.
80 minutes. Black and white.

¡Centinela alerta! (1936)
Production Company: Ricardo Urgoiti, Filmófono (Spain)
Executive Producer: Luis Buñuel
Directors: Jean Grémillon (uncredited), Luis Buñuel (uncredited)
Screenplay: Eduardo Ugarte, Luis Buñuel, based on the comedy *La alegría del batallón,* by Carlos Arniches
Cinematography: José María Beltrán
Editor: Jean Grémillon
Music: Fernando Remacha, lyrics by Daniel Montoro

Sound: León Lucas de la Peña
Cast: Angel Sampedro "Angelillo," Ana María Custodio, Luis Heredia, Mari-Tere, José María Linares Rivas, Raúl Cancio, Mary Cortés, Pablo Hidalgo, Emilio Portes, Pablo Alvarez Rubio, Mario Padreco.
90 minutes. Black and white.

España 1937/¡España Leal en Armas! (1937)
Production Company: Ciné Liberté (France)
Supervision: Luis Buñuel
Assembly of Material: Luis Buñuel
Cinematography: Roman Karmen, Manuel Villagas López
Commentary: Pierre Unik, Luis Buñuel, read by Gaston Modot
Editor: Jean Paul Dreyfus (Jean-Paul Le Chanois)
Music: Beethoven's Seventh and Eighth Symphonies
40 minutes. Black and white.

Triumph of Will (1939)
Production Company: Museum of Modern Art, Kenneth MacGowan (United States)
Director: Luis Buñuel
Commentary: Luis Buñuel
Editor: Luis Buñuel
Nine-reel montage composed of material from Leni Riefenstahl's *Triumph des Willens* (The Triumph of the Will, 1935), and Hans Bertram's *Vuurdoop* (Baptism of Fire, 1939)
Black and white.
NOTE: Although New York's Museum of Modern Art documents that Buñuel worked at the museum as part of the Office for Coordination of Inter-American Affairs, and it does have a short version of Leni Riefensthal's *Triumph of Will* in its archives, it has no documentation of Buñuel's participation on this film and will not confirm his work on it. On Feb. 5, 1982, Buñuel responded in rough English to MOMA film curator William Sloane about the work: "*The Triumph of Will* of Lenie (sic) Riefenstal (sic) and *The Conquest of Poland* (sic) — I don't remember the name of the author — were about 12 reels each one. Iris Barry asked me to make with both films a single one of about 12 reels. During the last war this work was sent to the American consulates of this continent on behalf of anti-Nazi propaganda. I have never heard about my work since 1948."

The Beast With Five Fingers (1946)
Production Company: Warner Bros.
Director: Robert Florey
Cinematography: Wesley Anderson
Editor: Frank Magee
Art Direction: Stanley Fleischer
Special Sequence: Luis Buñuel (uncredited)
Cast: Robert Alda, Andrea King, Peter Lorre, Victor Francen, J. Carrol Naish, Charles Dingle.
88 minutes. Black and white.

Gran Casino (En el Viejo Tampico) (1946)
Production Company: Ultramar Films, Películas Anáhuac, Oscar Dancigers (Mexico)
Director: Luis Buñuel

Screenplay: Mauricio Magdaleno, Edmundo Báez, based on the novel *El rugido del paraíso,* by Michel Weber
Cinematography: Jack Draper
Editor: Gloria Schoemann
Music: Manuel Esperón, songs: "Dueño de mi amor," by Manuel Esperón, "Adios, pampa mia," by Francisco Canaro and Mariano Mores, "El choclo," by A. G. Villoldo, "El reflector del amor," by Francisco Alonso, "La norteña," by F. Vigil.
Sound: Javier Mateos, José de Pérez
Art Direction: Javier Torres Torija
Cast: Libertad Lamarque (Mercedes Irigoyen), Jorge Negrete (Gerardo Ramírez), Mercedes Barba (Camelia), Agustín Isunza (Heriberto), Julio Villareal (Demetrio García), Alfonso Bedoya (El Rayado), Fernanda Albany (Nanette), Berta Linar (Raquel), José Baviera (Flavio), Francisco Jambrina (José Enrique), Charles Rooner (Van Eckerman), the "Los Calaveras" Trio, Ignacio Peón, Julio Ahuet, Juan García.
85 minutes. Black and white.
Synopsis: The story supposedly takes place before Mexico's petroleum industry was nationalized. After escaping from jail, three adventurers are hired by a petroleum company in Tampico. One of them, Gerardo Ramírez (Jorge Negrete), meets Camelia (Meche Barba), a rumba dancer at a casino owned by Fabio (José Baviera). Fabio wants to take over the oil wells belonging to Gerardo's boss and friend José Enrique (Francisco Jambrina), and he has José Enrique killed. When José's sister Mercedes (Libertad Lamarque) arrives in Tampico, she suspects Gerardo of her brother's murder. Mercedes is hired to sing at the casino. Fabio is in cahoots with the German Van Eckerman (Charles Rooner) to steal the oil wells. After her suspicions are lain to rest, Mercedes and Geraldo fall in love. Gerardo then wounds Fabio, killing his accomplice, who had been preparing a trap to murder him. In order to free Gerardo, Mercedes sells the oil wells to Van Eckerman. Before leaving Tampico, Gerardo, Mercedes, and their friends blow up the wells.

El gran calavera/The Great Madcap (1949)
Production Company: Ultramar Films, Fernando Soler, Oscar Dancigers (Mexico)
Director: Luis Buñuel
Assistant Director: Moises Delgado
Screenplay: Luis and Janet Alcoriza, based on the comedy by Adolfo Torrado
Cinematography: Ezequiel Carrasco
Editor: Carlos Savage, Luis Buñuel
Music: Manuel Esperón
Sound: Rafael Ruiz Esparza
Art Direction: Luis Moya, Dario Cabañas
Cast: Fernando Soler (Don Ramíro), Rosario Granados (Virginia), Andrés Soler (Ladislao), Rubén Rojo (Pablo), Gustavo Rojo (Eduardo), Maruja Grifell (Milagros), Francisco Jambrina (Gregorio), Luis Alcoriza (Alfredo), Antonio Bravo (Alfonso), Nicolás Rodríguez (Carmelito), Antonio Monsell (Juan, butler), María Luisa Serano, Juan Pulido, Pepe Martínez, José Chávez, Gerardo Pérez Martínez.
90 minutes. Black and white.
Synopsis: Ramiro (Fernando Soler) is a rich drunk whose behavior shocks his lazy, parasitic family. Dr. Gregorio (Francisco Jambrina) comes up with a plan to reform Ramiro: the family must make him believe he has been unconscious for an entire year, during which time the family has fallen into poverty. To carry out this scheme, the family moves to a poor neighborhood and everyone finds humble jobs. When Ramiro learns of the plan, he uses it in his

favor; not only does he change his ways, the family also changes. His children, Virginia (Rosario Granados) and Eduardo (Gustavo Rojo), become useful members of society. Virginia is going to marry the vain Alfredo (Luis Alcoriza), but the wedding is interrupted at the last moment by Virginia's real love, a working-class young man named Pablo (Rubén Rojo). In the end, the family returns to its wealthy lifestyle, much the better for their experience.

Los olvidados/The Young and the Damned (1950)
Production Company: Ultramar Films, Oscar Dancigers, Jaime Menasce (Mexico)
Director: Luis Buñuel
Screenplay: Luis Buñuel, Luis Alcoriza, Max Aub (uncredited), Pedro de Urdimalas (uncredited)
Cinematography: Gabriel Figueroa
Editor: Carlos Savage, Luis Buñuel
Music: Rodolfo Halffter, based on themes by Gustavo Pittaluga
Sound: José B. Carles, Jesús González Gancy
Art Direction: Edward Fitzgerald
Cast: Stella Inda (Pedro's Mother), Miguel Inclán (blind man), Alfonso Mejía (Pedro), Roberto Cobo (El Jaibo), Alma Delia Fuentes (Meche), Francisco Jambrina (farm school director), Efraín Arauz (Poxface), Javier Amezcua (Julián), Mario Ramírez (El Ojitos), Charles Rooner, Sergio Villareal, Jesús García Navarro, Jorge Pérez, Angel Merino.
88 minutes. Black and white.
Synopsis: In a poor Mexico City neighborhood, a young delinquent, "El Jaibo" (Roberto Cobo), forms a gang. They try to rob an old blind beggar, Don Carmelo (Miguel Inclán), but he wounds one of the boys by striking him with his cane. The gang later stones the blind man. One of its members, Pedro (Alfonso Mejía), whose mother shows him no affection, becomes El Jaibo's inseparable companion. At the market, Pedro meets a young peasant boy who has lost his father and takes him to the house where Meche (Alma Delia Fuentes) lives. The young peasant boy, nicknamed "El Ojitos" (Mario Ramírez), becomes blind Don Carmelo's helper. In Pedro's presence, El Jaibo kills a boy, Julián (Javier Amezcua), who he thinks betrayed him. The murder haunts Pedro and El Jaibo imposes a pact of silence. After fighting with his mother, Pedro gets a job at a knife-sharpening shop. El Jaibo seduces Pedro's mother (Stella Inda), then visits Pedro at work, stealing a knife. Pedro is accused of the robbery and is sought by the police. His mother takes him to the Youth Correctional Center, and the boy enters a farm school, whose director, in order to prove his trust in the boy, sends him out to buy some cigarettes with a fifty peso bill. El Jaibo steals the money from Pedro and runs off. Pedro looks for him, they argue, and fight. Pedro accuses El Jaibo of killing Julián. Don Carmelo tries to abuse Meche sexually, but is stopped by El Ojitos. El Jaibo finds Pedro and kills him in revenge for the betrayal. The police kill El Jaibo while trying to arrest him. Meche and her father throw Pedro's body on a garbage dump, while his mother looks for him everywhere.

Susana (Demonio y carne)/The Devil and the Flesh (1950)
Production Company: Sergio Kogan, Internacional Cinematográfica, S.A., Manuel Reachi (Mexico)
Director: Luis Buñuel
Screenplay: Luis Buñuel, Jaime Salvador, Rodolfo Usigli, based on a story by Manuel Reachi
Cinematography: José Ortiz Ramos
Editor: Jorge Bustos

Music: Raúl Lavista
Sound: Nicolás de la Rosa
Art Direction: Gunther Gerzso
Cast: Rosita Quintana (Susana), Fernando Soler (Don Guadalupe), Víctor Manuel Mendoza (Jesús), Matilde Palou (Doña Carmen), María Gentil Arcos (Felisa), Luis López Somoza (Alberto).
82 minutes. Black and white.
Synopsis: One stormy night, Susana (Rosita Quintana) escapes from a women's correctional center and arrives at the ranch of rich and honorable Don Guadalupe (Fernando Soler), who gives her shelter. At first, everyone thinks Susana is a good woman, but with her alluring beauty she immediately begins to disrupt the happy household, successively conquering the foreman, Jesús (Víctor Manuel Mendoza), the son, Alberto (Luis López Somoza), and finally the patriarch Don Guadalupe himself. His wife, Doña Carmen (Matilde Paloa), and an old servant, Felisa (María Gentil Arcos), can only look on indignantly as Susana sets the menfolk against each other. When he sees Doña Carmen whipping Susana, Don Guadalupe tells his wife she must leave the ranch, while Susana will stay. Finally, Jesús leads the police to Susana and she is returned to prison. Life at the ranch returns to its paradisal state once again.

Si Usted no puede, yo sí (1950)
Production Company: Ultramar Films, Oscar Dancigers (Mexico)
Director: Julián Soler
Screenplay: Luis Buñuel, Luis and Janet Alcoriza
Cinematography: José Ortiz Ramos
Editor: Carlos Savage
Music: Manuel Esperón
Art Direction: Edward Fitzgerald
Cast: Pepe Iglesias, Alma Rosa Aguirre, Fernando Soto "Mantequilla," Julio Villarreal.
95 minutes. Black and white.

La hija del engaño/Daughter of Deceict (1951)
Production Company: Ultramar Films, Oscar Dancigers (Mexico)
Director: Luis Buñuel
Screenplay: Luis and Janet Alcoriza, based on the play *Don Quintín el amargao,* by Carlos Arniches and José Estremera
Cinematography: José Ortiz Ramos
Editor: Carlos Savage, Luis Buñuel
Music: Manuel Esperón, songs: "Amorcito Corazón," "Jugando, Mamá, Jugando"
Sound: Eduardo Arjona
Art Direction: Edward Fitzgerald
Cast: Fernando Soler (Don Quintín), Alicia Caro (Marta), Fernando Soto (Mantequilla), Rubén Rojo (Paco), Nacho Contla (Jonrón), Amparo Garrido (María), Lily Aclemar (Jovita), Alvaro Matute (Julio), Roberto Meyer (Lencho García), Conchita Gentil Arcos (Toño).
80 minutes. Black and white.
Synopsis: Traveling salesman Don Quintín (Fernando Soler) is bitter because he believes that nothing comes out well for him. When he returns home unexpectedly and surprises his wife with another man, he throws her out of the house. In retaliation, she tells him that Marta is not his daughter, and Don Quintín leaves the little girl on the doorstep of the drunkard Lencho (Roberto Meyer), who takes her in and brings her up as his own daughter.

Disappointed that his good behavior has not been rewarded, Don Quintín buys a cabaret and treats everyone tyrannically. Marta (Alicia Caro) grows up and marries Paco (Rubén Rojo). Before dying, Don Quintín's ex-wife confesses that Marta really is his daughter, and Don Quintín wants to get his daughter back. One day he has a serious fight with Paco and at the last minute discovers that Paco is really his son-in-law. Reconciliation and happy ending... (Despite the fact he is happy to be a grandfather, Don Quintín has a momentary doubt that nothing good will come of it.)

Una mujer sin amor (Cuando los hijos nos juzgan)/A Woman Without Love (1951)
Production Company: Sergio Kogan, Internacional Cinematográfica, S.A. (Mexico)
Director: Luis Buñuel
Screenplay: Jaime Salvador, based on the novel *Pierre et Jean*, by Guy de Maupassant
Cinematography: Raúl Martínez Solares
Editor: Jorge Bustos
Music: Raúl Lavista
Sound: Rodolfo Benítez
Art Direction: Gunther Gerzso
Cast: Rosario Granados (Rosario), Julio Villareal (Carlos Montero), Tito Junco (Julio Mistral), Joaquín Cordero (Carlos Jr.), Xavier Loyá (Miguel), Elda Peralta (Dr. Luisa), Jaime Calpe (Carlitos), Miguel Manzano, Eva Calvo.
90 minutes. Black and white.
Synopsis: Antiquarian Carlos Montero (Julio Villarreal) is married to Rosario (Rosario Granados) and they have a son, Carlitos, who is driven from the house by his father's severity. Carlitos is taken in by the engineer Julio Mistral (Tito Junco). Julio and Rosario become lovers, and Rosario gives birth to Julio's son Miguel, who Montero raises as his own son. Miguel and Carlitos grow up together and both become doctors. Carlos Jr. (Joaquín Cordero) falls in love with Dr. Luisa (Elda Peralta), who is in love with Miguel (Xavier Loyá). When Julio dies, leaving Miguel his inheritance, Carlos Jr. becomes suspicious of his mother. Miguel and Luisa marry. Montero dies and leaves his clinic to both Carlos and Miguel. They fight and Rosario pulls them apart, telling them the truth about Miguel's father. The brothers reconcile, and Miguel and Luisa stay together while Rosario remains alone, rejected by Carlos.

Subida al cielo/Mexican Bus Ride (1951)
Production Company: Producciones Isla, Manuel Altolaguirre, María Luisa Gómez Mena (Mexico)
Director: Luis Buñuel
Screenplay: Manuel Altolaguirre, Juan de la Cabada, Luis Buñuel, Lilia Solano Galeana
Cinematography: Alex Phillips
Editor: Rafael Portillo, Luis Buñuel
Music: Gustavo Pittaluga, song: "La sanmarqueña," by Agustín Jiménez
Sound: Eduardo Arjona, Jesús González Gancy
Art Direction: José Rodríguez Granada, Edward Fitzgerald
Cast: Lilia Prado (Raquel), Carmen González (Albina), Esteban Márquez (Oliverio), Leonor Gómez (Mother), Luis Aceves Castañeda (Silvestre), Manuel Dondé (Don Eladio González), Roberto Cobo (Juan), Víctor Pérez (Felipe), Paz Villegas (Ester), Francisco Reiguera (Miguel Suárez), Roberto Meyer (Don Nemesio), Beatriz Ramos (expectant mother), Paula Rendón (Silvestre's mother), Pedro Elviro "Pitouto" (peg leg), Pedro Ibarra, Manuel Noriega, Chel López, Silvia Castro.

85 minutes. Black and white.

Synopsis: In a small Mexican coastal village, Oliverio Grajales (Esteban Márquez) and Albina (Carmen González) marry but can't enjoy their wedding night because Oliverio's mother Ester (Paz Villegas) is dying. Oliverio's brothers, Felipe (Víctor Pérez) and Juan (Roberto Cobo), conspire to keep the entire inheritance. In order to stop them, Ester begs Oliverio to find a friendly lawyer in another town to draw up a will. Oliverio takes a bus, driven by Silvestre (Luis Aceves Castañeda), and the journey is eventful: the sexy Raquel (Lilia Prado) seduces Oliverio at a mountainous point on the highway called *Subida al Cielo* (Gate to Heaven); a politician named Figueroa (Manuel Dondé) is booed by the town he represents, etc. Because of these delays, by the time Oliverio returns his mother has already died. Oliverio signs the will using his dead mother's fingerprint and the newlyweds' future is assured.

El bruto/The Brute (1952)
Production Company: Internacional Cinematográfica, Sergio Kogan (Mexico)
Director: Luis Buñuel
Screenplay: Luis Buñuel, Luis Alcoriza
Cinematography: Agustín Jiménez
Editor: Jorge Bustos, Luis Buñuel
Music: Raúl Lavista
Sound: Javier Mateos, Galdino Samperio
Art Direction: Gunther Gerzso
Cast: Pedro Armendáriz (Pedro, "the Brute"), Katy Jurado (Paloma), Rosita Arenas (Meche), Andrés Soler (Andrés Cabrera), Roberto Meyer (Don Carmelo), Beatriz Ramos, Paco Martínez, Gloria Mestre, Paz Villegas.
83 minutes. Black and white.

Synopsis: Landlord Andrés Cabrera (Andrés Soler) wants to evict the poor tenants from a tenement in order to sell the land. Led by Don Carmelo (Roberto Meyer), the tenants oppose him, so Cabrera hires Pedro "the Brute" (Pedro Armendáriz), who is in his debt. The Brute, who works at the Rastro slaughterhouse, terrorizes the tenants and beats Don Carmelo so brutally that he dies shortly afterwards. The Brute is seduced by Cabrera's lover, the coquettish Paloma (Katy Jurado). The tenants surprise the Brute and wound him. Carmelo's daughter Meche (Rosita Arenas) shelters the wounded man and the two fall in love. Jealous, Paloma tells Meche that the Brute killed her father. The Brute hits Paloma and she goes to Cabrera, telling him that the Brute has tried to rape her. Cabrera upbraids Pedro and tries to shoot him, but the Brute beats him to death. The police pursue Pedro and kill him.

Adventures of Robinson Crusoe/Robinson Crusoe (1952)
Production Company: Ultramar Films, Oscar Dancigers, OLMEC (United Artists), Henry F. Ehrlich (Mexico-United States)
Director: Luis Buñuel
Screenplay: Luis Buñuel, Phillip Ansel Roll (pseudonym for Hugo Butler), based on the novel by Daniel Defoe
Cinematography: Alex Phillips
Editor: Carlos Savage, Luis Buñuel, Alberto Valenzuela
Music: Luis Hernández Bretón, Anthony Collins
Sound: Javier Mateos
Art Direction: Edward Fitzgerald
Cast: Dan O'Herlihy (Robinson Crusoe), Jaime Fernández (Friday), Felipe de Alba (Captain

Oberzo), Chel López (Bosun), José Chávez (mutineer), Emilio Garibay (mutineer).
89 minutes. Color.
Synopsis: Robinson Crusoe (Dan O'Herlihy) is shipwrecked and reaches a desert island. He survives, constructing a hut and enclosure; he builds various objects, and cultivates the land. One day he meets a young savage, Friday (Jaime Fernández); at first he forces Friday to be his servant before establishing a friendship with him. The two fight some pirates, are rescued, and return to civilization.

El/This Strange Passion (1952)
Production Company: Ultramar Films, Oscar Dancigers (Mexico)
Director: Luis Buñuel
Screenplay: Luis Buñuel, Luis Alcoriza, based on the novel by Mercedes Pinto
Cinematography: Gabriel Figueroa
Editor: Carlos Savage, Luis Buñuel
Music: Luis Hernández Bretón
Sound: José D. Pérez, Jesús González Gancy
Art Direction: Edward Fitzgerald, Pablo Galván
Cast: Arturo de Córdova (Francisco Galván), Delia Garcés (Gloria), Luis Beristáin (Raúl), Aurora Walker (Doña Esperanza), Carlos Martínez Baena (Father Velasco), Rafael Banquells (Ricardo), Manuel Dondé (Pablo), Fernando Casanova (Beltrán), José Pidal, Roberto Maya.
100 minutes. Black and white.
Synopsis: The rich Francisco Galván (Arturo de Córdova), a man of honor, falls in love with Gloria (Delia Garcés) and marries her. Afterwards, he suddenly exhibits profound jealousy. When Francisco becomes violent, his wife complains to her mother (Aurora Walker) and to her husband's confessor (Carlos Martínez Baena), but they don't believe her. Raúl (Luis Beristáin), a friend of Francisco and Gloria's former boyfriend, does believe her. Gloria escapes from the house and Francisco searches for her. He thinks he sees her enter a church, accompanied by Raúl, and follows. In the church, he raves and attacks a priest. He is committed to an ayslum. Years later, he lives in apparent peace at a monastery. But at the end, we see him zig-zag down the path as during his paranoia attacks.

Abismos de pasión/Cumbres borrascosas/Wuthering Heights (1953)
Production Company: Producciones Tepeyac, Oscar Dancigers, Abelardo L. Rodríguez (Mexico)
Director: Luis Buñuel
Screenplay: Luis Buñuel, Julio Alejandro, Arduino Maiuri, Pierre Unik, based on the novel *Wuthering Heights*, by Emily Brontë.
Cinematography: Agustín Jiménez
Editor: Carlos Savage, Luis Buñuel
Music: Raúl Lavista, based on themes from *Tristan and Isolde,* by Richard Wagner
Sound: Eduardo Arjona, Galindo Samperio
Art Direction: Edward Fitzgerald, Raymundo Ortiz
Cast: Irasema Dilián (Catalina), Jorge Mistral (Alejandro), Lilia Prado (Isabel), Ernesto Alonso (Eduardo), Luis Aceves Castañeda (Ricardo), Francisco Reiguera (José), Hortensia Santoveña (María), Jaime González (Jorge).
90 minutes. Black and white.
Synopsis: After a ten-year absence, Alejandro (Jorge Mistral) returns to the country estate where his childhood sweetheart Catalina (Irasema Dilián) lives. As a child, Alejandro was

adopted by Catalina's parents; he now returns rich and ready to marry Catalina who, in the meantime, has married Eduardo (Ernesto Alonso) and is expecting his child. Catalina refuses to leave Eduardo. In revenge, Alejandro marries Eduardo's sister Isabel (Lilia Prado), whom he treats badly. He also treats Catalina's brother Ricardo (Luis Aceves Castañeda) like a servant because Ricardo had mistreated him in their childhood. Alejandro and Eduardo have a violent fight. Catalina confesses that she has always loved Alejandro and dies in childbirth. When Alejandro enters Catalina's tomb to kiss her corpse, Ricardo kills him. Catalina and Alejandro's souls unite in the afterlife.

La ilusión viaja en tranvía/Illusion Travels by Streetcar (1953)
Production Company: Clasa Films Mundiales, Armando Orive Alba (Mexico)
Director: Luis Buñuel
Screenplay: Luis Buñuel, Mauricio de la Serna, José Revueltas, Luis Alcoriza, Juan de la Cabada
Cinematography: Raúl Martínez Solares
Editor: Jorge Bustos, Luis Buñuel
Music: Luis Hernández Bretón
Sound: José D. Pérez
Art Direction: Edward Fitzgerald
Cast: Lilia Prado (Lupita), Carlos Navarro (Caireles), Fernando Soto "Mantequilla" (Tarrajas), Agustín Isunza (Papá Pinillos), José Pidal (Professor), Paz Villegas (Doña Mechita), Miguel Manzano, Conchita Gentil Arcos, Javier de la Parra, Guillermo Bravo Sosa, Felipe Montoyo, Fernando Soto.
90 minutes. Black and white.
Synopsis: Caireles (Carlos Navarro) and Tarrajas (Fernando Soto "Mantequilla") learn that the streetcar in which they have been working as driver and ticket taker for many years is going to be retired from service. They get drunk and decide to steal the streetcar and take it on a final nocturnal tour of the city. Along the way, they pick up diverse characters and have some surprising experiences: butchers from the Rastro slaughterhouse board the streetcar with pieces of meat, some pious women board carrying the image of a saint, children from an orphanage get on, etc. Meanwhile, they are pursued by Papá Pinillos (Agustín Isunza), a retired streetcar inspector who has taken it upon himself to expose them. Tarrajas' sister Lupita (Lilia Prado) helps the two friends. During the trip, which lasts until the following morning, Caireles and Tarrajas fight with some black marketeers. There is also a holiday celebration during which the tenants in the neighborhood perform a morality play. In the morning, the streetcar is returned to the train yard just in time. Caireles and Lupita become a couple.

El río y la muerte/The River and Death (1954)
Production Company: Clasa Films Mundiales, Amando Orive Alba (Mexico)
Director: Luis Buñuel
Screenplay: Luis Buñuel, Luis Alcoriza, based on the novel *Muro blanco sobre roca negra*, by Miguel Alvarez Acosta
Cinematography: Raúl Martínez Solares
Editor: Jorge Bustos, Luis Buñuel
Music: Raúl Lavista
Sound: José D. Pérez
Art Direction: Gunther Gerzso
Cast: Columba Domínguez (Mercedes), Miguel Torruco (Felipe Anguiano), Joaquín

Cordero (Gerardo Anguiano), Jaime Fernández (Rómulo Menchaca), Víctor Alcocer (Polo), Silvia Derbez (Elsa), Jorge Arriaga (Filogonio Menchaca), Humberto Almazán (Crescencio), Alfredo Varela, Jr. (Chinelas), José Elías Moreno, Carlos Martínez Baena, Miguel Manzona, Fernando Soto "Mantequilla," Manuel Dondé, Roberto Meyer, Chel López, José Muñoz.

90 minutes. Black and white.

Synopsis: In the coastal town of Santa Bibiana, all the men carry guns on their belts and the slightest misunderstanding can end in death. Young doctor Gerardo Anguiano (Joaquín Cordero) is hospitalized in Mexico City, inside an iron lung. He is visited by someone from the town, Rómulo Menchaca (Jaime Fernández), who slaps him and challenges him to a future duel. A flashback explains the origin of the feud between the Anguiano and Menchaca families: Felipe Anguiano (Miguel Torruco) was forced to kill Filogonio Menchaca (Jorge Arriaga). He flees to the desert, but secretly returns to marry his girlfriend Mercedes (Columba Domínguez). He is surprised by Polo Menchaca (Víctor Alcocer), who kills him and the vendetta is established. Gerardo is Felipe's son. End of flashback. Gerardo returns to the town and everyone, including his mother, hopes he will avenge his father's death. When a gunfight between Felipe and Rómulo seems inevitable, the two suddenly hug and bring to the feud to an end.

Ensayo de un crimen/The Criminal Life of Archibaldo de la Cruz/Rehearsal for a Crime (1955)
Production Company: Alianza Cinematográfica, Alfonso Patiño Gómez (Mexico)
Director: Luis Buñuel
Screenplay: Luis Buñuel, Eduardo Ugarte, based on the novel *Ensayo de un crimen*, by Rodolfo Usigli
Cinematography: Agustín Jiménez
Editor: Jorge Bustos, Luis Buñuel
Music: Jorge Pérez Herrera
Sound: Rodolfo Benítez
Art Direction: Jesús Bracho
Cast: Ernesto Alonso (Archibaldo de la Cruz), Miroslava (Lavinia), Rita Macedo (Patricia), Ariadna Welter (Carlota Cervantes), Rodolfo Landa (Alejandro Rivas), Leonor Llausás (nanny), Chabela Durán (nun), Andrea Palma (Sra. Cervantes), José María Linares Rivas (Willy Corduran), Carlos Riquelme, Eva Calvo, Carlos Martínez Buena, Antonio Bravo Sánchez.
91 minutes. Black and white.
Synopsis: As a child, while listening to a waltz on a music box, Archibaldo de la Cruz (Ernesto Alonso) sees his nanny (Leonor Llausás) killed by a stray bullet. Years later, he finds the music box at an antique shop. Its melody sparks an association linking death and eroticism, and he believes that his true vocation is to be a murderer. Unfortunately for him, all of his intended victims — a nun (Chabela Durán) and a tease (Rita Macedo) — die before he can kill them. Archibaldo becomes engaged to Carlota (Ariadna Welter), then discovers she is carrying on an affair with Alejandro (Rodolfo Landa). He fantasizes about killing her on their wedding night, but Alejandro beats him to it. He is fascinated with another woman, Lavinia (Miroslava), but can't kill her either; instead, he burns her in effigy. Despite all his failures, Archibaldo continues to see himself a murderer and confesses his "crimes" to the police, who tell him he is innocent and free to go. Archibaldo throws the music box into a lake, runs into Lavinia, and they go off arm in arm.

Cela s'appelle l'aurore (1955)
Production Company: Les Films Marceau, Laetitia Films, Insignia Films (France-Italy)
Director: Luis Buñuel
Screenplay: Luis Buñuel, Jean Ferry, based on the novel by Emmanuel Robles
Cinematography: Robert Lefebvre
Editor: Marguerite Renoir, Luis Buñuel
Music: Joseph Kosma
Sound: Antoine Petitjean
Art Direction: Max Douy
Cast: Georges Marchal (Dr. Valerio), Lucía Bosé (Clara), Gianni Esposito (Sandro), Julien Bertheau (Police Commissioner), Nelly Borgeaud (Angela), Jean-Jacques Delbo (Gorzone), Robert Levfort (Pietro), Brigitte Elloy (Magda), Henri Nassiet (Angela's father), Gaston Modot (peasant), Simone Paris (Madame Gorzone), Pascale Mazotti (Azzopardi), Marcel Peres.
102 minutes. Black and white.
Synopsis: Dr. Valerio (Georges Marchal), working for an industrial concern on a Mediterranean island, devotes himself to helping the workers and poor farmers. His wife, Angela (Nelly Borgeaud), suffers from nerves. Valerio has an affair with a beautiful Italian woman, Clara (Lucía Bosé). Valerio's worker friend Sandro (Gianni Esposito) kills his heartless employer, who had been indirectly responsible for Sandro's wife's death. Pursued by police commissioner Fasaro (Julien Betheau), Sandro hides at Valerio's house. Angela and her father break with Valerio because he is protecting a murderer, and Sandro leaves. He is discovered and commits suicide. Valerio, who tried to get Sandro to surrender peacefully, becomes indignant. He refuses to shake hands with Fasaro and leaves with Clara and three worker friends.

La mort en ce jardin/Death in the Garden/Evil Eden (1956)
Production Company: Producciones Tepeyac, Oscar Dancigers, Films Dismage, David Mage (Mexico-France)
Director: Luis Buñuel
Screenplay: Luis Buñuel, Raymond Queneau, Luis Alcoriza, Gabriel Arout, based on the novel by José André Lacour
Cinematography: Jorge Stahl, Jr.
Editor: Marguerite Renoir, Luis Buñuel
Music: Paul Misraki
Sound: José D. Pérez, Galino Samperio
Art Direction: Edward Fitzgerald
Cast: Simone Signoret (Djin), Georges Marchal (Shark), Charles Vanel (Castin), Michel Piccoli (Father Lizardi), Jorge Martínez de Hoyos (Captain Ferrero), Michele Girardon (María), Raúl Ramírez (Alvaro), Tito Junco (Chenko), Luis Aceves Casteñeda (Alberto), Alberto Pedret (lieutenant), Marc Lambert, Alia del Lago.
97 minutes. Color.
Synopsis: In an unnamed Latin American country, the miners at a diamond field revolt, despite the pacifist advice of the priest, Father Lizardi (Michel Piccoli). Among the rebels is the Frenchman Castin (Charles Vanel), father of a deaf girl, María (Michele Girardon). A European adventurer, Shark (Georges Marchal), is accused of bank robbery and thrown in jail, but he manages to escape and participates in the strike, blowing up the dynamite depository. The rebellion is quashed. Joined by the prostitute Djin (Simone Signoret), Lizardi, Castin, María, and Shark flee, pursued by Captain Ferrero (Jorge Martínez de Hoyos). In the

jungle, they find a downed airplane, whose rich contents enable them to have an elegant dinner party in the jungle. Crazed, Castin begins to shoot at his companions and kills Djin and Lizardi, before being killed by Shark. He and María manage to escape to freedom in a canoe.

Nazarín (1958)
Production Company: Producciones Barbachano Ponce, Manuel Barbachano Ponce (Mexico)
Director: Luis Buñuel
Screenplay: Luis Buñuel, Julio Alejandro, based on the novel by Benito Pérez Galdós
Cinematography: Gabriel Figueroa
Editor: Carlos Savage, Luis Buñuel
Music: "Dios nunca muere," waltz by Macedonio Alcalá, drums of Calanda
Sound: José D. Pérez
Art Direction: Edward Fitzgerald
Cast: Francisco Rabal (Nazarín), Marga López (Beatriz), Rita Macedo (Andara), Ignacio López Tarso (church thief), Ofelia Guilmain (Chanfa), Luis Aceves Casteñeda (parricide), Noé Murayama (El Pinto), Rosenda Monteros (La Prieta), Jesús Fernández (Ujo, the Dwarf), Pilar Pellicer (dying woman), Aurora Molina, David Reynoso, Ada Carrasco, Edmundo Barbero, Raúl Dantés, Antonio Bravo.
94 minutes. Black and white.
Synopsis: At the beginning of the century, the young priest Nazario (Francisco Rabal) lives in a poor Mexico City neighborhood helping his fellow human beings. After a bloody brawl, the prostitute Andara (Rita Macedo) hides from the police in Nazario's room. Beatriz (Marga López), who has been abandoned by her lover El Pinto (Noé Murayama), tries to hang herself. She fails and is comforted by Nazario. Andara burns her bloody clothes in Nazarín's room and starts a fire. The two women flee. After the fire, the police look for Nazario. Punished by the church, he decides to wander in the countryside, living on alms. He encounters Beatriz and Andara, who follow him because his prayers "miraculously" cured a dying girl. Nazarín admonishes a soldier who mistreats a peasant and, witnessing this, another priest considers Nazarín to be a "subversive element." Nazarín offers to work on a roadway crew in exchange for food; without realizing it, he sparks a dispute between the foreman and the workers. The three wandering pilgrims arrive at a plague-stricken village, where Nazarín unsuccessfully tries to save the soul of a dying woman (Pilar Pellicer). In another town, the dwarf Ujo (Jesús Fernández) falls in love with Andara. The villagers, considering Nazarín immoral, turn him over to the authorities. Andara and Nazarín are taken to the capital in chains, while El Pinto comes for Beatriz. En route, a thief and patricidal criminal (Luis Aceves Castañeda) mistreats Nazarín in jail while another thief, (Ignacio López Tarso), defends the priest, then asks him for his remaining money, and tells him that neither good nor evil deeds count for anything in this world. Accompanied by a guard, Nazarín continues his journey. He rejects a pineapple that a humble woman offers him, then reconsiders, accepts the fruit, and continues on.

La fièvre monte à El Pao/Los ambiciosos/Republic of Sin (1959)
Production Company: Cinematográfica Filmex, Gregorio Wallerstein, Films Borderie, Groupe des Quatre (Mexico-France)
Director: Luis Buñuel
Screenplay: Luis Buñuel, Luis Alcoriza, Louis Sapin, Charles Dorat, Henri Castillou, based on the novel by Henri Castillou
Cinematography: Gabriel Figueroa, Ignacio Romero

Editor: Rafael López Ceballos (Mexican version), James Cuenet (French version)
Music: Paul Misraki
Sound: William Robert Sivel (French version), Rodolfo Beníntez, Roberto Camacho (Mexican version)
Art Direction: Jorge Fernández, Pablo Galván
Cast: Gérard Philipe (Ramón Vásquez), María Félix (Inés Várgas), Jean Servais (Alejandro Gual), Tito Junco (Inclarte), Roberto Cañedo (Olivares), Domingo Soler (Professor Cárdenas), Luis Aceves Casteñeda (López), Miguel Angel Ferriz (Várgas), Raúl Dantés (García), Andrés Soler, Pilar Pellicer, Augusto Benedicto, Miguel Arenas, David Reynoso, Antonio Bravo, Armando Acosta.
97 minutes (France), 110 minutes (Mexico). Black and white.
Synopsis: In a South American dictatorship, Ramón Vázquez (Gérard Philipe) believes in the possibility of liberalizing the regime from the inside. Vázquez is secretary to the prison director, Mariano Vargas (Miguel Angel Ferriz); when Vargas is killed, the tyrant Barreiro (Andrés Soler) responds with harsh repression, carried out by Alejandro Gual (Jean Servais). Gual tries to seduce Vargas' widow, Inés (María Félix), but she becomes Ramón's lover instead. In order to save Ramón, Inés offers herself to Gual. Ramón's teacher Cárdenas (Domingo Soler) is jailed and Ramón's conscience bothers him. Inés tries to kill Gual, but is subdued and raped. Cárdenas dies in jail; Ramón puts down a revolt and becomes head of the regime. When Ramón orders the soldiers to arrest Inés, they shoot her and she dies. Despite his actions, Ramón only manages to reinforce the tyranny. But he compromises his situation when he orders that the prisoners be unchained.

The Young One/Island of Shame/*La joven* (1960)
Production Company: Producciones Omeca, George P. Werker (Mexico-United States)
Director: Luis Buñuel
Screenplay: Luis Buñuel, H.B. Addis (Hugo Butler), based on the novel *Travellin' Man*, by Peter Matthiesen
Cinematography: Gabriel Figueroa
Editor: Carlos Savage, Luis Buñuel
Music: Jesús Zarzosa, song: "Sinner Man," by Leon Bibb
Sound: José B. Carles, James L. Fields, Galdino Samperio
Art Direction: Jesús Bracho
Cast: Zacahary Scott (Miller), Bernie Hamilton (Traver), Kay Meersman (Evvie), Graham Denton (Jackson), Claudio Brook (Reverend Fleetwood).
95 minutes. Black and white.
Synopsis: Two people live on an island off the southern coast of the United States: Miller (Zachary Scott), the game warden, and Evvie (Kay Meersman), a young girl whose grandfather, Pee Wee the handyman, has just died. Miller seduces the girl. Fleeing a lynch mob for the supposed rape of a white woman, black clarinet player Traver (Bernie Hamilton) arrives on the island. After a fight, Miller subdues the black man and forces him to be his servant. Protestant minister Fleetwood (Claudio Brook) also arrives on the island, accompanied by the racist Jackson (Graham Denton). Taken prisoner by his pursuers, Traver is tied up. Evvie cuts the ropes, Jackson and Traver fight, and the black man humiliates his enemy by not killing him. The minister makes an agreement with Miller: if he allows the black man to go free, the minister promises to remain silent about Miller's seduction of Evvie. Miller helps the black man repair the launch and allows him to leave. Evvie and Miller plan to get married.

Viridiana (1961)
Production Company: Producciones Alatriste, Gustavo Alatriste, Uninci-Films 59, Pedro Portabella (Mexico- Spain)
Director: Luis Buñuel
Screenplay: Luis Buñuel, Julio Alejandro
Cinematography: José Fernández Aguayo
Editor: Pedro del Rey, Luis Buñuel
Music: Handel's Messiah, Beethoven's Ninth Symphony, selections by Gustavo Pittaluga
Art Direction: Francisco Canet
Cast: Silvia Pinal (Viridiana), Francisco Rabal (Jorge), Fernando Rey (Don Jaime), Margarita Lozano (Ramona), Victoria Zinny (Lucía), Teresa Rabal (Rita), José Calvo, Luis Heredia, Joaquín Roa, José Manuel Martín, Lola Gaos, Juan García Tienda, Maruja Isbert, Joaquín Mayol, Palmira Guerra, Sergio Mendizabal.
90 minutes. Black and white.
Synopsis: Just before taking her final vows, the novice Viridiana (Silvia Pinal) visits her uncle, Don Jaime (Fernando Rey). He is an old landowner who, since the death of his wife, lives retired on his neglected estate with his maid Ramona (Margarita Lozano), her small daughter Rita (Teresa Rabal), and the old man Moncho. Fascinated by his beautiful niece, who resembles his dead wife, Don Jaime tries unsuccessfully to convince her to live with him. Before her departure, Viridiana consents to her uncle's whim: to wear his dead wife's wedding dress. Aided by Ramona, Don Jaime drugs Viridiana and plans to rape her, but repents. Horrified by her uncle's plan, Viridiana decides to return to the convent. Don Jaime commits suicide, leaving his estate to Viridiana and his son, Jorge (Francisco Rabal), who arrives with his lover and begins to work the fields. Leaving the convent, Viridiana decides to exercise Christian charity by housing a group of beggars on her part of the property. Jorge sends his lover away and seduces Ramona. One night when the owners are away, the beggars enter the house and have an orgiastic dinner; they get drunk and fight. The owners return suddenly. The Cripple (José Manuel Martín) and the Leper (Juan García Tienda) knock Jorge out and try to rape Viridiana. Ramona arrives with the police. That night, after calm has been restored, Viridiana goes to see Jorge in his room and finds him sitting with Ramona. The three play cards.

*El ángel exterminador/*The Exterminating Angel (1962)
Production Company: Producciones Alatriste, Uninci, Films 59, Gustavo Alatriste (Mexico)
Director: Luis Buñuel
Screenplay: Luis Buñuel, Luis Alcoriza
Cinematography: Gabriel Figueroa
Editor: Carlos Savage, Luis Buñuel
Music: Scarlatti, Beethoven, Chopin, with incidental music by Raúl Lavista
Sound: José B. Carles
Art Direction: Jesús Bracho
Cast: Silvia Pinal (Leticia "the Valkyrie"), Enrique Rabal (Nobile), Jacqueline Andere (Alicia Roe), José Baviera (Leandro), Augusto Benedico (The Doctor), Luis Beristáin (Christian), Claudio Brook (Butler), Antonio Bravo (Russell), César del Campo (The Colonel), Rosa Elena Durgel (Silvia), Lucy Gallardo (Lucía Nobile), Enrique García Alvarez (Mr. Roc), Ofelia Guilmain (Juana Avila), Nadia Haro Oliva (Ana Maynar), Tito Junco (Raúl), Xavier Loyá (Francisco Avila), Xavier Massé (Eduardo), Angel Merino (Waiter), Ofelia Montesco (Beatrice), Patricia Morán (Rita), Berta Moss (Leonora), Patricia de Morelos (Blanca), Enrique del Castillo, Pancho Córdova, Luis Lomeli.

95 minutes. Black and white.

Synopsis: Edmundo (Enrique Rabal) and Lucía Nobile (Lucy Gallardo) give an elegant dinner party at their mansion. For no reason, the cook and other servants have suddenly become frightened and fled, leaving the butler Julio (Claudio Brook) in charge of everything. Blanca (Patricia de Morelos) plays a sonata on the piano and from that moment on, the guests, without knowing why, can't leave the room. The following morning they have only coffee for breakfast. The guests, now virtual prisoners, are puzzled and irritated; they fight and blame Nobile for the strange situation. Russell (Antonio Bravo) gets sick and dies; he is "buried" in a three-door wardrobe. Two lovers, Beatriz (Ofelia Montesco) and Eduardo (Javier Massé), hide behind the second door to make love; then they commit suicide. The third compartment is used as a lavatory. Without food, hygiene, or privacy, life becomes unbearable in the drawing room; incidents explode, a bear roams through the house, etc. Outside, family members knock frantically at the gates of the mansion, unable to get in. By chance, Leticia (Silvia Pinal) discovers the key to their escape: everyone must repeat the same gestures they made during the first performance of the sonata. The characters leave the room and later celebrate a Mass to give thanks. At the end, they discover that no one can leave the church.

Le journal d'une femme de chambre/Diary of a Chambermaid (1963)
Production Company: Speva Films-Ciné Alliances Filmsonor, Dear Film Produzione, Serge Silberman, Michel Safra (France-Italy)
Director: Luis Buñuel
Screenplay: Luis Buñuel, Jean-Claude Carrière, based on the novel by Octave Mirbeau
Cinematography: Roger Fellous
Editor: Louisette Hautecoeur
Sound: Antoine Petitjean, Robert Kambourakis
Art Direction: Georges Wakhevitch, Arlette Lalande
Cast: Jeanne Moreau (Célestine), Georges Géret (Joseph), Michel Piccoli (M. Monteil), Françoise Lugagne (Mme. Monteil), Jean Ozenne (M. Rabour), Daniel Ivernal (Captain Mauzer), Gilberte Geniat (Rose), Bernard Musson (Sacristain), Jean-Claude Carrière (Priest), Muni (Marianne), Claude Jaeger (Judge), Dominique Sauvage (Claire).
98 minutes. Black and white.
Synopsis: In the 1920s, the chambermaid Célestine (Jeanne Moreau) goes to work for the Monteils, a provincial bourgeois family. The pater familias has a foot fetish; Monteil Jr. (Michel Piccoli), who is rejected sexually by his pious wife (Françoise Lugagne), courts Célestine, who also rejects him. He then declares his *amour fou* to the other maid, Marianne (Muni), who is old and ugly. The priest (Jean-Claude Carrière) has a strong influence over Mrs. Monteil, preaching against "sins of the flesh." A neighbor, the retired Captain Mauzer (Daniel Ivernal), throws trash into Monteil's garden in order to upset them. The game warden Joseph (Georges Géret), who is a reactionary brute, rapes and murders a young girl. Célestine sleeps with him, discovers that he is the murderer and informs the police. She later marries Captain Mauzer and becomes a bourgeois. Joseph gets out of prison and buys a bar, from whose door he delights in watching a right-wing demonstration.

En este pueblo no hay ladrones/There Are No Thieves in This Town (1964)
Production Company: Grupo Claudio, Alberto Isaac (Mexico)
Director: Alberto Isaac
Screenplay: Alberto Isaac, Emilio García Riera, based on the story by Gabriel García Márquez

Cinematography: Carlos Carbajal
Editor: Carlos Savage
Music: Nacho Méndez
Cast: Julián Pastor, Rocío Sagaón, Mario Castillón, Graciela Enríquez, Luis Vicens, Antonio Alcalá, Alfonso Arau, Héctor Ortega, María Antonieta Domínguez, Argentina Morales, Juan Rulfo, Gabriel García Márquez, José Luis Cuevas, Abel Quezada, Leonora Carrington, Carlos Monsiváis, Arturo Ripstein, Luis Buñuel (as priest).
90 minutes. Black and white.

Llanto por un bandido/Time for a Bandit (1964)
Production Company: Agata Films, Atlantica Cinematográfica, Meditérranée Cinéma (Spain-Italy-France)
Director: Carlos Saura
Screenplay: Carlos Saura, Mario Camus
Cinematography: Juan Julio Baena
Editor: Pedro del Rey
Music: Carlos Rustichelli
Art Direction: Enrique Alarcón
Cast: Francisco Rabal, Lea Massari, Phillipe Leroy, Lino Ventura, Manuel Zarzo, Silvia Soler, Antonio Prieto, Luis Buñuel (as the executioner).
101 minutes. Color.

Simón del desierto/Simon of the Desert (1965)
Production Company: Producciones Alatriste, Gustavo Alatriste (Mexico)
Director: Luis Buñuel
Screenplay: Luis Buñuel, Julio Alejandro
Cinematography: Gabriel Figueroa
Editor: Carlos Savage, Luis Buñuel
Music: "Pilgrims Hymn," by Raúl Lavista, drums of Calanda
Sound: James L. Fields
Cast: Claudio Brook (Simón), Hortensia Santoveña (Simón's mother), Silvia Pinal (Temptress), Jesús Fernández (dwarf), Enrique Alvarez Félix (Brother Mathias), Luis Aceves Castañeda (priest), Enrique García Alvarez, Antonio Bravo, Eduardo MacGregor, Francisco Regueira, Enrique del Castillo, Enrique García Alvarez.
43 minutes. Black and white.
Synopsis: Simon (Claudio Brook), an anchorite, lives atop a column in the desert during the Middle Ages. He is visted by monks, soldiers, and the common people. Rich people give him a higher column. Simon's mother (Hortensia Santoveña) lives in a small cabin at the foot of the column. Simon restores the hands of a handicapped artisan (Enrique del Castillo) who, without being suprised by the miracle, gives his daughter a slap and leaves. The Devil or "Temptress" (Silvia Pinal) tempts Simon, adopting various forms. The monk Trifón (Luis Aceves Castañeda) slanders Simon, saying that he secretly eats well; God punishes him with an epileptic fit. The monk Daniel (Eduardo MacGregor) warns Simon that the barbarians are closing in. The Devil, furious for failing to tempt him, reappears in a traveling coffin and transports Simon to the twentieth century to a New York discotheque.

Belle de jour (1966)
Production Company: Henri Baum, Paris Film Production-Five Films, Robert and Raymond Hakim (France-Italy)

Director: Luis Buñuel
Screenplay: Luis Buñuel, Jean-Claude Carrière, based on the novel by Joseph Kessel
Cinematography: Sacha Vierney
Editor: Louisette Hautecoeur
Sound: René Longuet
Art Direction: Robert Clavel
Cast: Catherine Deneuve (Séverine), Jean Sorel (Pierre), Michel Piccoli (Husson), Geneviève Page (Anaïs), Francisco Rabal (Hippolyte), Pierre Clementi (Marcel), Françoise Fabian (Charlotte), Maria Latour (Mathilde), Francis Blanche (M. Adolphe), François Maistre (The Professor), Macha Meril (Renée), Muni, Dominique Dandrieux, Bernard Fresson, Brigitte Parmentier, Claude Cerval, Michel Charrel, Iska Khan, Marcel Charvey.
100 minutes. Color.
Synopsis: Séverine (Catherine Deneuve), the beautiful and frigid wife of a young doctor, Pierre (Jean Sorel), fantasizes about surrendering herself to various degrading sexual acts. The couple's liberal friend Husson (Michel Piccoli) gives Séverine the address of a brothel run by Anaïs (Geneviève Page). Séverine begins to carry on a double life: a decent wife during the rest of the day and, in the afternoons, a deluxe prostitute. At the brothel she meets various clients with special tastes. A young gangster, Marcel (Pierre Clementi), falls in love with her. Marcel shoots Pierre, leaving him crippled, and later dies in a shootout with the police. Husson tells Pierre about Séverine's afternoon activities. Pierre rises from his wheelchair, cured, but this may be only another of Séverine's fantasies.

La voie lactée/The Milky Way (1969)
Production Company: Serge Silberman, Greenwich Films, Fraia Films (France-Italy)
Director: Luis Buñuel
Screenplay: Luis Buñuel, Jean-Claude Carrière
Cinematography: Cristian Matras
Editor: Louisette Hautecoeur, Luis Buñuel
Sound: Jacques Gallois
Art Direction: Pierre Guffroy
Cast: Paul Frankeur (Pierre), Laurent Terzieff (Jean), Alain Cuny (Man in Cape), Edith Scob (Virgin Mary), Bernard Verley (Jesus), François Maistre (Crazy Priest), Claude Cerval (Brigadier, at Restaurant), Julien Bertheau (Maître d'), Jean-Claude Carrière (Priscillian), Pierre Clementi (Angel of Death), Claudine Berg, Georges Marchal.
100 minutes. Color.
Synopsis: Two hitchhikers, Pierre (Paul Frankeur) and Jean (Laurent Terzieff), on a pilgrimage to Santiago de Compostela, have various adventures that go beyond time and space: a man in a cape (Alain Cuny) tells them they must beget children with a prostitute in Santiago de Compostela; at an inn they meet a crazy priest, steal a ham and are surprised by a Civil Guard, who lets them go free; in a forest they encounter Priscillian (Jean-Claude Carrière) and his sect in one of their mystic orgies; they watch a theological duel between a Jesuit and a Jansenist, the exhumation of the remains of a heretic bishop, various miracles, and they meet a prostitute (Delphyne Seyrig), who wants to beget children with them, etc. There are other episodes: a nun is crucified by other members of her order; the Virgin Mary (Edith Scob) tells Jesus (Bernard Verley) not to shave off his beard; the Wedding of Canaan is shown; sight is miraculously restored to the blind; the Marquis de Sade (Michel Piccoli) tortures Justine, etc. The film deals with historical heresies concerning six Catholic dogmas or mysteries: the Eucharist, the Nature of Christ, the Trinity, the Origin of Evil, the Immaculate Conception, Free Will.

Tristana (1970)
Production Company: Época Film, Talía Film, Selenia Cinematográfica, Les Films Corona (Spain-Italy-France)
Director: Luis Buñuel
Screenplay: Luis Buñuel, Julio Alejandro, based on the novel by Benito Pérez Galdós
Cinematography: José F. Aguayo
Editor: Pedro del Rey, Luis Buñuel
Sound: José Nogueira
Art Direction: Enrique Alarcón
Cast: Catherine Deneuve (Tristana), Fernando Rey (Don Lope), Franco Nero (Horacio), Lola Gaos (Saturna), Jesús Fernández (Saturno), Antonio Casas (Don Cosme), Sergio Mendizábal (headmaster), José Calvo (bellringer), Vicente Soler, Fernando Cabrian, Juan José Menéndez, Candida Losada, María Paz Pondal, Antonio Ferrandis, José María Caffarel, Joaquín Pamplona.
100 minutes. Color
Synopsis: Don Lope (Fernando Rey) is a mature playboy from Toledo, idle, liberal, anticlerical, and a bit of a Don Juan. He is the guardian of an orphan girl, Tristana (Catherine Deneuve), whom he seduces. Tristana accepts the situation passively until one day she meets a painter, Horacio (Franco Nero), and runs off with him. Don Lope is left with her rich inheritance. Tristana falls ill and comes home. Her leg has to be amputated and replaced by an artificial one. Horacio returns to Toledo and Don Lope asks him to visit Tristana; finally the painter and the girl fight and he leaves. Meanwhile, Tristana becomes more and more reserved, but gives special attention to the young deaf mute, Saturno (Jesús Fernández). Don Lope ages and adapts to social conventions. One night when Don Lope has a heart attack, Tristana pretends to phone the doctor. She opens the window to let in the cold winter air and Don Lope dies.

Le charme discret de la bourgeoisie/The Discreet Charm of the Bourgeoisie (1972)
Production Company: Serge Silberman, Greenwich Films (France-Spain)
Director: Luis Buñuel
Screenplay: Luis Buñuel, Jean-Claude Carrière
Cinematography: Edmund Richard
Editor: Hélène Plemiannikov
Sound: Guy Villette
Art Direction: Pierre Guffroy
Cast: Fernando Rey (Rafael Acosta, Ambassador of Miranda), Delphine Seyrig (Simone Thevenot), Stephane Audran (Alice Senechal), Bulle Ogier (Florence), Jean-Pierre Cassel (Senechal), Paul Frankeur (Thevenot), Julien Bertheau (bishop), Milena Vukotic (maid), Claude Pieplu (colonel), Michel Piccoli (minister), Muni (peasant), Maria Gabrille Maione (revolutionary).
106 minutes. Color.
Synopsis: The ambassador of Miranda (Fernando Rey), Mr. and Mrs. Thevenot (Paul Frankeur, Delphine Seyrig) and Mrs. Thevenot's sister Florence (Bulle Ogier) are all invited to dinner at the home of friends, the Senechals (Jean-Pierre Cassel, Stephane Audrau), but they arrive on the wrong day. Instead, the five go to a restaurant, where they can't eat because the owner has died that afternoon. The ambassador uses his diplomatic pouch to smuggle cocaine, which Thevenot and Senechal sell. Another dinner with the Senechals is called off because the hosts sneak off to make love. A bishop (Julien Bertheau) asks the Senechals for a job as gardener. At a restaurant, Mrs. Thevenot, Mrs. Senechal, and Flor-

ence are approached by a lieutenant, who tells them about his childhood; they discover they can't order anything. The ambassador and Mrs. Thevenot unsuccessfully attempt to make love. A woman revolutionary tries to kill the ambassador, but she's disarmed and taken away. Military maneuvers interrupt another dinner at the Senechals' house and the sergeant recounts a dream. At another frustrated dinner, the characters suddenly discover they are on stage, in a theater set; at a formal cocktail at the colonel's home, the guests ask the ambassador offensive questions until he shoots the host. The bishop hears the confession of a dying man; when he learns the man had murdered his parents, he shoots him. During lunch, the police suddenly arrive and arrest everyone for drug trafficking. In jail, the ghost of Brigadier Sangrante appears; the brigadier had formerly tortured prisoners. Freed, the ambassador and his friends attempt to dine once again when an assault team suddenly bursts in and shoots everyone (the ambassador's dream sequence). On three occasions, we see the characters walking down a highway, apparently going nowhere.

Le moine/The Monk (1972)
Production Company: Maya Films, Comacico, Intercontinental Production, Peri Productions, Tritone Cinematográfica, Studio Films (France-Italy-Germany)
Director: Ado Kyrou
Screenplay: Luis Buñuel, Jean-Claude Carrière, based on the novel *The Monk,* by Matthew Gregory Lewis
Cinematography: Sacha Vierny
Music: Ennio Morricone
Cast: Franco Nero, Mathalie Delon, Nicol Williamson, Elizabeth Wiener, Najda Tiller, Eliana de Santis, Denis Manuel.
90 minutes. Color.

Le fantôme de la liberté/The Phantom of Liberty (1974)
Production Company: Serge Silberman, Greenwich Films (France)
Director: Luis Buñuel
Screenplay: Luis Buñuel, Jean-Claude Carrière
Cinematography: Edmond Richard
Editor: Hélène Plemiannikov
Sound: Guy Villette
Art Direction: Pierre Guffroy
Cast: Adriana Asti (nurse), Monica Vitti (mother), Jean-Claude Brialy (father), Adolfo Celi (doctor), Melina Vujotic, Jean Rochefort, Michel Lonsdale, I. Carrière (girl with postcards), Bernard Verley (French dragon), Philippe Brigaud (man in park), Hélène Perdrière (aunt), Pierre-François Pistorio (nephew), Michel Lousdale (masochist), Anne-Marie Deschott (sadist), François Maistre (teacher), V. Blanco (missing girl), Pierre Lary (killer-poet), Julien Bertheau (police prefect), Michel Piccoli, Serge Silberman, José Bergamín, José Luis Barros, Luis Buñuel.
103 minutes. Color.
Synopsis: During Napoleon's invasion of Toledo, a captain of the French dragoons (Bernard Verley) kisses the statue of a kneeling woman and is struck by the statue of a knight. At a park, a suspicious-looking man (Philippe Brigaud) gives some postcards to a little girl (I. Carrière): though they are assumed to be pornographic, the postcards turn out to be photos of famous Parisian monuments. The girl's parents (Jean-Claude Brialy, Monica Vitti) are shocked. Suffering from insomnia, the father watches a series of animals parade through his bedroom, followed by a mailman who deposits a letter. The next day he

recounts this experience to the doctor (Adolfo Celi), showing him the letter as proof. The nurse (Adriana Asti) leaves Paris because her father is dying; en route she runs into some soldiers who use tanks to hunt a fox; then she meets various characters at an inn: some priests, a musician and a dancer, an older woman and her nephew (Hélène Perdrière, Pierre-François Pistorio) who are lovers, and a masochistic hatmaker (Michel Lousdale), who is married to a sadistic woman (Anne-Marie Deschott). The next day, during a class at the policemen academy, the teacher (François Maistre) lectures about social conventions and gives an example of an elegant social gathering where the guests eat in secret and defecate in public. In another episode, the police and family members frantically search for a little girl (V. Blanco) who is supposedly missing...yet at no time is she out of the sight of those who look for her. The action passes to the top of a Paris skyscraper where the "killer-poet" (Pierre Lary) murders 18 persons with a high-powered rifle. He is arrested, condemned to death, and then set free. The police commissioner (Julien Bertheau) who is and isn't the police commissioner (he meets another one), relates a memory of his late sister and afterwards receives a phone call from her, from the beyond. Later he goes with his police force to quell an assault on the zoo by an angry crowd. Like the Spanish protesters at the beginning of the film, the crowd shouts: "Long live chains, death to liberty!"

Cet obscur objet du désir/That Obscure Object of Desire (1977)
Production Company: Greenwich Films, Les Films Galaxie, Incine, Serge Silberman (France-Spain)
Director: Luis Buñuel
Screenplay: Luis Buñuel, Jean-Claude Carrière, based on the novel *La femme et le pantin*, by Pierre Loüys
Cinematography: Edmond Richard
Editor: Hélène Plemiannikov, Luis Buñuel
Art Direction: Pierre Guffroy, Pierre Bartlet
Cast: Fernando Rey (Mathieu), Carole Bouquet (Conchita), Angela Molina (Conchita), Julien Bertheau (Judge Edouard), André Weber (Martin), Milena Vukotic (woman in train), Bernard Musson (police inspector), María Asquerino (Conchita's mother), David Rocha, Muni, Isabelle Sadoyan, Ellen Bahl, Jacques Debary, Valérie Bianco, Claude Jaeger, Augusta Carrière, Jean-Claude Montalban, Lita Peiró, André Lacombe.
103 minutes. Color.
Synopsis: On a railway trip from Seville to Madrid, the mature gentleman Mathieu (Fernando Rey) recounts his misfortunes with the dancer Conchita (played alternately by Angela Molina and Carole Bouquet) to a group of traveling companions, who had watched Mathieu douse the woman with a bucket of cold water shortly before the train departed. With Conchita, Mathieu's feelings have gone from desire to frustration, from tenderness to violence. She arouses him, but when she appears ready to give herself to him, she is wearing an unremovable girdle. Parallel to this story are a series of terrorist attacks that don't seem to disturb the protagonists greatly or even the course of the plot, though Mathieu is robbed. At the end of the trip, Conchita douses Mathieu with a bucket of cold water. The film ends with them walking together through a shopping arcade where they observe a woman stitching a blood-stained torn piece of cloth in a shop window. As they walk away, a bomb blast is heard.

SELECTED BIBLIOGRAPHY

Included here are a few of the more pertinent books by and about Luis Buñuel and his films, with an emphasis on published screenplays and personal writings, augmented by a selection of more notable reference works. While much has been published on Buñuel in various languages, the focus here is on editions in English, except when the work is not available in any other form.

SCRIPTS:

Belle de jour, Simon & Schuster, New York, 1971.

L'Age d'Or & Un Chien Andalou: Films by Luis Buñuel, trans. Marianne Alexandre, Simon & Schuster, New York, 1968.

La ilusión viaja en tranvía, Obras completas de Juan de la Cabada, Universidad de Sinaloa, Culiacán, Mexico, 1981.

La voie lactée and *Simon du Désert*, l'Avant-Scène, No. 94-95, Paris, 1969.

Las Hurdes (Terre sans pain), l'Avant-Scène, No. 36, Paris, 1964.

Le charme discret de la bourgeoisie, l'Avant-Scène, No. 135, Paris, 1973.

Le fantôme de la liberté, l'Avant-Scène, No. 151, Paris, 1974.

Le journal d'une femme de chambre, Editions de l'Avant-Scène, Paris, 1971.

Le moine, Luis Buñuel and Jean-Claude Carrière, Eric Losfeld, Paris, 1971.

Subida al cielo, Obras completas de Juan de la Cabada, Universidad de Sinaloa, Culiacán, Mexico, 1981.

The Exterminating Angel, Nazarín, Los olvidados: Three Films by Luis Buñuel, trans. Nicholas Fry, Simon & Schuster, New York, 1972.

Three Screenplays: Viridiana, The Exterminating Angel, Simon of the Desert, Orion Press, New York, 1969.

Tristana, Simon & Schuster, New York, 1971.

WRITINGS BY BUÑUEL:

Buñuel, Luis, *My Last Sigh*, trans. Abigail Israel, Vintage Books, New York, 1984.

Buñuel, Luis, *Obra Literaria,* introduction and notes by Agustín Sánchez Vidal, Editorial Heraldo de Aragón, Zaragoza, 1982.

BOOKS ABOUT BUÑUEL:

Aranda, Francisco, *Luis Buñuel, A Critical Biography*, Da Capo Press, New York, 1976.

Aub, Max, *Conversaciones con Buñuel*, Aguilar, Madrid, 1984.

C. de Rojo, Alba, ed., *Buñuel: Iconografía Personal*, Fondo de Cultura Económica /Universidad de Guadalajara, Mexico City, 1988.

Durgnat, Raymond, *Luis Buñuel*, University of California Press, Berkeley, 1977.

Edwards, Gwynne, *The Discreet Art of Luis Buñuel*, Marion Boyars, Boston, 1982.

Kirou, Ado, *Luis Buñuel: An Introduction*, Simon & Schuster, New York, 1963.

Mellen, Joan, *The World of Luis Buñuel: Essays in Criticism*, Oxford University Press, New York, 1978.

Rucar de Buñuel, Jeanne, and Martín del Campo, Marisol, *Memorias de una mujer sin piano*, Alianza Editorial Mexicana, Mexico City, 1990.

Sánchez Vidal, Agustín, *Luis Buñuel, Obra Cinematográfica*, Ediciones J.C., Madrid, 1984.

FRANKLIN PIERCE COLLEGE LIBRARY

00073506

DATE DUE

MAR 0 3 2003			

GAYLORD — PRINTED IN U.S.A.